McGraw-Hill Language Arts

Preparation and Practice for the ITBS, SAT-9, and TerraNova

Grade 2

Teacher's Edition

McGraw-Hill School Division

The Princeton Review

This booklet was written by The Princeton Review, the nation's leader in test preparation. The Princeton Review helps millions of students every year prepare for standardized assessments of all kinds. Through its association with McGraw-Hill, The Princeton Review offers the best way to help students excel on the ITBS, SAT-9, and TerraNova tests.

The Princeton Review is not affiliated with Princeton University or Educational Testing Service.

McGraw-Hill School Division
A Division of The McGraw·Hill Companies

Copyright © McGraw-Hill School Division, a Division of the Educational and Professional Publishing Group of The McGraw-Hill Companies, Inc.

All rights reserved. Permission granted to reproduce for use with McGRAW-HILL LANGUAGE ARTS. No other use of this material or parts thereof, including reproduction, distribution, or storage in an electronic database, permitted without the prior written permission of the publisher, except as provided under the United States Copyright Act of 1976.

McGraw-Hill School Division
Two Penn Plaza
New York, New York 10121

Printed in the United States of America

ISBN 0-02-244942-6

2 3 4 5 6 7 8 9 047 04 03 02 01

ITBS

Teacher Introduction................................. p. T3
Student and Class Diagnostic Charts.................. p. T12
Student Introduction................................. p. T17
Warm-Up Test... p. 17
On Your Mark! Get Set! Go! Exercises................. p. 25
Practice Testp....................................... p. 87
On Your Mark! Get Set! Go! Review.................... p. T19

SAT-9

Teacher Introduction................................. p. T27
Student and Class Diagnostic Charts.................. p. T36
Student Introduction................................. p. T41
Warm-Up Test... p. 109
On Your Mark! Get Set! Go! Exercises................. p. 117
Practice Test.. p. 179
On Your Mark! Get Set! Go! Review.................... p. T43

TERRANOVA

Teacher Introduction................................. p. T49
Student and Class Diagnostic Charts.................. p. T58
Student Introduction................................. p. T63
Warm-Up Test... p. 203
On Your Mark! Get Set! Go! Exercises................. p. 211
Practice Test.. p. 273
On Your Mark! Get Set! Go! Review.................... p. T65

Index.. p. Index 1

ITBS

TEACHER INTRODUCTION

WHY *PREPARATION AND PRACTICE FOR THE ITBS* IS THE BEST PREPARATION FOR STUDENTS

Welcome to the Teacher Edition of *Preparation and Practice for the ITBS* for grade 2!

By completing each section of this book, students will:

- Increase their knowledge and understanding of language arts skills
- Become familiar with the types of questions that will be asked on the test
- Become accustomed to the style of the test
- Become better writers and speakers
- Learn test-taking techniques and tips that are specifically designed to help students do their best on the ITBS
- Feel comfortable on the day of the exam

Parts of This Book

There are eight sections of this Teacher Edition:

Teacher Introduction

The Teacher Introduction familiarizes you with the purpose and format of *Preparation and Practice for the ITBS*. It also describes the ITBS sections and questions on the test that pertain to language arts skills.

Student and Class Diagnostic Charts

This section consists of two charts. A student and a class diagnostic chart are included for the Warm-Up Test. These charts may be used to gauge student performance and to determine the skills with which students will need the most practice as they prepare for the ITBS.

Student Introduction

This section contains some tips and explanations for students as they begin their preparation for the ITBS. Extra annotations are included for teachers to help you further explain what is expected of students and to encourage them as they begin their test preparation.

Warm-Up Test

This diagnostic test reveals students' strengths and weaknesses so that you may customize your test preparation accordingly. The skill tested in each question of the Warm-Up Test directly correlates to a skill reviewed in one of the thirty On Your Mark! Get Set! Go! practice exercises.

On Your Mark! Get Set! Go!

This section consists of 30 practice exercises. Each exercise focuses on a specific language arts skill or test-taking strategy. On Your Mark! introduces and explains the skill. Get Set! provides an example question that tests the skill. (You should go over this question as a class. Get Set! is designed to bridge the gap between On Your Mark! and the test-like questions in Go!) Go! contains questions—similar to ITBS questions—that test the skills introduced in the exercise. Have students complete these questions on their own.

Practice Test

The Practice Test is a shortened version of the actual ITBS. The Practice Test only contains a portion of the questions that will appear on the actual test so that students are not tapped of energy on the day of the actual ITBS. The Practice Test includes questions from each section: listening, word analysis, and language. The test provides students with a simulated test-taking experience. Make sure you tell students that the actual ITBS will be longer.

On Your Mark! Get Set! Go! Review

This section is *not* included in the Pupil Edition. This review section is an overview of the skills contained in On Your Mark! Get Set! Go! Similar skills are grouped together.

Index

The index is a brief listing of where you can look to find exercises about specific skills.

How to Use This Book

This book has been designed so that you may customize your ITBS test preparation according to your class's needs and time frame. However, we recommend that you begin your test preparation as early in the school year as possible. This book will yield your students' best ITBS scores if you diagnose your students' strengths and weaknesses early and work toward helping them achieve their best performance. Please note that preparing students for a test such as the ITBS is a process. As much preparation as possible should take place in the classroom and be discussed as a class.

Warm-Up Test

Have students complete the Warm-Up Test in class. It should be administered as early in the school year as possible. By doing so, students will gain familiarity with the types of questions and the specific skills tested on the ITBS *before* they begin working through the skill-specific exercises in this book. Use the student and class diagnostic charts to grade the tests. The results of the Warm-Up Test reveal students' strengths and weaknesses and allow you to focus your test preparation accordingly.

On Your Mark! Get Set! Go!

We recommend that you review an On Your Mark! Get Set! Go! exercise after completing each chapter in your McGraw-Hill language arts textbook. It is best to go through the On Your Mark! Get Set! Go! section throughout the year so that students can digest the material properly. Consider reviewing On Your Mark! and Get Set! as a class. The Go! section may be assigned as homework or completed by students individually in class. Having students complete Go! individually will provide the best simulated preparation for the ITBS. After students have completed the Go! exercises, go over the correct answers as a class. The Princeton Review's research and experience shows this in-class work to be an essential element in effective test preparation.

Practice Test

The Practice Test should be administered in the weeks prior to the actual exam. Testing conditions should be simulated. For example, no two desks should be placed directly next to each other, students should have two pencils at their disposal, the room should be quiet, and so on.

On Your Mark! Get Set! Go! Review

Use this review in the few days leading up to the actual exam. Its purpose is to solidify the On Your Mark! Get Set! Go! skills students have learned throughout the school year. Because this section is in the Teacher Edition only, you may want to photocopy it and review the skills as a class. Or, you may simply want to keep the information to yourself and make sure students are prepared to answer questions based on the material. If students need additional review, consult the On Your Mark! Get Set! Go! exercises that correlate to the skills. You will find the practice exercise-skill correlation information in the index.

About the Teacher Pages

Each page of the Pupil Edition is reproduced in this Teacher Edition, either reduced or full-size. Each reduced Pupil Edition page has teacher wrap. Teacher wrap consists of a **column** and a **box**.

- The column serves as a guide for you as you present the material on the Pupil Edition page in an interactive way. Guiding prompts and notes are included to ensure that information pivotal to the exercise is covered.

- The box includes teaching tips and extra activities. The extra activities are often fun, game-like activities for your class. These activities give students the opportunity to learn or apply ITBS-related skills in a variety of ways.

Teacher wrap pages are punctuated with six icon types that help guide you through the Pupil Edition.

 This icon correlates the teacher wrap to the information in the On Your Mark! section of the Pupil Edition page.

 This icon reminds you to go over the example question in the Get Set! section of the Pupil Edition page.

 This icon reminds you to go over each question on the Go! pages of the Pupil Edition.

 This icon provides a point of emphasis for you to make concerning the exercise on the Pupil Edition page.

 This icon identifies an extra activity.

 This icon reminds you to read any text that follows to the students.

About the Annotated Pages

Some pages in the Teacher Edition include full-size Pupil Edition pages. These occur in the Student Introduction, the Warm-Up Test section, and the Practice Test section.

All of these full-size reproductions are highlighted with teacher annotations. These annotations, which appear in magenta ink, provide the following:

- **Teacher Script**

A small magenta megaphone will appear directly before the script you need to read aloud.

- **Correct Answers**

The correct answer to each question is filled in with magenta ink.

- **Question Analyses**

Sometimes an annotation offers further explanation of a specific question.

- **Extra Tips**

Certain annotations provide you with extra teaching tips specific to the skill tested on the Pupil Edition page.

- **Hints**

Some annotations offer hints that you can give to your students when they are working through the questions in the exercise or test sections.

Introduction to the ITBS

ITBS stands for Iowa Test of Basic Skills. It is a standardized test administered every year by students throughout the country. Talk to your school's test administrator to get the exact testing date for this school year.

The ITBS is a multiple-choice test that assesses students' skills in reading, language arts, mathematics, social studies, science, and information sources. This book covers the language arts section of the ITBS, which consists of three parts:

- **Listening**
- **Word Analysis**
- **Language**

The specific number of questions for each skill discussed above is broken down as follows on the actual ITBS:

Skill	Listening	Word Analysis	Language
Number of Items	31	32	54

Timing

The ITBS is *not* timed in grade 2. However, the ITBS that students will take in the years to come *will* be timed. Therefore, students might benefit if you integrate timing into their test-taking situations. Students should take approximately twenty-five minutes to complete the listening section, fifteen minutes to complete the word analysis section, and thirty-five minutes to complete the language section of the actual ITBS.

How Language Arts Skills Are Tested on the ITBS

Listening

Students are asked to identify the picture that represents the best answer to the question. For this section, you will read something aloud to students.

EXAMPLE:

You will say: This lesson will let you show how well you understand the way that people use language. We will start with a sample question. Look at the three pictures for the sample question and listen carefully. Tonia gave Renee a present that she can only use when it is raining. Fill in the circle under the picture that shows what Tonia gave Renee.

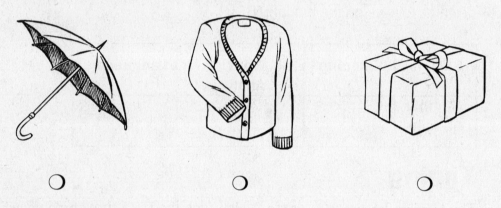

Word Analysis

There are several different types of word analysis questions.

- **Initial Sound:** You will say a word out loud and students must pick the word that begins with the same sound.

- **Letter Substitution:** Students will be given a word and three pictures. They must identify the picture that can be named by changing the first letter or letters of the word.

- **Vowel Sounds:** 1) Students will be given three pictures. You will say a word and students will choose the picture whose name has the same vowel sound as the word. 2) You will say a word and students must pick the written word with the same vowel sound.

- **Word Building:** 1) Students are given three pictures and a word with missing letters. Students must pick the letters that will complete the word shown in the picture. 2) Students are given a word and must choose the suffix that can be added to make another word.

- **Silent Letters:** Students must pick out the word that contains a silent letter.

Language

There are several different types of language questions.

- **Word Classification:** Students are given four words and must choose the word that does not fit with the other three.
- **Spelling:** Students are given three words and must choose which of the three words is spelled incorrectly.
- **Capitalization:** Students must choose the part of the sentence that contains a capitalization error.
- **Punctuation:** Students must choose the part of a sentence that contains a punctuation error.
- **Usage and Expression:** 1) Students must choose the part of a sentence that uses the incorrect form of a verb, pronoun, noun, or adjective. 2) Students must choose the part of a sentence that includes a double negative. 3) Students must choose the part of a sentence that uses incorrect subject-verb agreement.

STUDENT AND CLASS DIAGNOSTIC CHARTS

How to Use the Student Diagnostic Chart

The Student Diagnostic Chart on page T15 should be used to score the Warm-Up Test in this book. The chart is designed to help you and your individual students determine the areas in which they need the most practice as they begin their preparation for the ITBS. You will need to make enough copies of the chart for each of your students.

There are two ways to use the Student Diagnostic Chart:

- You can collect the finished Warm-Up Tests from each student and fill out one chart for each student as you grade the tests.
- You can give one copy of the Student Diagnostic Chart to each student and have students grade their own tests as you read aloud the correct answer choices.

Note: Correct answer choices are marked in the Warm-Up Test of this Teacher Edition.

How to Fill Out the Student Diagnostic Chart

For each question number, there is a blank column labeled "Right or Wrong." An "R" or a "W" should be placed in that column for each question on the Warm-Up Test. By looking at the chart upon completion, students will understand which questions they answered incorrectly and to which skills these incorrect answers corresponded. The exercise from the On Your Mark! Get Set! Go! section that teaches the skill is also noted. You should encourage students to spend extra time going over the corresponding exercises covering the skills with which they had the most trouble. The charts will also help you determine which students need the most practice and what skills gave the majority of the students trouble. This way, you can plan your students' ITBS preparation schedule accordingly.

How to Use the Class Diagnostic Chart

The Class Diagnostic Chart on page T16 should be used to record your class's performance on the Warm-Up Test in this book. The chart is designed to help you determine what areas your class needs to practice most as they begin the preparation for the ITBS. The Class Diagnostic Chart is strictly for your own use. You should not share it with students.

How to Fill Out the Class Diagnostic Chart

Under the "Name" column, you should write the names of each of your students. Then you should use the completed Student Diagnostic Charts to help you fill out the Class Diagnostic Chart. Fill out one row for each student.

For each question on the Warm-Up Test, there is a corresponding row in the Class Diagnostic Chart. The row is labeled with the question number and the exercise number of the correlating On Your Mark! Get Set! Go! exercise. If a student gets a question wrong, you should mark an "X" in the box underneath that question number. After completing a column for one student, add up all of the "Xs" and put a total for that student in the "Total" row on the top of the page. When you have filled out a column for each student, you should total up the "Xs" for each question. Put the totals in the "Total" row on the right-hand side of the page. Assessing both "Total" columns will help you determine two things: 1) which students are having the most trouble individually, and 2) which questions are giving the class as a whole the most trouble.

You should use the information gathered in the Class Diagnostic Chart to determine which skills to spend the most time reviewing and which students need the most individual practice and guidance.

Student Diagnostic Chart

Question #	Correct Answer	Right or Wrong	Exercise #	Skill
1	3rd		1	End Marks
2	2nd		2	Capitalizing Sentences
3	2nd		3	Capitalizing Names of People
4	2nd		4	Capitalizing Days of the Week
5	3rd		5	Capitalizing Places
6	1st		6	Vowels
7	1st		8	Forming Plurals
8	1st		9	Verbs
9	3rd		10	Terms of Respect
10	1st		11	Abbreviations
11	2nd		12	Punctuating Dates
12	2nd		13	Vowel Sounds with R
13	1st		15	Verb Tense
14	1st		16	Irregular Verbs
15	2nd		17	Double Negatives
16	3rd		18	Suffixes
17	1st		19	Pronouns
18	1st		20	Silent Letters
19	1st		21	Adjectives that Compare
20	3rd		22	Quotation Marks
21	1st		23	Short and Long /E/
22	3rd		25	/C/ and /G/ Sounds
23	1st		26	Adjectives
24	1st		27	Adding Endings
25	2nd		28	Drawing Conclusions
26	1st		29	Classifying Words
27	1st		30	/Ph/, /ch/, and /tch/ Sounds

Introduction • Preparation and Practice for the ITBS, SAT-9, and TerraNova • Grade 2

Class Diagnostic Chart

		Name																				Total

Spelling: Q1-Ex. 1, Q2-Ex. 2, Q3-Ex. 3, Q4-Ex. 4, Q5-Ex. 5

Capitalization: Q1-Ex. 8, Q2-Ex. 9, Q3-Ex. 10, Q4-Ex. 8, Q5-Ex. 9

Punctuation: Q1-Ex. 13, Q2-Ex. 14, Q3-Ex. 15, Q4-Ex. 16, Q5-Ex. 17, Q6-Ex. 18

Usage and Expression: Q1-Ex. 20, Q2-Ex. 22, Q3-Ex. 22, Q4-Ex. 23, Q5-Ex. 24, Q7-Ex. 26, Q8-Ex. 27, Q9-Ex. 28, Q10-Ex. 20

Total

Introduction • Preparation and Practice for the ITBS, SAT-9, and TerraNova • Grade 2

© McGraw-Hill School Division

STUDENT INTRODUCTION

What is the ITBS?

The Iowa Tests of Basic Skills (ITBS) is a multiple-choice test that helps you and your teacher find out how much you have learned in school so far. Now's your chance to show off what you know about reading and writing!

> This may be the first time students are preparing to take a standardized test. Explain to them that test-taking does not have to be a stressful experience. Instead, it is an opportunity for them to demonstrate what they have learned in reading and writing. Emphasize to students that this workbook will allow them to practice these skills so that each of them will do his or her best on the ITBS.

> Instilling a positive attitude about test-taking in students from the beginning will help them get more out of the practice exercises and approach the ITBS with confidence.

Does the ITBS measure how smart I am?

No, definitely not. The ITBS tests how well you can use the skills you've learned in class.

> Ease test-taking anxiety by assuring students that the ITBS *does not* measure their intelligence. Instead, it measures their ability to use the skills that they have learned in school.

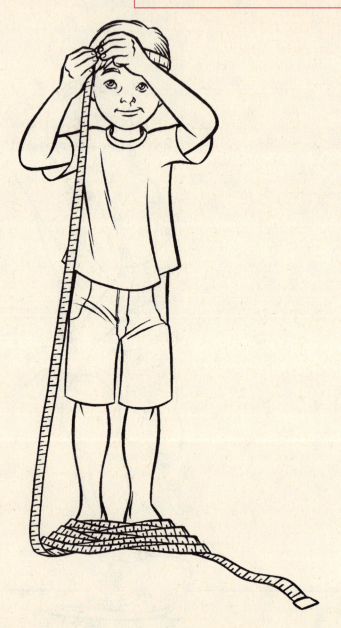

Can I study for the ITBS?

You can answer practice questions. You can also learn some tips that will help you do your best.

Just like riding a bike or playing the violin, studying for the ITBS takes practice. The more you practice, the better you will do!

Remind students that the ITBS measures what they have been learning in school. Instead of studying for the exam, students need to review the concepts that they have learned in school and learn some test-taking tips. The exercises and activities in this workbook are designed to provide such practice. To emphasize this point, have students discuss how practicing leads to improvement. For example, ask students to name several activities (e.g., sports, music, art) in which they participate. Then, ask them to discuss how they practice for these activities. Has practice helped them improve their skills? How?

Here's how you will practice for the ITBS:

✓ You'll take a Warm-Up Test.

✓ You'll brush up on your reading and writing skills in On Your Mark! Get Set! Go!

✓ You'll take a Mini-Practice Test. After all of your practicing, you'll know exactly what to expect when you take the real ITBS.

> Let students know that they'll be completing these book sections over an extended period of time so that they do not feel overwhelmed.

Practice Like a Superstar

Ask questions. Ask your teacher if you don't understand why an answer is wrong.

Learn from your mistakes. Notice the things you have trouble with, and find out how to answer the questions correctly.

Read as much as you can. Read everything and anything you can get your hands on. Read signs as you pass by them. Read stories aloud. Listen to others read stories aloud to you.

Answering questions incorrectly can be as valuable as answering questions correctly in preparing for a standardized test. Make sure students understand that it is okay to make mistakes. The important thing is to learn from their mistakes.

Pay Attention to the Directions

The directions tell you how to answer the question. Sometimes you will read directions on your own. Other times, the teacher will read them to you. Always make sure you understand the directions.

> Reinforce the importance of listening to all directions carefully. The directions will often provide important information about how to answer the questions.

Read Questions and Answer Choices Slowly and Carefully

Always read all the words in the questions and all the words in the answer choices carefully. Read every answer choice, even if you think you already found the correct answer!

Let students in on a little secret: Standardized tests often contain answer choices that are designed to distract the students from the correct answer. Therefore, students need to read and compare all of the answer choices in order to figure out which is the best choice.

Get Rid of the Wrong Answer Choices First

✓ Every time you answer a question, read each answer choice, one by one.

✓ After you read each answer choice, decide whether you think the answer choice is right or wrong.

✓ If you still have more than one answer choice left over, guess! Try not to leave a question blank.

Process of elimination is one of the most important strategies students can use to increase their success on standardized tests. You may want to illustrate this concept by playing some sort of guessing game with students. For example, write down four things (e.g., types of sports) on index cards. Share the items with students, and then have one student choose one card. Ask the rest of the class to guess the chosen card. Keep track of the number of guesses. Repeat the game with three cards, two cards, and finally, one card. This should illustrate to students how the chances of guessing correctly increase as the number of choices decreases.

Watch Yourself

Don't spend too much time on one question.

Going too slowly is no good—you'll leave more questions blank than you need to.

Don't rush through the test.

Going too quickly is no good, either—you'll only make silly mistakes, like misunderstanding the directions.

The ITBS is not a timed for second graders, but it will be timed for older grades. Therefore, it is important to reinforce to students the importance of working carefully and efficiently. They should try to answer each question. However, they shouldn't spend too much time answering a question that is difficult for them. This might prevent them from reaching questions that they can answer correctly.

Mark Your Answer Choices Correctly

When you find the answer to a question, fill in the bubble that goes with the answer choice you have found.

 Do NOT fill in half of the bubble. This is wrong.

 Do NOT place a checkmark over the bubble. This is wrong.

 Do NOT scribble inside the bubble. This is wrong.

 DO fill in the bubble completely. This is correct!

Now you try filling in the bubble correctly.

On the test, how should you fill in the bubble?
○ You should fill in half of the bubble.
○ You should scribble inside the bubble.
○ You should completely fill in the bubble.

Explain to students that it is important to fill in the bubbles correctly so that they get credit for their correct answers. Because a machine scores the test, it will not be able to read bubbles that are only partially filled.

Warm-Up Test

📣 *Each of the stories in questions 1 through 5 contains a mistake in punctuation or capitalization. Read the stories to yourself as I read them aloud to you. For each story, fill in the bubble next to the part of the story that contains a mistake in punctuation or capitalization.*

Warm-Up Test

Read each story from the Pupil's Edition page aloud, pausing between questions for students to mark their answers.

1. ○ Tell me if the pants
   ○ are too small. I can
   ● get you another pair

   A period goes at the end of a sentence.

2. ○ Don't forget to put the
   ● ice tray away. you don't
   ○ want it to melt again!

3. ○ The peaches on that tree
   ● are new. I think that bert's
   ○ sister will pick them tomorrow.

   The first letter of a proper noun is always capitalized.

4. ○ I have piano lessons on
   ● tuesday. I can't come
   ○ over for dinner that night.

   The days of the week are always capitalized.

5. ○ The wind was so bad last
   ○ night that three trees fell
   ● down on baker Street.

   Names of streets are always capitalized.

6.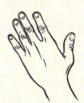

   h_nd

   ● a
   ○ o
   ○ i

   📣 *Now look at the picture of a hand in question 6. Fill in the bubble next to the letter that completes the word hand.*

7. ● Was there some moneys
   ○ in the drawer? I think
   ○ I left it there last week.

   📣 *Now look at question 7. Read the story to yourself while I read it aloud. Fill in the bubble next to the part of the story that has a mistake in the use of a word.*

GO ON ➡

> Each of the stories in questions 8 through 11 contains a mistake in punctuation, capitalization, or the use of a word. Read the stories to yourself as I read them aloud to you. For each story, fill in the bubble next to the part of the story that contains a mistake. Let's look at question 8.

Warm-Up Test

8 ● The path were full of
○ horses and bikes. We
○ walked around them.

> *Path* is singular, so *was* agrees with it.

9 ○ I liked my teacher this
○ year a lot, but my favorite
● is still mr. Washburn.

> *Mr.* is a title and should be capitalized.

10 ● BJ told me to read this
○ book carefully so that I
○ do not miss the funny parts.

> Place periods after letters in an abbreviation.

11 ○ I need to be done by
● May 5 2001. That is the
○ date that my report is due.

> Place a comma between the day and year.

12 ○ girl
● part
○ port

> Look at question 12. Fill in the bubble next to the word that contains the same vowel sound as the word *car* . . . *car*.

13 ● The gift will be waiting
○ on the steps when I
○ got home yesterday.

> *Yesterday* is a clue that a past tense verb is needed.

14 ● I goed outside to enjoy
○ the sun. I think it is
○ going to rain tomorrow.

> *Went* is the past tense of *go*.

15 ○ Tell me if you like this
● kind of cake. I don't never
○ have to make it again.

> Avoid double negatives.

> Each story in questions 13 through 15 contains a mistake in the use of one or more words. Read the stories to yourself while I read them aloud. Fill in the bubble next to the part of the story that has a mistake.

Warm-Up Test

> Look at question 16. The word in the shaded box is quick. Fill in the bubble next to the ending that can be added to quick to make it a new word.

16 quick
- ○ able
- ○ ful
- ● ly

17
- ● Me and Tabitha both
- ○ collect stamps. Sometimes
- ○ we trade with each other.

> Look at question 17. Read the story to yourself while I read it aloud. Fill in the bubble next to the part of the story that has a mistake in the use of a word.

> Look at question 18. Fill in the bubble next to the word that contains a silent letter. Pale is the best choice for this item. Technically the e in pale is not considered silent because of its role in forming the long /a/ sound.

18
- ● pale
- ○ loop
- ○ open

19
- ● It is most darkest if I
- ○ turn off the bathroom
- ○ light and the one outside.

Do not need *most* with *darkest*

20
- ○ I leaned over the rail.
- ○ Pam saw the edge and said,
- ● I don't think I can look.

Need quotation marks for direct quote

> Each story in question 18 and 19 contains a mistake. Read the stories to yourself while I read them aloud. Fill in the bubble next to the part of the story that has a mistake.

GO ON →

Warm-Up Test

> Look at question 23. Read the story to yourself while I read it aloud. Fill in the bubble next to the part of the story that has a mistake in the use of a word.

21 ● week
    ○ late
    ○ for

> Look at question 21. Fill in the bubble next to the word that has the same vowel sound as the word leaf . . . leaf.

22 ○ great
    ○ gap
    ● gym

> Look at question 22. Fill in the bubble next to the word that has the same beginning sound as the word jump . . . jump.

23 ● This here hat looks
    ○ like it will fit. You can
    ○ wear it to the park.

24 ● tradeing
    ○ cards
    ○ bench

> Look at question 24. Which of the words is spelled wrong? Fill in the bubble next to the word that is misspelled.

Warm-Up Test

25 ○

●

○

> Look at question 25. Listen carefully as I read a story to you: Melinda was enjoying her weekend. She had gone to the park, watched a movie, and written a letter to a friend. Now look at the three pictures. Fill in the bubble next to the picture that shows something Melinda did on the weekend.

26 ● eyes
○ look
○ see

> Look at question 26. Fill in the bubble next to the word that is different from the other two.

27 ● elephant
○ grape
○ pace

> Look at question 27. Fill in the bubble next to the word that makes an /f/ sound.

On Your Mark, Get Set, Go!

Exercise 1
END MARKS

 Go over each type of end mark with your students.

On the board, write several sentences and ask students to choose the end mark for each. Some sentences you might use are:

- *I want a dog(.)*
- *Go to the store(.)*
- *What are you doing(?)*
- *Oh my goodness(!)*

Discuss with students how they decided on the end marks. For example, how did they know where to put a question mark? Answer any questions students have.

 Go over the example question as a class.

Exercise 1

ON YOUR MARK!
End Marks

A **statement** is a sentence that tells something. It ends with a period.

I have to go home.

A **command** is a sentence that tells someone to do something. It also ends with a period.

Please shut the door.

A **question** is a sentence that asks something. It ends with a question mark.

What time is it?

An **exclamation** is a sentence that shows strong feeling. It ends with an exclamation mark.

What a great time I had!

 GET SET!

Let's look at an example.

Find the punctuation error in the example below.

○ Do you know where
○ Cara went She was in the
○ kitchen a minute ago.

(2nd) is **correct!** This line is missing a question mark. A question mark must come at the end of a sentence that asks something. A question mark belongs after *went*. Do you know where Cara went?

TEACHING TIP

As extra practice with end marks, create a worksheet with several different sentences. Don't include the end marks. Make sure the worksheet contains statements, commands, questions, and exclamations. Have students insert the end marks for homework or extra credit.

GO!

1. ○ There is a meeting after
   ○ school today. We need to
   ● go to the big classroom

2. ● Wait Don't touch the
   ○ seat yet. I don't think
   ○ the paint is dry.

3. ○ Is there a note on the
   ● door Maybe that will
   ○ tell us where Fran went.

4. ○ I asked Amira about
   ● the race She said that the
   ○ winner will get a goldfish.

5. ● Why is school
   ○ closed today? Did
   ○ we have a snowstorm

6. ○ The window is very
   ○ big. I can see all the
   ● way across the lake

7. ● Stop Always look
   ○ both ways before
   ○ you cross the street.

8. ○ Marty cleaned off
   ○ the table. Now we
   ● can start to set it

 Go over each question on this page as a class.

Each of the stories in questions 1 through 8 contains a mistake in punctuation. Read the stories to yourself as I read them aloud to you. For each story, fill in the bubble next to the part of the story that contains a mistake in punctuation. Let's look at question 1.

(Read each story from the Pupil Edition page aloud, pausing between questions for students to mark their answers.)

Questions 1, 4, 6, and 8

Period—Statement

Questions 2 and 7

Exclamation Mark—Exclamation

Questions 3 and 5

Question Mark—Question

On this page, questions 2 and 7 might also be considered commands with periods needed. Remind students that, for the purposes of this test section, they will only need to identify where punctuation is needed. They will not be asked to provide the punctuation.

Exercise 2
CAPITALIZING BEGINNING OF A SENTENCE

 Go over the sentence capitalization rule with your students.

Explain that a sentence is a complete idea. On the board, write some complete sentences and some incomplete sentences. Ask students to tell you which should be capitalized. Some examples you might use are:

- *dogs are cute animals*
- *cute animals*
- *it is a rainy day*
- *sunny days*
- *she went to the park*
- *to the ballgame*

Discuss with students how they decided which sentences were complete and needed a capital letter. Answer any questions students have.

 Go over the example question as a class.

Exercise 2
 ON YOUR MARK!
Capitalizing the Beginning of a Sentence

A **sentence** is a set of words that tells a complete idea.
 I walk in the park.

If words do not tell a complete idea, they are not a sentence.
 in the park

A sentence always begins with a **capital letter**. A capital letter means the start of a new idea.
 Are you ready? I want to go out. It is so warm and sunny!

 GET SET!
Let's look at an example.

Find the capitalization error in the example below.
○ I want to use the yellow
○ mug. it is pretty and has
○ lots of gold stars on it.

(2nd) is **correct!** There is an error in the second line. The word *it* begins a sentence. *It* must be capitalized.

 ### EXTRA ACTIVITY

To give students more practice with capitalizing sentences, write a paragraph or two containing several sentences on the board. Include some capitalization errors at the beginning of some sentences. Have students come up to the board and circle the capitalization errors.

 Go over each question on this page as a class.

Each of the stories in questions 1 through 8 contains a mistake in capitalization. Read the stories to yourself as I read them aloud to you. For each story, fill in the bubble next to the part of the story that contains a mistake in capitalization. Let's look at question 1.

(Read each story from the Pupil Edition page aloud, pausing between questions for students to mark their answers.)

Explain to students that the first letter immediately following a period, question mark, or exclamation mark will always be capitalized.

Question 1
My
Question 2
Follow
Question 3
Dad
Question 4
This
Question 5
The
Question 6
It's
Question 7
Let's
Question 8
We

Exercise 3

CAPITALIZING THE NAMES OF PEOPLE

 Go over the difference between common and proper nouns with your students.

Discuss how these types of nouns are used when referring to people.

Explain that a common noun refers to a general person:

- *boy*
- *girl*
- *aunt*

Explain that a proper noun refers to a specific person:

- *Juan*
- *Sarah*
- *Aunt Bessie*

A common noun, such as *girl*, can refer to any girl, so it is not capitalized. A proper noun, on the other hand, such as *Sarah*, is capitalized because it refers to a particular girl.

 TEACHING TIP

Make sure students understand that *I* is always capitalized.

 Go over the example question as a class.

Exercise 3

 ON YOUR MARK!

Capitalizing Names of People

A **common noun** is a general name for a person, place, or thing. Common nouns are <u>not</u> capitalized.

A **proper noun** is the name of a specific person, place, or thing. Proper nouns are always capitalized.

The word *David* is the name of a specific person. It is always capitalized.

The pronoun *I* is not a proper noun, but it is always capitalized.

You and I will go to the playground at recess.

 GET SET!

Let's look at an example.

Find the capitalization error.
○ The oatmeal cookies
○ were baked by
○ gregory's sister.

(3rd) is **correct!** There is an error in this line. The word *Gregory's* is a proper noun. It must be capitalized.

 EXTRA ACTIVITY

Make a worksheet with a list of several "people" nouns and hand it out to your class. Do not capitalize the proper nouns. Have students write "common" or "proper" next to each noun. Then have them fix the capitalization mistakes for each proper noun.

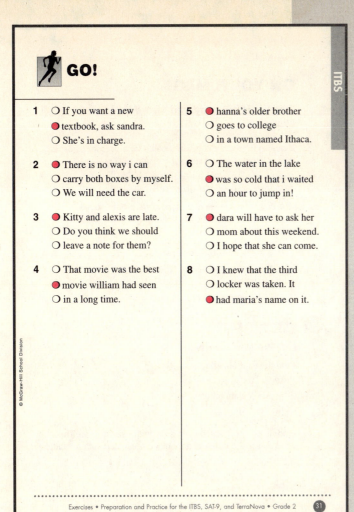

GO!

1. ○ If you want a new
   ● textbook, ask sandra.
   ○ She's in charge.

2. ● There is no way i can
   ○ carry both boxes by myself.
   ○ We will need the car.

3. ● Kitty and alexis are late.
   ○ Do you think we should
   ○ leave a note for them?

4. ○ That movie was the best
   ● movie william had seen
   ○ in a long time.

5. ● hanna's older brother
   ○ goes to college
   ○ in a town named Ithaca.

6. ○ The water in the lake
   ● was so cold that i waited
   ○ an hour to jump in!

7. ● dara will have to ask her
   ○ mom about this weekend.
   ○ I hope that she can come.

8. ○ I knew that the third
   ○ locker was taken. It
   ● had maria's name on it.

 Go over each question on this page as a class.

Each of the stories in questions 1 through 8 contains a mistake in capitalization. Read the stories to yourself as I read them aloud to you. For each story, fill in the bubble next to the part of the story that contains a mistake in capitalization. Let's look at question 1.

(Read each story from the Pupil Edition page aloud, pausing between questions for students to mark their answers.)

Question 1
Sandra

Question 2
I

Question 3
Alexis

Question 4
William

Question 5
Hanna's

Question 6
I

Question 7
Dara

Question 8
Maria's

Exercise 4
CAPITALIZING DAYS OF THE WEEK AND MONTHS

 Go over the difference between common and proper nouns with your students.

Discuss how these types of nouns are used when referring to months and days.

Explain that a common noun refers to a general time. The words *month* and *day* are not capitalized because they are not referring to a particular time. For example:

- I plan to go on vacation for a month. I will leave on a sunny day.

Explain that a proper noun refers to a specific day or month and therefore must be capitalized. For example:

- I plan to go on vacation next June. I will leave on the first Saturday.

 Go over the example question as a class.

Exercise 4

 ## ON YOUR MARK!
Capitalizing Days of the Week and Months

A **common noun** is a general name for a person, place, or thing. Common nouns are <u>not</u> capitalized.

A **proper noun** is the name of a specific person, place, or thing. Proper nouns are always capitalized.

The *days of the week* and *months* are proper nouns because they name specific things. They must begin with a capital letter.

> I go to the zoo on **Tuesdays**.
> In **November**, we have a birthday party for my grandmother.
> On **Saturday** he painted our house.

 ### GET SET!
Let's look at an example.

Find the capitalization error.
○ We are going on a trip
○ in july. We are bringing
○ the dog with us.

(2nd) is **correct!** There is an error in the second line. The word *July* is the name of a month. It must start with a capital letter.

 ### TEACHING TIP

Write the names of all of the days of the week and all of the months of the year on the board. Make sure students are familiar with each of them. For extra practice, have students write a short paragraph about their favorite day of the week or month of the year. Check their paragraphs for capitalization mistakes.

GO!

1. ○ If we get our homework
   ○ done, we can rent a movie
   ● and make popcorn on friday.

2. ○ My favorite day of the
   ● week is sunday. I like
   ○ to eat a big breakfast.

3. ○ This month is always busy
   ○ in my mom's office. I will
   ● be glad when april is over.

4. ○ The pool stays open late
   ○ during the summer. In
   ● september it closes early.

5. ○ This year my birthday is
   ● on a wednesday. I wish I
   ○ didn't have to go to school.

6. ● In october, my aunt
   ○ always takes me to pick
   ○ apples and pumpkins.

7. ○ I need to finish the book
   ● by monday. Then I can
   ○ start writing my report.

8. ○ Where I live, the coldest
   ● month is january. It costs
   ○ a lot to heat the house.

Exercises • Preparation and Practice for the ITBS, SAT-9, and TerraNova • Grade 2

 Go over each question on this page as a class.

Each of the stories in questions 1 through 8 contains a mistake in capitalization. Read the stories to yourself as I read them aloud to you. For each story, fill in the bubble next to the part of the story that contains a mistake in capitalization. Let's look at question 1.

(Read each story from the Pupil Edition page aloud, pausing between questions for students to mark their answers.)

Have students pay careful attention to questions 2 and 3. In question 2, the word *day* is not capitalized because it is a common noun. The mistake is in the second line. *Sunday* should be capitalized because it is a specific day of the week. In question 3, the word *month* is not capitalized because it is a common noun. The mistake is in the third line. *April* should be capitalized because it is a specific month.

Exercise 5

CAPITALIZING PLACES

 Go over the difference between common and proper nouns with your students.

Discuss how these types of nouns are used when referring to places.

Explain that a common noun refers to a general place and should not be capitalized. For example:

- street
- city
- country
- island
- avenue
- state

Explain that a proper noun refers to a specific place and therefore must be capitalized. For example:

- Puritan Street
- Hollywood
- France
- Ellis Island
- Bennaville Avenue
- Florida

A common noun, such as *state*, can refer to any state, so it is not capitalized. A proper noun, on the other hand, such as *Florida*, is capitalized because it refers to a particular state.

 Go over the example question as a class.

Exercise 5

 ON YOUR MARK!

Capitalizing Places

A **common noun** is a general name for a person, place, or thing. Common nouns are <u>not</u> capitalized.

A **proper noun** is the name of a specific person, place, or thing. Proper nouns are always capitalized.

Streets, cities, and countries are all proper nouns. They must start with a capital letter.

> My favorite doctor works on **Trolley Street**.
> There are very tall buildings in **New York City**.
> We go to **Holland** every summer.

TIP: If a proper noun contains more than one word, all the major words are capitalized. For example, the United States of America

  GET SET!

Let's look at an example.

Find the capitalization error.
○ My brother is visiting
○ new orleans. He is
○ at a big music concert.

(2nd) is **correct!** There is an error in the second line. *New Orleans* is a proper noun. It must be capitalized.

TEACHING TIP

Emphasize the tip box on the Pupil Edition page. Write more examples on the board. Some examples include:

- *United Kingdom*
- *District of Columbia*
- *Republic of Congo*

GO!

1. ○ If we have enough time
   ○ this winter, my mom
   ● said we will go to maine.

2. ● maryland usually doesn't
   ○ get much snow, so we
   ○ were surprised this winter.

3. ○ I've never gone on
   ○ an airplane, so I have
   ● never been to hawaii.

4. ○ I would rather go
   ● to the virgin islands
   ○ where it will be warm.

5. ○ You will probably pass
   ● pickford Street on the
   ○ way to the mall.

6. ● There is a hill on jackson
   ○ Avenue. It is very hard to
   ○ get up it on a bike.

7. ○ This summer my sister
   ● is going to chile to teach
   ○ English and travel, too.

8. ○ There is block party this
   ○ weekend to celebrate
   ● summer. It's on dore Drive.

 Go over each question on this page as a class.

 Each of the stories in questions 1 through 8 contains a mistake in capitalization. Read the stories to yourself as I read them aloud to you. For each story, fill in the bubble next to the part of the story that contains a mistake in capitalization. Let's look at question 1.

(Read each story from the Pupil Edition page aloud, pausing between questions for students to mark their answers.)

To help students recognize proper nouns that refer to places, it might be useful to make a list of states, familiar cities, and so on, and hand it out to your class. Looking at maps and pointing out the capitalization of specific places might also help.

Exercise 6
VOWELS

 Go over the difference between long vowels and short vowels with your students.

Explain that vowels are considered "long" or "short" on the basis of their sound.

Have students look at the list in the middle of the Pupil's Edition page that compares short and long vowels sounds. Have one student say *cat* out loud. Then have another student say *cave*. Discuss how the two sounds are different, even though they contain the same vowel. Follow this routine for the rest of the words listed.

 TEACHING TIP

Make sure students understand that a silent /e/ often comes at the end of a word with a long vowel sound.

 Go over the example question as a class.

Exercise 6

 ON YOUR MARK!
Vowels

The letters *a*, *e*, *i*, *o*, and *u* are called **vowels**. We call vowels *long* or *short* depending on how we say them.
Long vowels sound like we say them in the alphabet.
  c*a*ve, w*e*, d*i*ve, n*o*te, fl*u*te
Look at the words above again. Notice how many words with long vowels in them end with an *e* that is silent.
  cav*e*, div*e*, not*e*, flut*e*
Short vowels do not sound like we say them in the alphabet. Compare the word pairs below to hear the difference.

Short:	c*a*t	w*e*t	b*i*t	m*o*p	s*u*nk
Long:	c*a*ve	w*e*	d*i*ve	n*o*te	fl*u*te

 GET SET!
Let's look at an example.
Which word has the same vowel sound as the word *set*?
○ wave
○ nest
○ feet

(1st) is **wrong**. *Set* has a short *e* sound, but *wave* has a long *a* sound.
(2nd) is **correct!** *Nest* and *set* both have a short *e* sound.
(3rd) is **wrong**. *Feet* has a long *e* sound, but *set* has a short *e* sound.

  EXTRA ACTIVITY

Here are some more words you can write on the board to demonstrate the difference between long and short vowel sounds. Have students read the words aloud.

- *bin*   *bite*
- *rat*   *rate*
- *met*   *me*
- *rod*   *rode*
- *bun*   *dune*

GO!

1. ● came
   ○ looked
   ○ left

2. ○ would
   ○ like
   ● late

3. ● sell
   ○ very
   ○ white

4. ● feel
   ○ high
   ○ places

5.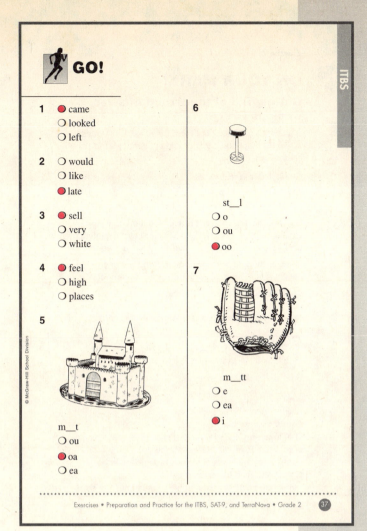
   m__t
   ○ ou
   ● oa
   ○ ea

6. st__l
   ○ o
   ○ ou
   ● oo

7. m__tt
   ○ e
   ○ ea
   ● i

Go over each question on this page as a class.

Question 1
Look at question 1. Fill in the bubble next to the word with the same vowel sound as date.

Question 2
Look at question 2. Fill in the bubble next to the word with the same vowel sound as cape.

Question 3
Look at question 3. Fill in the bubble next to the word with the same vowel sound as bell.

Question 4
Look at question 4. Fill in the bubble next to the word with the same vowel sound as meal.

Question 5
Look at the picture of the moat in question 5. Fill in the bubble next to the letters that complete the word moat.

Question 6
Look at the picture of the stool in question 6. Fill in the bubble next to the letter or letters that complete the word stool.

Question 7
Look at the picture of the mitt in question 7. Fill in the bubble next to the letter or letters that complete the word mitt.

Exercise 7

GETTING RID OF THE WRONG ANSWER CHOICES FIRST

 Explain to students that ruling out wrong answers is an important test-taking skill.

Have students read the top section of the Pupil Edition page or read it aloud to them. Point out that ruling out wrong answers will help them do the following:

- Move through the test more quickly
- Increase their chances of finding the correct answer
- Score higher on the test

By getting rid of wrong answer choices, students will feel more confident that the answer they choose is the best answer.

 Go over the example question as a class. Have students raise their hands and explain why each answer choice is correct or incorrect.

Exercise 7

 ON YOUR MARK!
Getting Rid of the Wrong Answer Choices First

Sometimes you might not know the answer to a question. When this happens, try to get rid of as many wrong answer choices you can.

○ The beach is really fun,
○ but sometimes I like to
● swim in candice's pool.

Look at the 1st answer choice. Are there any capitalization errors? No. The first word of the sentence is capitalized, as it should be. Get rid of this answer choice.

Look at the 2nd answer choice. Are there any capitalization errors? No. Get rid of this answer choice.

Look at the 3rd answer choice. Are there any capitalization errors? Yes! *Candice* is a specific name, so it should be capitalized. This answer choice is correct!

 GET SET!
Let's look at an example.

Find the capitalization error.
○ My best friend, Anna, is
○ moving to the other side
● of town next may.

(1st) is **wrong.** Every word that should be capitalized is capitalized. Rule this answer choice out.
(2nd) is **wrong.** None of these words needs to be capitalized. Rule this answer out.
(3rd) is **correct!** *May* is a proper noun. It must be capitalized.

  EXTRA ACTIVITY

Play *Twenty Questions* with your students to help them understand the importance of ruling out wrong answers. Have one student think of a famous person. The other students can raise their hand and ask "yes" or "no" questions about the famous person until they find out the correct answer. By doing so, students will begin to understand how ruling out wrong answers leads them closer to the correct answer. For example, if a student asks: "Is it a boy?" and the answer is "no," then the next student will know not to guess a famous male. They are one step closer to determining the correct answer.

GO!

1. ● Hurry Pick up
   ○ your toys before
   ○ our mom gets home.

2. ● Talia lent me this book.
   ○ she thinks that I will like
   ○ the part about the class trip.

3. ○ My mom always reads
   ● the newspaper, and i like
   ○ to look at the comics.

4. ○ The car isn't ready yet.
   ○ We can pick it up on the
   ● way home on thursday.

5. ○ Those tomatoes are very
   ○ sweet. They are from
   ● the country of israel.

6.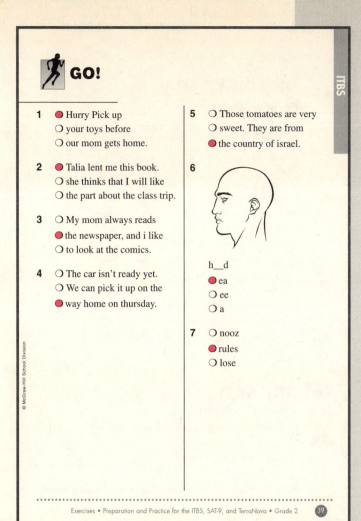

   h__d
   ● ea
   ○ ee
   ○ a

7. ○ nooz
   ● rules
   ○ lose

 Go over each question on this page as a class.

This page tests skills that students learned in Exercises 1 through 6. Students should try to get rid of wrong answer choices as they work through questions 1 through 7.

📣 *Look at questions 1 through 7. Fill in the bubble next to the answer you choose.*

Question 1

📣 *Find the punctuation error in question 1.*

Questions 2, 3, 4, and 5

📣 *Look at questions 2 through 5. Find the capitalization errors.*

Question 6

📣 *Look at the picture of the head in question 6. Fill in the bubble next to the letter or letters that complete the word head.*

Question 7

📣 *Look at question 7. Fill in the bubble next to the word with the same sound as tools.*

Exercise 8
FORMING PLURALS

 Go over each rule for forming plurals with your students.

Write some singular words on the board and have students use the rules to make them plural. Some examples you might use are:

- chicken
- shelf
- canary
- half
- life
- goose

Talk to your students about how they decided on the plurals of these words. How did they know whether to add -s, -es, -ies, or to change the spellings of the word? How did they know when to change an *f* to a *v*?

 Go over the example question as a class.

 ## ON YOUR MARK!
Forming Plurals

One person, place, or thing is a **singular noun**. More than one person, place, or thing is a **plural noun**.

Add an *-s* or an *-es* to most singular nouns to form a plural noun.

  river + s = rivers
  dish + es = dishes

When a noun ends in a *consonant* and *y*, change the *y* to *i* and add *-es* to form a plural noun.

  berry - y + i + es = berries

When a noun ends in *-f*, the *f* changes to a *v*.

  calf → calves
  wife → wives

Some nouns change their spelling to become plural nouns:

singular	plural
man	men
woman	women
foot	feet

 ### GET SET!
Let's look at an example.

Find the part of the story that has a mistake.
○ We spent all morning with my
○ mom in the yard. By lunch
○ we had whole pile of weedes.

(3rd) is **correct!** This line is wrong. The plural of *weed* is *weeds*.

 ### EXTRA ACTIVITY

Make a worksheet of several nouns. Have students change these nouns into their correct plural forms.

GO!

1. ○ There were so many
   ● flys in the yard that
   ○ I had to come inside.

2. ○ By the afternoon we
   ○ had collected enough
   ● leafs to jump into a pile.

3. ○ People say that cats have
   ● nine lifes. That is why they
   ○ can make scary jumps.

4. ● Four deers walked up to
   ○ the car as we were making
   ○ dinner near the tent.

5. ○ My dog, Tipper, always
   ● burys her bones in the
   ○ backyard near the pond.

6. ● Some blue birdes are very
   ○ hard to find. I have only
   ○ seen one in my life.

7. ○ We left the tigers to see
   ○ if we could find the
   ● area with all the ponys.

8. ○ Each person gets four
   ● trys. Does that sound
   ○ like a fair way to play?

 Go over each question on this page as a class.

Each of the stories in questions 1 through 8 contains a mistake in spelling. Read the stories to yourself as I read them aloud to you. For each story, fill in the bubble next to the part of the story that contains a misspelled word. Let's look at question 1.

(Read each story from the Pupil Edition page aloud, pausing between questions for students to mark their answers.)

Question 1
Fly ends in *y*, so students must drop the *ys* and add *-ies*.

Question 2
Plural is formed by dropping the *fs* and adding *-ves*.

Question 3
Plural is formed by dropping the *fs* and adding *-ves*.

Question 4
Deer stays the same in singular and plural form.

Question 5
Point out to students that the spelling mistake in question 5 involves a verb, not a noun. Make sure they understand that the same spelling rules apply to both verbs and nouns.

Question 6
Add *-s* to bird

Questions 7 and 8
Questions seven and eight follow the same rule as question one: drop the *ys* and add *-ies*.

Exercise 9
SUBJECTS AND VERBS

 Go over singular and plural subjects and singular and plural verbs with your class.

Tell students that these parts of the sentence need to match up; if there is a singular subject, the sentence must have a singular verb and vice versa.

Write several subjects and verbs on the board, mixing up the verb agreement. Some examples you might use are:

- *Mike walk down the street.*
- *Many people calls out my name.*
- *Several cats walks into the store.*
- *I are all right.*

Have students correct these sentences and discuss with them why they were incorrect to begin with. If students have any questions about how to make the subjects and verbs agree, now is a good time to answer them. Tell students that a lot of noun-verb agreement is about training their ears in order to know what sounds right.

 Go over the example question as a class.

Exercise 9

 ON YOUR MARK!
Subjects and Verbs

The **subject** of a sentence tells who or what does something.
  Ryan asks a question.

An **action verb** tells what someone or something is doing.
  *Ryan **asks** a question.*

The subject and the verb in a sentence must agree. That means a singular subject must take a singular verb, and a plural subject must take a plural verb.

Singular subjects are subjects that tell about one person or thing. Just add *-s* or *-es* to the verb to make the singular verb form.

  Singular verb: listen + s   She **listens** to him.

Plural subjects are subjects that tell about more than one person or thing. Add nothing to a present tense verb to make the plural verb form.

  Plural verb: listen   The kids **listen** to him.

 GET SET!
Let's look at an example.

Find the part of the sentence where a word is used incorrectly.
 I likes to eat my cereal
 with blueberries, milk,
○ and bananas.

(1st) is **correct!** The first line has an error in it. The verb *likes* does not agree with the subject *I*. A singular subject, *I*, must have a singular verb, *like*.

★ EXTRA ACTIVITY

Have each student pair up with another student. Have the first student come up with one singular and one plural noun. Have the second student supply singular or plural verbs that agree with the nouns given by the first student.

GO!

1. ● You sets the alarm
   ○ wrong. I was late to
   ○ ballet class yesterday.

2. ○ I put the boxes in the
   ● yard. They is next to
   ○ the bird house.

3. ○ We can have dinner
   ○ before the movie.
   ● There are plenty of time.

4. ○ The vases are full of
   ● lowers. Now we needs
   ○ to get some water.

5. ○ The teacher is ready.
   ○ The most exciting
   ● class begin now.

6. ○ Aunt Lanni and Uncle Tim
   ○ are on their way over.
   ● They always brings gifts.

7. ● The bananas turns
   ○ brown if we
   ○ do not eat them.

8. ● I are learning to sew.
   ○ I want to make a scarf
   ○ for Mom's birthday.

Go over each question on this page as a class.

Each of the stories in questions 1 through 8 contains a mistake in the use of a word. Read the stories to yourself as I read them aloud to you. For each story, fill in the bubble next to the part of the story that contains a mistake. Let's look at question 1.

(Read each story from the Pupil Edition page aloud, pausing between questions for students to mark their answers.)

Question 1

You is singular, so the verb should be *set*.

Question 2

They is plural, so the verb should be *are*, not *is*.

Question 3

There is plenty of time.

Question 4

We is plural, so the verb should be *need*, not *needs*.

Question 5

The word is *class*, not *classes*, so it is singular—*begins*, not *begin*.

Question 6

They is plural, so the verb should be *bring*, not *brings*.

Question 7

Bananas is plural, so the verb should be *turn*, not *turns*.

Question 8

I is never used with a plural verb.

Exercise 10
CAPITALIZING TERMS OF RESPECT

 Go over the terms of respect on this page with your students.

Write some of these terms on the board without capitalizing them. Some examples you might include are:

- *I am going to dr. Parker's office later toay.*
- *Have you seen ms. Brown lately?*
- *Mother and mr. Martinez had lunch today.*
- *Mr. Jefferson and Ms. Haversham are my favorites.* (No mistake)

 Go over the example question as a class.

 Exercise 10
ON YOUR MARK!
Capitalizing Terms of Respect

Some names have special titles to show respect. **Terms of respect** are always capitalized.

*I am going see **Dr.** Kraskow today.*

Other terms of respect include: Ms., Miss, Mrs., Jr., and Mr.

*I see **Ms.** Perkins in the window.*
*I like it when **Mr.** Roth gives me candy.*
***Miss** Laker and I are watching the dogs this afternoon.*
*Jamal and Rob, **Jr.**, are sitting in back.*

 GET SET!
Let's look at an example.

Find the capitalization error.
○ I am playing chess with
○ ms. Richter later. We
○ are meeting at the park.

(2nd) is **correct!** The second line has a mistake in it. *Ms.* is a term of respect. It must be capitalized.

 EXTRA ACTIVITY

Have students make a list of their favorite teachers, dentists, doctors, parents' friends, and so on, using the appropriate term of respect for each individual. Tell them to pay attention to capitalization as they write. Check their lists for correct use of capitalization in titles.

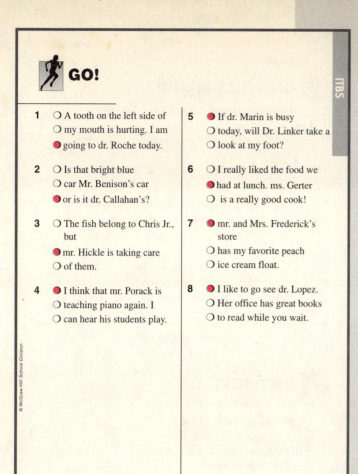

 Go over each question on this page as a class.

📣 *Each of the stories in questions 1 through 8 contains a mistake in capitalization. Read the stories to yourself as I read them aloud to you. For each story, fill in the bubble next to the part of the story that contains a mistake in capitalization. Let's look at question 1.*

(Read each story from the Pupil Edition page aloud, pausing between questions for students to mark their answers.)

Question 1
Dr. Roche

Question 2
Dr. Callahan's

Question 3
Mr. Hickle

Question 4
Mr. Porack

Question 5
Dr. Marin

Question 6
Ms. Gerter

Question 7
Mr. and Mrs. Frederick's

Question 8
Dr. Lopez

Exercise 11
ABBREVIATIONS

 Go over each of the abbreviations listed on the Pupil Edition page.

Make sure students notice that, in each case, all of the letters in the abbreviation are also in the longer word.

Write several abbreviations on the board, leaving out the periods and capital letters. Have students help you insert the correct punctuation and capitalization where necessary. Some examples you might use are:

- *Maple rd*
- *dr Smith*
- *Pete sr*
- *william j clinton*
- *b b King*
- *apt 4*

After the corrections have been made, have students tell you the longer way of spelling the more common abbreviations.

 Go over the example question with the class.

Exercise 11

 ON YOUR MARK!
Abbreviations

An **abbreviation** is a short way of writing a word. Abbreviations start with a capital letter and end with a period.

*The biggest tree in my neighborhood is on Paxton **Street**.*

or

*The biggest tree in my neighborhood is on Paxton **St**.*

Here are how some other words are abbreviated:

Junior → Jr.
Doctor → Dr.
Avenue → Ave.
Apartment → Apt.

Sometimes an abbreviation is for more than one word. In that case, each letter must be capitalized and end with a period.

Thomas John → T.J.
United States → U.S.

 GET SET!

Let's look at an example.

Find the punctuation error.
○ On Baker Ave there is
○ a yellow dog. It always
○ barks when I walk by.

(1st) is **correct!** The first line has a mistake. The abbreviation for *Avenue* is *Ave*. It must end in a period.

 EXTRA ACTIVITY

Tell students to look for abbreviations in picture books and stories. Have them bring the books and stories to class. Point out the abbreviations that the students found, and read a few of the stories to the class.

GO!

1. ○ I live at the corner of
   ● Burberry Dr and
   ○ Lansdowne Rd.

2. ● I went to NY with my
   ○ class. I have never seen
   ○ such tall buildings.

3. ○ I rang the doorbell for
   ● Apt 3 and nobody came
   ○ to the door. I'll try again.

4. ○ I have been playing
   ● with BJ and John Jr.
   ○ for seven years.

5. ○ My stepfather told
   ● me I cannot watch tv
   ○ after school any more.

6. ● Fern Dr runs all the way
   ○ around the lake. Fern Dr.
   ○ takes five minutes to walk.

7. ○ My family moved to
   ○ the third floor last year.
   ● Now we live in Apt 2.

Exercises • Preparation and Practice for the ITBS, SAT-9, and TerraNova • Grade 2   47

 Go over each question on this page as a class.

Each of the stories in questions 1 through 7 contains a mistake in punctuation. Read the stories to yourself as I read them aloud to you. For each story, fill in the bubble next to the part of the story that contains a mistake in punctuation. Let's look at question 1.

(Read each story from the Pupil Edition page aloud, pausing between questions for students to mark their answers.)

Question 1
Dr in this case represents *Drive* and needs a period.

Question 2
New York has been shortened to *NY*, so each word that has been shortened gets a period after it.

Question 3
Apartment has been shortened to *Apt,* so there should be a period after the *t*.

Question 4
B.J.

Question 5
Though *tv* is not a normal abbreviation (the proper shortened form is TV), students should note that the form used here is incorrect.

Question 6
Dr in this case represents *Drive* and needs a period.

Question 7
Apartment has been shortened to *Apt,* so there should be a period after the *t*.

Exercises • Preparation and Practice for the ITBS, SAT-9, and TerraNova • Grade 2   47

Exercise 12
PUNCTUATING DATES

 Go over the punctuation rules for writing dates with your class.

Write some more examples on the board to give students practice with this rule. Some sentences you might write are:

- *Opening day for fishing is going to be April 1 2001.*
- *I couldn't wait till that movie came out on December 12 2000.*
- *On January 15, 1989, my sister was born.* **(correct)**

Have students tell you which sentences are incorrect. Ask them to help you fix the errors.

 Go over the example question with the class.

Exercise 12

 ON YOUR MARK!

Punctuating Dates

A date must have a comma between the day and the year.
  I am having a birthday party on **May 20, 2001.**
  This milk is good until **January 1, 2002.**
  That building was built on **June 24, 1976.**
  My great-grandparents got married on **April 10, 1906.**

All of the dates in the box above have a comma between the day and the year.

 GET SET!

Let's look at an example.

Which part of the story has a mistake in it?
○ There is a garage sale
○ on April 4 2000. I am going
○ to look for baseball cards.

(2nd) is **correct!** The second line has a mistake in it. There must be a comma between the day, *April 4*, and the year, *2000*. *April 4, 2000.*

 EXTRA ACTIVITY

As practice for comma placement, have students write several of their favorite dates on a piece of paper—their birth date, dates of holidays, and so on. Make sure they are placing commas between the day and the year.

GO!

1. ○ The bridge
   ○ will be closed May 1, 2004
   ● to March 17 2005.

2. ○ The door said that the
   ○ building was built on
   ● March 10 1898.

3. ○ We will stay
   ● until January 1 2002
   ○ or February 1, 2002.

4. ○ The play was first shown
   ● on April 14 1954. My
   ○ mom saw it back then.

5. ○ If the house isn't done by
   ● November 1 2000, I will
   ○ have to stay with Grandma.

6. ○ Please visit me
   ○ on December 9, 2000 or
   ● December 10 2000.

7. ○ That store opened on
   ○ May 5, 1935 and closed
   ● April 17 1997.

8. ● On June 3 2002, I have
   ○ a party to go to. My
   ○ sister is graduating!

 Go over each question on this page as a class.

 Each of the stories in questions 1 through 8 contains a mistake in punctuation. Read the stories to yourself as I read them aloud to you. For each story, fill in the bubble next to the part of the story that contains a mistake in punctuation. Let's look at question 1.

(Read each story from the Pupil Edition page aloud, pausing between questions for students to mark their answers.)

For each question on this page, a comma is missing between the day and the year.

Exercise 13

VOWEL SOUNDS WITH THE LETTER *R*

 Go over the example words on the Pupil Edition page, demonstrating the different sounds.

Write some other words on the board and have students match these words with the corresponding word group on their page. Some words you might use are:

- *bar (car, star)*
- *tear (wear, bear)*
- *shirt (turn, bird, perfect)*
- *shore (store, torn)*

 Go over the example question as a class.

Exercise 13

 ON YOUR MARK!

Vowel Sounds with the Letter *R*

If the letter *r* comes after a vowel, the sound of the vowel changes.

For example:

- Some words that have an *r* after the letter *a* sound like the words *car* or *star*.
- Some words that have an *r* after the letter *o* sound like the words *store* or *torn*.
- Some words that have an *r* after the letters *i*, *u*, or *e* sound like the words *bird*, *turn*, or *perfect*.
- Words that have an *r* after the letters *ea* sometimes sound like the words *ear* or *fear*. Words with *ear* can also sound like *wear* or *bear*.

 GET SET!

Now let's try an example.

Which word has the same middle sound as the word <u>short</u>?
○ more
○ main
○ treat

(1st) is **correct!** The *or* in *more* sounds like the *or* in *short*.

(2nd) is **wrong.** The *ai* in *main* does not sound like the *or* in *short*.

(3rd) is **wrong.** The *ea* in *treat* does not sound like the *or* in *short*.

 EXTRA ACTIVITY

Have students come up with as many words as they can think of that have an *-r* after a vowel. Then have them group their words according to the different vowel sounds.

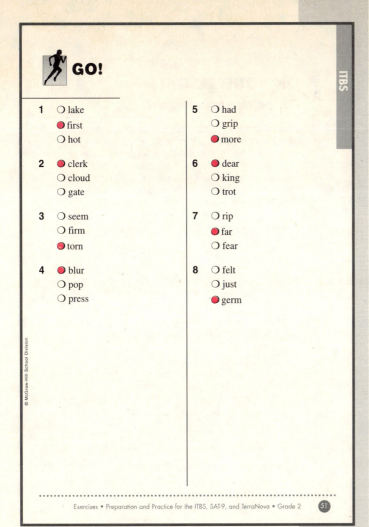

 Go over each question on this page as a class.

Question 1

📢 *Look at question 1. Fill in the bubble next to the word with the same vowel sound as turn.*

Question 2

📢 *Look at question 2. Fill in the bubble next to the word with the same vowel sound as word.*

Question 3

📢 *Look at question 3. Fill in the bubble next to the word with the same vowel sound as cord.*

Question 4

📢 *Look at question 4. Fill in the bubble next to the word with the same vowel sound as stir.*

Question 5

📢 *Look at question 5. Fill in the bubble next to the word with the same vowel sound as shore.*

Question 6

📢 *Look at question 6. Fill in the bubble next to the word with the same vowel sound as cheer.*

Question 7

📢 *Look at question 7. Fill in the bubble next to the word with the same vowel sound as star.*

Question 8

📢 *Look at question 8. Fill in the bubble next to the word with the same vowel sound as bird.*

Exercise 14
FIX THE MISTAKES YOURSELF

 It is important that students be able to correct mistakes in paragraphs.

Explain to students that if they fix mistakes in their head as they read through the ITBS, they will most likely improve their overall scores. Mistakes that are easy to find in a stand-alone sentence may be more difficult when hidden in a larger paragraph. Students must be able to read carefully to find these mistakes.

 Go over the example paragraph with the class, pointing out the errors:

- *Mr* needs a period
- *store* spelled incorrectly
- *goes* should be *go*
- *loafs* should be *loaves*
- comma between *Woo* and *Jr.*
- *jr* should be capitalized and followed by a period.
- comma after *Jr.*

Point out to students that the need for a comma between *Woo* and *Jr.* is not something that will be tested on the ITBS this year.

Exercise 14

 ON YOUR MARK!
Fix the Mistakes Yourself

When you take the ITBS, try correcting the errors you see as you read them. If you think about how you would write the words as you are reading them, you may be able to find the errors and correct them. This is especially helpful to you on punctuation questions, when errors might be so small they are hard to spot—like a missing period or an incorrectly placed comma.

GET SET!
Let's look at an example. Read the paragraph below.

> Mr Woo owns a stor down the street from our apartment. My mother and I goes there to buy loafs of bread if we run out. Sometimes his son, Paul Woo jr works behind the counter.

Now write the paragraph in the lines below. Try to correct the errors you see.

_____
_____
_____
_____
_____
_____
_____
_____

 EXTRA ACTIVITY

Write another short paragraph on the board and ask students to make corrections on it. An example paragraph you might use is:

I often see Ms Johnson out walking her dog. She goes very fast because her dog pull her along. She flys past dr Smith's office and keeps going down cherry street. We never even gets the chance to wave.

GO!

1. ○ It's our puppy's
   ○ birthday. He was born
   ● on February 11 2000.

2. ● I think that Seaside Ave
   ○ is the nicest area of town.
   ○ I like the trees there.

3. ○ There is a lot of dust in
   ● here. I think that dr. Tam
   ○ is fixing the office door.

4. ● My glasses is in the
   ○ bedroom. Can you go
   ○ and get them for me?

5. ○ We were walking on the
   ● trail. Jeb saw berrys
   ○ growing on a bush.

6. ○ There is a secret road. It
   ○ runs from the back of my
   ● yard to mrs. Dhulpa's.

7. ● My sister make me
   ○ necklaces with pretty
   ○ and colorful beads.

 Go over each question on this page as a class.

The questions on this page cover the skills learned in Exercises 1 through 13. Tell students to read carefully and look closely for mistakes. They should try to fix mistakes in their head as they read along with you.

Each of the stories in questions 1 through 7 contains a mistake in punctuation, capitalization, or the use of a word. Read the stories to yourself as I read them aloud to you. For each story, fill in the bubble next to the part of the story that contains a mistake. Let's look at question 1.

(Read each story from the Pupil Edition page aloud, pausing between questions for students to mark their answers.)

Question 1
Comma between *11* and *2000*

Question 2
Period after *Ave*

Question 3
Dr. should be capitalized.

Question 4
Glasses gets a plural verb—*are.*

Question 5
Drop the *ys* and add *-ies*.

Question 6
Mrs. should be capitalized.

Question 7
Sister is singular and should be followed by the singular verb *makes*.

Exercise 15
VERB TENSE

 Go over the examples of present, past, and future tense verbs with the class.

To give students more practice with verb tense, write some examples on the board. Some examples you might use are:

- *Yesterday, we ___ some cake.* (ate, eat, will eat)
- *Right now, I ___ very tired.* (was, will be, am)
- *Tomorrow, I ___ to the movie.* (went, will go, go)

Go over the answers to these example sentences as a class, discussing how the correct verb choice is based on *when* the action in the sentence takes place.

 Go over the example question with the class.

Exercise 15
ON YOUR MARK!
Verb Tense

A verb tense tells when action takes place.

Verbs in the **present tense** tell about actions that happen now.
  *Susan **walks** in front of my house.*

Verbs in the **past tense** tell about actions that happened before now. Add *-ed* to verbs to form the past tense.
  *We **closed** the windows yesterday.*

Verbs in the **future tense** tell about actions that will happen later. Add the word *will* before the verb.
  *Darin **will take** his dog to the park tomorrow.*

> **TIP:** When you are using a verb, think about when the action happens. Make sure you use the correct verb tense.

 ## GET SET!
Let's try an example.

Which part of the story has a mistake in verb tense?
○ Last Monday there will be
○ a bake sale. Our class
○ needed money for our trip.

(1st) is **correct!** The verb should be in the past tense, not the future tense. *Last Monday there **was** a bake sale.*

TEACHING TIP

Tell students to look for a clue in the sentence that tells them when the action is taking place. Some of these clue words and phrases include:

- *Yesterday*
- *Today*
- *Last week*
- *Tomorrow*
- *Last year*

Ask students which tense goes with each of these words or phrases.

Go over each question on this page as a class.

Each of the stories in questions 1 through 8 contains a mistake in the use of a word. Read the stories to yourself as I read them aloud to you. For each story, fill in the bubble next to the part of the story that contains a mistake. Let's look at question 1.

(Read each story from the Pupil Edition page aloud, pausing between questions for students to mark their answers.)

Question 1

Clue: *was*

Question 2

Clue: *had*

Question 3

Clue: *yesterday*

Question 4

Clue: *tomorrow*

Question 5

Clue: *last week*

Question 6

Clue: *says*

Question 7

Clue: *last night*

Question 8

Clue: *last Friday night*

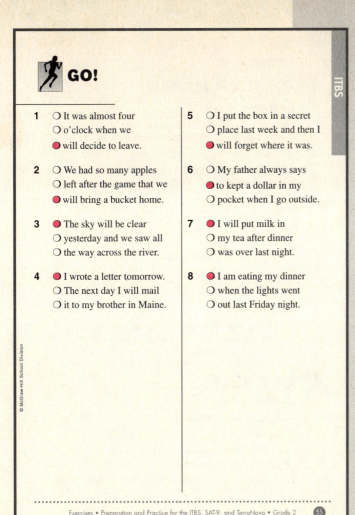

GO!

1. ○ It was almost four
   ○ o'clock when we
   ● will decide to leave.

2. ○ We had so many apples
   ○ left after the game that we
   ● will bring a bucket home.

3. ● The sky will be clear
   ○ yesterday and we saw all
   ○ the way across the river.

4. ● I wrote a letter tomorrow.
   ○ The next day I will mail
   ○ it to my brother in Maine.

5. ○ I put the box in a secret
   ○ place last week and then I
   ● will forget where it was.

6. ○ My father always says
   ● to kept a dollar in my
   ○ pocket when I go outside.

7. ● I will put milk in
   ○ my tea after dinner
   ○ was over last night.

8. ● I am eating my dinner
   ○ when the lights went
   ○ out last Friday night.

Exercise 16
IRREGULAR VERBS

 Go over the irregular verbs on the Pupil Edition page.

Explain that irregular verb spellings need to be memorized. Once students get used to how these verbs look and sound in the past tense, they will not make mistakes when they write them or answer questions about them.

Write some examples of irregular verbs on the board—some used correctly, some not—and have students make corrections where they find mistakes. Some examples you might use are:

- *The dog bited me on the leg.*
- *They drinked all the water.*
- *I met her at the cafe.* (correct)
- *We writed down everything.*
- *I readed the entire book before dinner.*
- *I knew he would come to the party.* (correct)

Go over each sentence with the class and discuss the corrections students suggest.

 Go over the example question as a class.

 Exercise 16

ON YOUR MARK!
Irregular Verbs

Verbs in the **past tense** tell about actions that happened before now. Add *-ed* or *-d* to most verbs to make them past tense.

walk → walked   tie → tied

Some verbs do not follow the *-ed* rule. These verbs are called **irregular verbs**. They have special spellings in the past tense.

Here are some examples of irregular verbs:

present	past
bite →	bit
meet →	met
see →	saw
run →	ran
drink →	drank
write →	wrote

TIP: The verb *read* does not change its spelling when it is in the past tense, but it is said differently. The past tense of *read* is said like the word *red*.

 GET SET!

Let's look at an example.

Find the mistake in the story.
○ My aunt likes to get mail.
○ I writed her a long letter
○ and sent it to her yesterday.

(2nd) is **correct!** *Write* is an irregular verb. The past tense of the verb *write* is *wrote*.

 EXTRA ACTIVITY

Make a worksheet with several sentences. Leave a blank where the past tense verb should be. At the end of each sentence, give the students two choices: the verb adding *-ed* and the irregular past tense verb. Have the students write the correct answer in the blank. This can be used as homework or as a classroom activity.

GO!

1. ○ I loved the sweater as
   ○ soon as I saw it. I
   ● buyed it right away

2. ○ I looked out of the
   ○ window for an hour
   ● before I seed the bird.

3. ● Reena thinked all day
   ○ about her report and
   ○ then she started to write.

4. ○ Allegra ran out into the
   ● field and catched the ball.
   ○ She almost dropped it.

5. ○ We needed more milk.
   ○ I put on my sweat pants
   ● and runed to the store.

6. ● The balls are keeped
   ○ in the closet. We play
   ○ indoor soccer with them.

7. ○ It took me a long time
   ○ to start the book, but I
   ● readed it in a week.

8. ● I had never meeted
   ○ Mr. Pickford before. He
   ○ was very friendly.

 Go over each question on this page as a class.

Each of the stories in questions 1 through 8 contains a mistake in the spelling of a past tense verb. Read the stories to yourself as I read them aloud to you. For each story, fill in the bubble next to the part of the story that contains a misspelled verb. Let's look at question 1.

(Read each story from the Pupil Edition page aloud, pausing between questions for students to mark their answers.)

Question 1

Buy is an irregular verb and becomes *bought* in the past tense.

Question 2

saw

Question 3

thought

Question 4

caught

Question 5

ran

Question 6

kept

Question 7

Read is an irregular verb; it is spelled the same way but pronounced differently in the past tense.

Question 8

met

Exercise 17

DOUBLE NEGATIVES

 Go over the concept of double negatives with the class.

Explain that double negatives should never be used in writing.

Write some examples of double negatives on the board and ask students to identify and change them. Some examples you might write are:

- He doesn't have no money.
- I don't see no deer.
- Nothing isn't ever going to happen.
- None of them hasn't got no sense.

Discuss the double or triple negatives in these sentences and how they should be corrected as a class.

 TEACHING TIP

Make sure students understand the information about contractions noted in the tip box on the Pupil Edition page.

 Go over the example question as a class.

Exercise 17

 ON YOUR MARK!
Double Negatives

A **double negative** is when a sentence has two negative words.

Mary has **not** got **no** ride to school.

Never use double negatives. It's hard to understand the meaning of sentences that have double negatives.

Negative words are words such as:

- Nothing
- Nowhere
- No one
- No
- Never
- None

> **TIP:** Some negative words are hard to notice because they are in the form of a contraction. For example, *don't* and *isn't* are both negative words because they have the word *not* in them.

 GET SET!
Let's look at an example.

Find the error in the story.
● My sister does not never
○ pick up the phone. She says
○ she doesn't hear it ring.

(1st) is **correct!** The first line has an error in it. *Does not* and *never* are both negative words. That is a double negative.

 TEACHING TIP

Constantly remind students to listen to how they and the people around them speak. Have them pay attention to grammatical errors in their speech and practice eliminating them. A good way to do this would be to assign a short two- or three-sentence speech that the students must give to the rest of the class. As each student speaks, keep a list of the grammatical errors the student makes and speak with each student individually about making improvements.

GO!

1. ○ Dana did not stop looking for her ring.
   ○ She says that it
   ● isn't nowhere in the house.

2. ● If I do not see nobody
   ○ sitting in the car, I will
   ○ go check inside the house.

3. ● There wasn't nothing to
   ○ see. Dr. Grate said that the
   ○ stars might not be out tonight.

4. ● I did not bring none
   ○ lunch. Karen gave me
   ○ her extra tuna sandwich.

5. ○ Lisa didn't make her bed.
   ● There was not none time
   ○ before she left for school.

6. ○ Clara will not have to buy
   ○ a card. There
   ● are not none in the store.

7. ● I don't want nothing
   ○ else with my juice. I
   ○ had none with lunch today.

8. ○ You need to finish the
   ○ whole room. There should
   ● not be none left to paint.

 Go over each question on this page as a class.

 Each of the stories in questions 1 through 8 contains a mistake in the use of a word or words. Read the stories to yourself as I read them aloud to you. For each story, fill in the bubble next to the part of the story that contains a mistake. Let's look at question 1.

(Read each story from the Pupil Edition page aloud, pausing between questions for students to mark their answers.)

Question 1

isn't anywhere

Question 2

do not see anybody

Question 3

was nothing, or

wasn't anything

Question 4

did not bring any

Question 5

wasn't any time, or

was no time

Question 6

are not any, or

are none

Question 7

don't want anything

Question 8

not be any

Exercises • Preparation and Practice for the ITBS, SAT-9, and TerraNova • Grade 2

Exercise 18
SUFFIXES

 Go over the definition of a suffix with students.

Review the examples on the Pupil Edition page and write some additional words on the board. Ask students to add suffixes. Some words you might use are:

- danger
- help
- quick
- big

Ask students to use the new words they created from the above examples in a sentence.

 TEACHING TIP

Make sure students understand that certain suffixes do not fit with certain words. For example, *tall + -en* doesn't make a new word. Encourage students to think about whether or not the word sounds correct. Have they heard or read the word before?

 Go over the example question with the class.

 Exercise 18

ON YOUR MARK!
Suffixes

A **suffix** is a word part that is added to the end of a word. A suffix changes the meaning of a word.

Suffix	Word	Example
-er	tall + er = taller	I am **taller** than he is.
-less	fear + less = fearless	The animal was **fearless**.
-ly	slow + ly = slowly	Chris walked **slowly**.
-ful	care + ful = careful	Be **careful**!
-ous	fame + ous = famous	The actor is **famous**.
-en	soft + en = soften	Please **soften** your voice.

TIP: Sometimes the root word changes when a suffix is added.
Fame + ous = famous   Beauty + ful = beautiful

GET SET!
Let's look at an example.
Find the ending that makes a new word.
   wonder
○ ate
● ful
○ ly

(1st) is **wrong**. *Wonderate* is not a word.
(2nd) is **correct!** *Wonderful* is a word that means full of wonder.
(3rd) is **wrong**. *Wonderly* is not a word.

 EXTRA ACTIVITY

For further practice on adding suffixes, make a list of thirty words and hand it out to students. Have them make as many new words for each word as possible by adding suffixes. The student who makes the most new words by correctly adding suffixes wins a gold star.

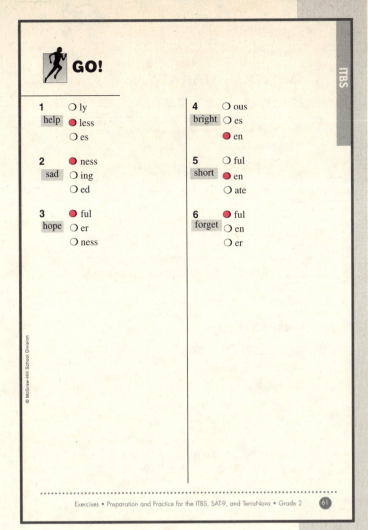

 Go over each question on this page as a class.

Question 1

📣 Look at question 1. The word in the shaded box is help. Fill in the bubble next to the ending that can be added to help to make it a new word.

Question 2

📣 Look at question 2. The word in the shaded box is sad. Fill in the bubble next to the ending that can be added to sad to make it a new word.

Question 3

📣 Look at question 3. The word in the shaded box is hope. Fill in the bubble next to the ending that can be added to hope to make it a new word.

Question 4

📣 Look at question 4. The word in the shaded box is bright. Fill in the bubble next to the ending that can be added to bright to make it a new word.

Question 5

📣 Look at question 5. The word in the shaded box is short. Fill in the bubble next to the ending that can be added to short to make it a new word.

Question 6

📣 Look at question 6. The word in the shaded box is forget. Fill in the bubble next to the ending that can be added to forget to make it a new word.

Exercises • Preparation and Practice for the ITBS, SAT-9, and TerraNova • Grade 2   61

Exercise 19
PRONOUNS

 Explain to students that pronouns are special words that take the place of nouns in sentences.

Go over the two types of pronouns, object and subject, with your class. Write sentences on the board and have students tell you which pronouns are object pronouns and which are subject pronouns. Some examples you might use are:

- She *likes to play games.* (subject)
- *I took* him *to the baseball field.* (object)
- We *are nice people.* (subject)
- *Juanita is in love with* him. (object)
- *Where are you taking* them*?* (object)

 TEACHING TIP

Point out that the pronoun *you* fits in every category. *You* is both an object and a subject pronoun and can be used as a singular or a plural. Also, remind students that *I* always comes second when there are two nouns in a subject.

 Go over the example question as a class.

Exercise 19

 ON YOUR MARK!
Pronouns

A **pronoun** is a word that you use instead of one or more nouns.
Subject pronouns take the place of nouns in the subject.

   Harriet *takes the bus.* → **She** *takes the bus.*

Some subject pronouns are *I, you, he, she, it, you, we,* and *they.*
Object pronouns take the place of nouns that come after the verb.

   He walked by **Susan**. → *He walked by* **her**.

Some object pronouns are *me, you, him, her, it, you, us,* and *them.*
Always name yourself last when telling about another person (or other people) and yourself.

   CORRECT: *Bonnie Jean and* **I** *are watering the plants.*
   WRONG: **I** *and Bonnie Jean are watering the plants.*
   CORRECT: *The cat sits with* **grandma and me**.
   WRONG: *The cat sits with* **me and grandma**.

 GET SET!
Let's look at an example.

Find the error.
○ I and Amy are blowing
○ up balloons for our
○ party this afternoon.

(1st) is **correct!** There is an error in the first line. Always put yourself last. *Amy and I are blowing up balloons for our party this afternoon.*

 EXTRA ACTIVITY

Give students worksheets containing the following sentences, or write them on the board. Students must choose the pronoun that correctly fits in the sentence.

- *Jenny gave the ball to (he/him).*
- *(I and James/ James and I) ran along the stream.*
- *(They/ Them) told their mother about (we/us).*
- *(She/Her) walked toward (I/me).*
- *The dog shook itself off all over (me and John/John and me).*

GO!

1. ● Her and my mom are
   ○ at the record store.
   ○ It is having a sale.

2. ○ They got the lamp for
   ● Lucie and I. It is from a
   ○ small town in Italy.

3. ○ I'm going to bring two.
   ○ That way there will be one
   ● for Wendy and one for she.

4. ● Me and Rod will
   ○ take the bird on
   ○ vacation with us.

5. ○ I have time for one more
   ○ round. How about Pam
   ● against me and you?

6. ● I and Nancy play
   ○ four square with her
   ○ every day at recess.

7. ○ Mom sat down at
   ○ the round table with
   ● me and Ernesto.

8. ○ It is almost time for
   ○ Jason's speech. I hope that
   ● him does a good job.

 Go over each question on this page as a class.

Each of the stories in questions 1 through 8 contains a mistake in the use of a word. Read the stories to yourself as I read them aloud to you. For each story, fill in the bubble next to the part of the story that contains a mistake. Let's look at question 1.

(Read each story from the Pupil Edition page aloud, pausing between questions for students to mark their answers.)

Question 1
This calls for a subject pronoun—*she*, not *her*.

Question 2
This calls for an object pronoun—*me*, not *I*.

Question 3
This calls for an object pronoun—*her*, not *she*.

Question 4
This calls for a subject pronoun—*I*, not *me*. The *I* should come after *Rod*.

Question 5
Me should always come second when there are two objects.

Question 6
I should always go second when there are two subjects.

Question 7
Me should always come second when there are two objects.

Question 8
This calls for a subject pronoun—*he*, not *him*.

Exercise 20
SILENT LETTERS

 Go over the explanation of silent letters with the class.

To demonstrate that the letters are silent, you might pronounce the silent letters the first time you read the example words, then leave the letters silent the second time you read them. This way, students will begin to see why the letters are not pronounced.

Remind students that when one vowel is needed to make the long sound for another vowel (e.g., *ai, oa, i_e*), the second vowel is *not* considered to be a silent letter.

Write some other words containing silent letters on the board. Have students point out which letters are silent. Some examples you might use are:

- *talk*
- *crumb*
- *wrong*
- *knife*
- *bright*

 Go over the example question with the class.

Exercise 20

ON YOUR MARK!
Silent Letters

Sometimes a word is spelled with a letter that you cannot hear when you say the word. These words have **silent letters**.

The word *walk* has a silent *l*.
The word *climb* has a silent *b*.
The word *know* has a silent *k*.
The word *write* has a silent *w*.
The word *gnaw* has a silent *g*.
The word *ghost* has a silent *h*.
The word *night* has a silent *gh*.

 ## GET SET!
Let's look at an example.

Find the word that has a silent letter.
○ wish
○ wrist
○ pet

(1st) is **wrong.** You pronounce every letter in *wish*.
(2nd) is **correct!** *Wrist* has a silent *w*.
(3rd) is **wrong.** You pronounce every letter in *pet*.

  ### EXTRA ACTIVITY

Play a game with students! Have them form pairs and give them five minutes to come up with as many words as they can that include silent letters. The pair that comes up with the most in the time allotted wins the game.

GO!

1. ● wrap
   ○ wait
   ○ wonder

2. ○ feel
   ● comb
   ○ lot

3. ○ kind
   ○ kitchen
   ● know

4. ○ brand
   ● lamb
   ○ board

5. ○ wake
   ○ wool
   ● write

6. ● tomb
   ○ try
   ○ treat

7. ○ keep
   ● knee
   ○ cart

8. ○ week
   ● wring
   ○ wag

 Go over each question on this page as a class.

📣 *For questions 1 through 8, fill in the bubble next to the word that contains a silent letter.*

Question 1

Wait does not have a silent letter because the *i* is needed to make the long *a* sound.

Question 2
Silent /b/

Question 3
Silent /k/

Question 4
Silent /b/

Question 5

The vowel combinations *a_e* (*wake*), *oo*, (*wool*), and *i_e* (*write*) do not contain silent letters because of the way one vowel affects the sound of the other. The silent letter in this question is the *w* in *write*.

Question 6
Silent /b/

Question 7
Silent /k/

Question 8
Silent /w/

Exercises • Preparation and Practice for the ITBS, SAT-9, and TerraNova • Grade 2

Exercise 21

USING ADJECTIVES THAT COMPARE

 Go over the definition of "adjective" with the class.

On the board, create two columns: comparative adjectives (compare two nouns) and superlative adjectives (compare more than two nouns). Using the examples on the Pupil Edition page as guides, ask students for additional examples. Write their examples in the appropriate columns.

Explain that some adjectives that are used to compare do *not* follow the usual pattern (*-er, -est*). Go over the examples provided on the Pupil Edition page. Call on students to create sentences with each of the words. Answer any questions students have.

 Go over the example question as a class.

Exercise 21

ON YOUR MARK!
Using Adjectives that Compare

Adjectives are words that are used to describe nouns.
 Buddy is **tall**.
To compare two nouns:
• Using a short adjective, just add *-er* to the adjective.
 Buddy is **taller** than Christopher.
• Using a long adjective, just put *more* before the adjective.
 Daisies are **more beautiful** than tulips.
To compare more than two nouns:
• Using a short adjective, add *-est* to the adjective.
 Buddy is the **tallest** person in his class.
• Using a long adjective, just put *most* before the adjective.
 Daisies are the **most beautiful** flowers of all.

> **TIP:** Never use both a suffix and *more* or *most* to compare nouns.
> **WRONG:** The soup is **more hotter** than the bread.
> **CORRECT:** The soup is **hotter** than the bread.

 GET SET!
Let's look at an example.
Which part of the story has a mistake in it?
 Kara ran fastest
○ than Gina, but not
○ faster than Pat.

(1st) is **correct!** Only two nouns, Kara and Gina, are being compared. The adjective should be *faster*.

 EXTRA ACTIVITY

Give students worksheets of the following sentences or write them on the board. Students must choose the adjective that correctly fits in the sentence.

• *David is (taller/tallest) than Peter.*

• *This painting is (more prettier/ prettier) than that one.*

• *The brown horse is (faster/ more faster) than the white one.*

• *Today has been (funner/ more fun) than yesterday.*

GO!

1. ○ The second movie was
   ● shortest than the first,
   ○ but no shorter than the last.

2. ○ I waited for the bus
   ○ longer than Rick. I waited
   ● the longest of everyone.

3. ○ Is Grandma's cake sweet?
   ○ Do you think it tastes
   ● more sweeter than the pie?

4. ● The most highest hill
   ○ in the park is higher than
   ○ the hill at Bear Lake.

5. ● My pants are more whiter
   ○ than your pants, but dirtier
   ○ than William's pants.

6. ○ The games this
   ○ year were most
   ● excitingest of all

7. ○ Everyone yell as loud
   ○ as they can so we can
   ● tell who is the most loudest.

8. ○ I like my blue pants better
   ○ than my black ones. They
   ● are more comfortabler.

 Go over each question on this page as a class.

 Each of the stories in questions 1 through 8 contains a mistake in the use of a word or words. Read the stories to yourself as I read them aloud to you. For each story, fill in the bubble next to the part of the story that contains a mistake. Let's look at question 1.

(Read each story from the Pupil Edition page aloud, pausing between questions for students to mark their answers.)

Question 1

Only two things are being compared—*er* is needed rather than *-est*.

Questions 3 through 8

These violate the "no suffix and *most*" and "no suffix and *more*" rules from the previous page.

Exercise 22
QUOTATION MARKS

 Go over the correct and incorrect uses of quotations marks with the class.

To give students extra practice using quotation marks, write the following sentences on the board:

- *I am never going back there, he said.*
- *He told me, "he was never going back there."*
- *I love scrambled eggs, said the woman at the counter.*
- *The woman at the counter was talking about "loving scrambled eggs."*

Go over each sentence with the class and ask them to point out the mistakes. Have students come to the board and correct the errors.

 Go over the example question with the class.

 Exercise 22

ON YOUR MARK!
Quotation Marks

Use **quotation marks** to show that someone is speaking.
   I hear Mom saying, "I am late for work this morning."
   Julie is screaming, "It's snowing outside!"
   "Is the dog still wet?" Inna asked.

Quotation marks come at the beginning and end of a person's exact words.

CORRECT:	Jake told me that **Gary is right**.
	Jake said, **"Gary is right."**
WRONG:	Jake told me that, **"Gary is right."**
	Jake said, **Gary is right**.

 ## GET SET!

Let's look at an example.

Find the error.

● Go to the game tonight,
○ Darby said. She is the
○ best soccer player.

(1st) is **correct!** There is an error in the first line. There must be quotation marks around Darby's exact words. It should read: *"Go to the game tonight," Darby said. She is the best soccer player.*

 ### EXTRA ACTIVITY

Have students write a two- or three-sentence story with at least one quotation. The stories can be about anything they want. Check their stories for correct use of punctuation and capitalization in their quotation.

GO!

1. ● Toby said, Don't leave!"
   ○ She wanted to show
   ○ everyone her new truck.

2. ● "I think the mail is here,
   ○ yelled Sam. They had
   ○ been waiting all day.

3. ○ Ms. Locke turned on the
   ● light and yelled,
   "Surprise!
   ○ I was very surprised!

4. ● There are only three left,
   ○ Diana told us. We should
   ○ share them with everyone.

5. ● Maricella said, I know how."
   ○ She is very good at
   ○ fixing things that break.

6. ● I'll bring the cake,"
   ○ said Robert. Now we
   ○ only need forks to eat it.

7. ○ Jess saw the box and said,
   ● What is inside this?
   ○ I knew he wanted a dog.

8. ● I don't like the music,
   ○ Sadie told us. She went
   ○ into the other room.

 Go over each question on this page as a class.

 Each of the stories in questions 1 through 8 contains a mistake in punctuation. Read the stories to yourself as I read them aloud to you. For each story, fill in the bubble next to the part of the story that contains a mistake. Let's look at question 1.

(Read each story from the Pupil Edition page aloud, pausing between questions for students to mark their answers.)

Each question on this page contains a direct quotation that is missing the beginning quotation mark, the end quotation mark, or both quotation marks.

Exercise 23
SHORT *E* AND LONG *E*

 Go over the difference between the sounds and spellings of short versus long /e/.

Choose some students to read the example words on the Pupil Edition page aloud. Then ask them to suggest extra examples for each sound and spelling. Some examples might be:

- *bread*
- *met*
- *reef*
- *heat*
- *city*
- *honey*
- *piece*

Ask students to determine which words contain the long /e/ sound and which contain the short /e/ sound.

 Go over the example question as a class.

Exercise 23

 ON YOUR MARK!

Short *E* and long *E*

Words with a short *e* sound:
With *ea*: *head*
With *e*: *fed*

Words with a long *e* sound:
With *ee*: *meet*
With *ea*: *treat*
With *y*: *kitty*
With *ey*: *money*
With *ie*: *chief*

 GET SET!
Let's look at an example.

Which word has the same vowel sound as the word <u>teach</u>?
○ sore
○ toad
○ see

(3rd) is **correct!** The word *teach* and the word *see* both have a *long e* sound.

 EXTRA ACTIVITY

Create a worksheet. Write a sentence leaving an /e/ word out. Give three choices of spelling at the end of the sentence. The students must choose the *e* word that is spelled correctly and write it in the blank. This can be used as a homework activity to give students extra practice spelling /e/ words. An example might be:

Theresa was in the (lead, leed, leid) at the beginning of the race.

GO!

1. ● lead
   ○ great
   ○ bite

2. ○ can
   ● hardly
   ○ best

3. ● ahead
   ○ need
   ○ pea

4. ○ joke
   ○ look
   ● reef

5. ○ keep
   ○ like
   ● red

6. ● feed
   ○ tape
   ○ let

7. ○ plate
   ● dirty
   ○ date

8. ○ jot
   ○ peek
   ● wet

 Go over each question on this page as a class.

Question 1

📣 *Look at question 1. Fill in the bubble next to the word with the same vowel sound as red.*

Question 2

📣 *Look at question 2. Fill in the bubble next to the word with the same vowel sound as steam.*

Question 3

📣 *Look at question 3. Fill in the bubble next to the word with the same vowel sound as jet.*

Question 4

📣 *Look at question 4. Fill in the bubble next to the word with the same vowel sound as green.*

Question 5

📣 *Look at question 5. Fill in the bubble next to the word with the same vowel sound as lent.*

Question 6

📣 *Look at question 6. Fill in the bubble next to the word with the same vowel sound as cheap.*

Question 7

📣 *Look at question 7. Fill in the bubble next to the word with the same vowel sound as feet.*

Question 8

📣 *Look at question 8. Fill in the bubble next to the word with the same vowel sound as bed.*

Exercise 24

PACING YOURSELF

 Review with the class the tips for pacing oneself on the ITBS.

Go over each of the three main points on the Pupil Edition page with students, and describe how each one of these tips will help them pace themselves on the ITBS.

Let students know it is important for them to find the pace at which they can answer the most questions correctly.

The two most important ways for students to improve their ideal pace are:

- **Practice:** The more students practice on tests that are similar to the ITBS, the more familiar the test will be and the more quickly they will be able to work through the questions.

- **Reading:** Reading improves spelling, punctuation, and just about every other aspect of language arts. If students are comfortable with the skills, they will be able to move through the test more comfortably.

Tell students that a good method to follow when they get stuck on a question is to choose the answer they feel is best and return to the question later if they have time at the end of the test.

 Go over the example question with the class.

Exercise 24

 ON YOUR MARK!
Pacing Yourself

Pacing yourself means using the time you have to complete as many questions as you can without rushing or spending too much time on one question. Here are some tips that help you work at a careful but steady pace:

- **Do not get stuck on one question.** If you cannot answer a question and you have been trying for a while, take your best guess and move on.
- **Know the directions.** When you take the practice tests, listen to the directions that your teacher reads so that on the real exam you already understand them.
- **Relax.** Don't worry if you don't know an answer. The ITBS is just one way to measure your skills. The calmer you are, the more likely you are to answer the questions correctly!

 GET SET!

Let's look at an example.

Which suffix can be used with the word in the gray box?

- ○ ful
- ● est
- ○ ous

(1st) is **wrong.** *Darkful* is not a word.
(2nd) is **correct!** *Darkest* is a word!
(3rd) is **wrong.** *Darkous* is not a word.

 TEACHING TIP

You might tell students to trust their instincts on questions—especially on questions that rely on their ability to use their ears for the language. If something sounds or looks wrong, it probably is. Remind them, too, to find the correct answer by eliminating answer choices that are obviously incorrect.

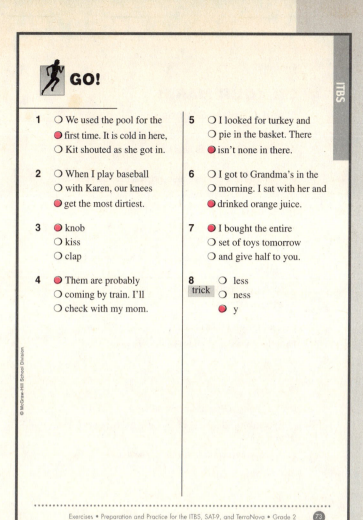

 Go over each question on this page as a class.

Questions 1 and 2

📣 *Each of the stories in questions 1 and 2 contains a mistake. Read the stories to yourself as I read them aloud to you. For each story, fill in the bubble next to the part of the story that contains a mistake. Let's look at question 1.*

(Read the stories for questions 1 and 2 from the Pupil Edition page aloud, pausing between questions for students to mark their answers. Remind students to pace themselves as they work through these questions. You might want to give the students a set amount of time to complete this exercise.)

Question 3

📣 *Look at question 3. Fill in the bubble next to the word that contains a silent letter.*

Questions 4 through 7

📣 *Each of the stories in questions 4 through 7 contains a mistake. Read the stories to yourself as I read them aloud to you. For each story, fill in the bubble next to the part of the story that contains a mistake. Let's look at question 4.*

(Read the stories for questions 4 through 7 from the Pupil Edition page aloud, pausing between questions for students to mark their answers.)

Question 8

📣 *Look at question 8. The word in the shaded box is trick. Fill in the bubble next to the ending that can be added to trick to make it a new word.*

Exercise 25

C AND G LETTER SOUNDS

 Go over the hard and soft /c/ and /g/ letter sounds with the class.

For extra practice with these sounds, write some more words on the board that contain both hard and soft /c/ and /g/ sounds. Some examples you might use are:

- *circle*
- *girl*
- *cell*
- *hedge*
- *clap*
- *gap*
- *curl*
- *grab*
- *gentle*

Have the students group these words according to the ones that have the same sounds. Discuss as a class which of these words makes the hard or soft /c/ and /g/ sounds.

 Go over the example question as a class.

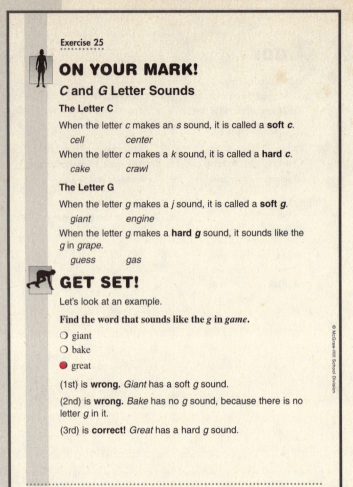

 TEACHING TIP

Give students a list of words containing the soft /c/ and /g/ sounds. Have them keep the list in their desks and add to it each time they come across a new word with either of the sounds.

GO!

1. ○ taste
   ● space
   ○ lazy

2. ● cup
   ○ chair
   ○ lace

3. ● get
   ○ gym
   ○ took

4. ○ clip
   ○ gum
   ● gem

5. ● cape
   ○ beach
   ○ race

6. ○ paws
   ○ has
   ● grace

7. ● gate
   ○ read
   ○ leap

8. ○ was
   ○ his
   ● niece

Go over each question on this page as a class.

Question 1
Look at question 1. Fill in the bubble next to the word with the same ending sound as rice.

Question 2
Look at question 2. Fill in the bubble next to the word with the same beginning sound as can.

Question 3
Look at question 3. Fill in the bubble next to the word with the same beginning sound as give.

Question 4
Look at question 4. Fill in the bubble next to the word with the same beginning sound as jelly.

Question 5
Look at question 5. Fill in the bubble next to the word with the same beginning sound as car.

Question 6
Look at question 6. Fill in the bubble next to the word with the same ending sound as case.

Question 7
Look at question 7. Fill in the bubble next to the word with the same beginning sound as garbage.

Question 8
Look at question 8. Fill in the bubble next to the word with the same ending sound as ice.

Exercise 26

ADJECTIVES

 Go over the adjectives on this page with the class, making a distinction between singular and plural.

To give students extra practice with this concept, write the following words on the board:

- *bird*
- *bush*
- *dogs*
- *ball*
- *people*

Have students put these words into sentences, using the adjectives *this, that, these*, or *those* in each one to describe the nouns listed. Discuss their sentences as a class.

 TEACHING TIP

Go over the tip box on the Pupil Edition page with students.

 Go over the example question as a class.

Exercise 26

ON YOUR MARK!
Adjectives

An **adjective** is a word that describes a noun.
Some adjectives tell *which* noun.

- Use the adjectives *this* and *that* to tell which noun.
  This house is close to mine.
  There are red leaves on **that tree**.

- Use the adjectives *these* and *those* to tell which noun when there is more than one.
  These shoes fit well.
  I want to use **those cups**.

> **TIP:** Do not use *this, that, these,* and *those* with *there* and *here*.
> **WRONG: This here** book is mine.
> **CORRECT: This** book is mine.

GET SET!
Let's look at an example.

Find the error.
○ I told Margie to
○ read the book on
● these brown table.

(2nd) is **correct!** There is an error in the second line. The table is singular, but the adjective is plural. *These* should be *this*.

76   Exercises • Preparation and Practice for the ITBS, SAT-9, and TerraNova • Grade 2

 EXTRA ACTIVITY

Have students revisit the sentence-writing activity above. Have them change the plural nouns to singular nouns and vice versa and change the adjectives to match the nouns.

GO!

1. ● This here car is the
   ○ fastest. We should take
   ○ it on our summer trip.

2. ○ If you want to find
   ○ out, you can read
   ● this books.

3. ○ It is getting really cold
   ○ outside. It is a good idea
   ● to bring this here coat.

4. ● I like that there dog
   ○ a lot. Maybe my dad
   ○ will let me keep her.

5. ○ The color of the room
   ● is green. Only this
   ○ colors will match.

6. ● This here game has been
   ○ the longest. The other ones
   ○ were much more fun.

7. ○ Let's go back to the
   ● first store where those
   ○ bread looked fresh.

8. ○ If we eat steak for
   ○ dinner, we need to use
   ● these here plates.

 Go over each question on this page as a class.

Each of the stories in questions 1 through 8 contains a mistake in the use of a word or words. Read the stories to yourself as I read them aloud to you. For each story, fill in the bubble next to the part of the story that contains a mistake. Let's look at question 1.

(Read each story from the Pupil Edition page aloud, pausing between questions for students to mark their answers.)

Question 1

Remind students not to use *this* with *here* when describing a noun.

Question 2

This should be *these*.

Question 3

Remind students not to use *this* with *here* when describing a noun.

Question 4

Never use *that* and *there* together.

Question 5

The word *colors* is plural, so the word *these* should be used.

Question 6

Remind students not to use *this* with *here* when describing a noun.

Question 7

Those should be *that*.

Question 8

Never use *these* and *here* together.

Exercise 27

ADDING -ED, -ING, -S, AND -LY

 Go over the rules for adding -ed, -ing, -s, and -ly as a class.

To further enforce these rules, write some other words on the board. Have students add the indicated endings using the rules discussed on the Pupil Edition page. Some examples you might use are:

- trot (-ed)
- pop (-ed)
- dive (-ing)
- fox (-s)
- pouch (-s)
- snappy (-ly)

 Go over the example question with the class.

Exercise 27

 ON YOUR MARK!

Adding -ed, -ing, -s, and -ly

Sometimes when you add endings to words, the spelling of the word does not change. Other times, the spelling of the word does change. Here are the rules when spellings change:

Adding -ed and -ing:

If the word ends in one consonant, double it and add -ed or -ing.

hop + ed ⟶ hopped

If the word ends in a silent e, drop the e and add -ed or -ing.

ride + ing ⟶ riding

Adding -s:

If the word ends in s, sh, ch, x or z, add an -es.

push + s ⟶ pushes

Adding -ly:

If the word ends in a y, change the y to an i and add -ly.

happy + ly ⟶ happily

 GET SET!

Let's look at an example.

Which word is NOT spelled correctly?
○ pull
○ start
○ ageing

(3rd) is **correct!** *Aging* is spelled wrong. *Age* ends in an *e*, so you must drop the *e* and then add -*ing*.

78   Exercises • Preparation and Practice for the ITBS, SAT-9, and TerraNova • Grade 2

  TEACHING TIP

Tell students to acquaint themselves with what these kinds of words look like when they are spelled properly. This way the students will be able to recognize these words when they are spelled incorrectly.

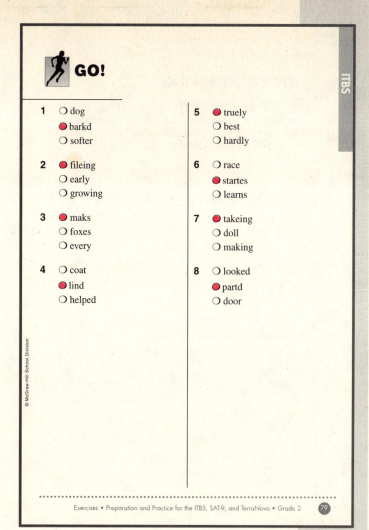

 Go over each question on this page as a class.

For questions 1 through 8, fill in the bubble next to the word that is misspelled.

Questions 1 and 8

Rule: If a word ends in two different consonants, just add -ed and do not drop any letters.

Questions 2 and 7

Rule: If a word ends in silent /e/, drop the e and add -ing.

Question 3

Rule: If a word ends in a silent /e/, just add -s and do not drop any letters.

Question 4

Rule: If a word ends in a silent /e/, just add -d and do not drop any letters.

Question 5

Rule: If a word ends in a silent /e/, drop the e and add -ly.

Question 6

Rule: If a word ends in two different consonants, just add -s and do not drop any letters.

The rules in questions 1, 3, 4, 5, 6, and 8 are not discussed on the previous page. Make sure students are comfortable with them before moving on. Also, give students extra practice with the following:

- adding -ed and -ing to words ending in one consonant (stop—stopped, stopping)

- adding -es to words ending in s, sh, ch, x, or z

- adding -ly to word ending in y

Exercise 28
DRAWING CONCLUSIONS

 Explain to students what it means to draw a conclusion.

Tell students that for these types of questions, they will look for clues in a picture. The clues will help them make a decision about what might be happening in the picture.

Encourage students to think about the facts in a picture before drawing a conclusion.

 Go over the example question as a class. Point out to students that the glasses might help Tara see better in the dark, but they won't provide any light.

Exercise 28
ON YOUR MARK!
Drawing Conclusions

In the ITBS, you will be able to answer questions based on words you read and pictures you look at. This is called drawing conclusions, or making decisions based on facts.

Here is what you know by looking at this picture:

Fact	Conclusion
Birthday sign	It is the girl's birthday.
Bow around puppy's neck	The dog is a present to the girl.
Smiling girl	The girl is happy.

GET SET!
Let's look at an example. Listen carefully.

The lights went off in Tara's house. Which picture shows something she can use to light her room?

○   ○   ○

(1st) is **wrong.** *Eyeglasses* won't light Tara's room.
(2nd) is **correct!** A *flashlight* would light Tara's room.
(3rd) is **wrong.** A *bed* won't light Tara's room.

★ EXTRA ACTIVITY

Have students draw their own pictures that tell a small story. Then, have students exchange the drawings with a partner. The partner can guess what is happening in the picture.

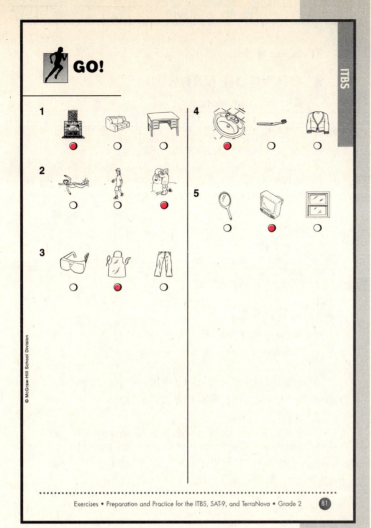

 Go over each question on this page as a class.

Question 1

📣 *Look at question 1. Listen carefully as I read a story to you:* Joey was cold. He wanted to warm up. *Now look at the three pictures. Fill in the bubble next to the picture that shows something Joey could use to warm up.*

Question 2

📣 *Look at question 2. Listen carefully as I read a story to you:* It was wintertime. Even though it was cold, Marguerite wanted to play outside. *Now look at the three pictures. Fill in the bubble next to the picture that shows something Marguerite might do outside.*

Question 3

📣 *Look at question 3. Listen carefully as I read a story to you:* Saleem was watching his father. His father was baking a cherry pie. *Now look at the three pictures. Fill in the bubble next to the picture that shows what Saleem's father is probably wearing.*

Question 4

📣 *Look at question 4. Listen carefully as I read a story to you:* Ling had been playing in the mud. He was dirty and wanted to wash his hands. *Now look at the three pictures. Fill in the bubble next to the picture that shows something Ling might use to wash his hands.*

Question 5

📣 *Look at question 5. Listen carefully as I read a story to you:* Patricia was looking at birds. They were flying from the tree in her backyard. *Now look at the three pictures. Fill in the bubble next to the picture that shows what Patricia was looking at when she saw the birds.*

Exercise 29
CLASSIFYING WORDS

 Go over the definition of classification with students.

To give students some practice with this concept, write these words on the board and have students put them into three different groups:

- brick
- goldfish
- planets
- metal
- trout
- stars
- wood
- bass
- moons

As a class, go over how the students grouped the words above. Explain to students that by understanding how words are grouped together, they will be able to choose words that *don't* belong in a group.

 Go over the example question as a class.

Exercise 29

 ON YOUR MARK!
Classifying Words

Some questions on the ITBS ask you to put words into groups. This is called **classifying words**. Words that have things in common are put in the same group.

These words belong in the same group because they are all **colors**:

  red, blue, green

These words belong in the same group because they are all **verbs**:

  jump, send, find

These words belong in the same group because they are all **rooms**:

  kitchen, bathroom, bedroom

 GET SET!

Let's look at an example.

Which word is different than the other three?
○ finger
○ mouth
○ car
○ leg

(3rd) is **correct!** *Car* is different than the other three. *Finger*, *mouth*, and *leg* are all parts of the body.

 EXTRA ACTIVITY

Bring several objects to class. Put four objects on a table in the front of the classroom. One object should not belong with the other three. Have students pick the object that doesn't belong. They should be able to explain why it doesn't belong. Some objects you might consider are books, types of clothing, types of food, and so on.

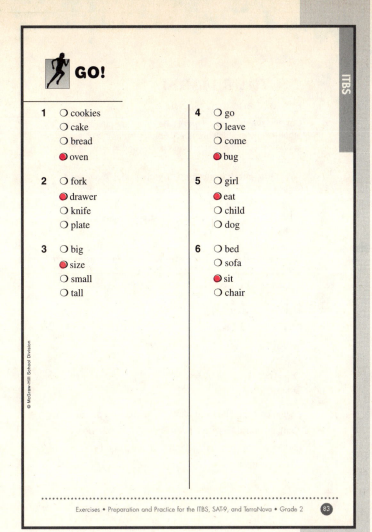

 Go over each question on this page as a class.

📣 *For questions 1 through 6, fill in the bubble next to the word that is different from the other three.*

Question 1

An *oven* is an appliance; the others are baked goods.

Question 2

A *drawer* holds the other three items.

Question 3

Size is a noun; the others are adjectives.

Question 4

Bug is a noun; the others are verbs.

Question 5

Eat is a verb; the others are nouns.

Question 6

Sit is a verb; the others are nouns.

Exercise 30

PH, CH, AND TCH SOUNDS

 Go over the sounds these letters make when they're grouped together.

To provide students with some extra familiarity with these kinds of words, write some extra examples on the board. Some examples you might use are:

- graph
- chart
- patch
- chicken
- phone
- catch
- stitch
- alphabet

Pick a different student to pronounce each of the words above.

 Go over the example question as a class.

Exercise 30

 ON YOUR MARK!

Ph, ch, and tch Sounds

Certain letters sound different when they are next to each other than when they are apart. For example, the *ch* sound in *choice* sounds different than the *c* sound in *cape* or the *h* sound in *Henry*.

When the letters *p* and *h* are together, they make an *f* sound.

   phone   alphabet

When the letters *c* and *h* are together, they make a *ch* sound.

   chore   which

When the letters *t*, *c*, and *h* are together, they make a *ch* sound.

   watch   itch

 GET SET!

Let's look at an example.

Which word makes an *f* sound?
- ○ photo
- ○ pail
- ○ tap

(1st) is correct! The word *photo* starts with an *f* sound.

(2nd) is wrong. The word *pail* starts with a *p* sound.

(3rd) is wrong. The word *tap* ends with a *p* sound.

  TEACHING TIP

Tell students that whenever they see a word spelled with a *ph*, it is always going to make the /f/ sound, never the /p/ sound.

GO!

1. ● fetch
   ○ face
   ○ cat

2. ○ crate
   ● lunch
   ○ take

3. ○ place
   ○ lap
   ● paragraph

4. ○ hat
   ○ case
   ● latch

5. ● touch
   ○ cash
   ○ face

6. ● phrase
   ○ how
   ○ plate

7. ○ lock
   ○ wake
   ● notch

8. ○ kiss
   ● pinch
   ○ push

Go over each question on this page as a class.

Question 1
Look at question 1. Fill in the bubble next to the word that makes a /ch/ sound.

Question 2
Look at question 2. Fill in the bubble next to the word that makes a /ch/ sound.

Question 3
Look at question 3. Fill in the bubble next to the word that makes an /f/ sound

Question 4
Look at question 4. Fill in the bubble next to the word that makes a /ch/ sound.

Question 5
Look at question 5. Fill in the bubble next to the word that makes a /ch/ sound.

Question 6
Look at question 6. Fill in the bubble next to the word that makes an /f/ sound.

Question 7
Look at question 7. Fill in the bubble next to the word that makes a /ch/ sound.

Question 8
Look at question 8. Fill in the bubble next to the word that makes a /ch/ sound.

Practice Test

LISTENING

🔊 *This lesson will show how well you understand the way that people use language. We will start with a sample question. Look at the three pictures and listen carefully.* Tonia gave Renee a present that she can only use when it is raining. *Fill in the bubble under the picture that shows what Tonia gave Renee. [Pause.] The first picture is a drawing of an umbrella. Fill in the bubble under this picture because you can only use an umbrella in the rain.*

🔊 *Look at the pictures for question 1.* It is snowing outside. Ruth and her father are staying home to bake cookies together. *Fill in the bubble under the picture that shows what Ruth and her father are doing. [Pause.] Look at the pictures for question 2.* Troy is going camping this weekend with his mom. *Fill in the bubble under the picture that shows what Troy is doing this weekend.*

GO ON ➡

LANGUAGE

S1
- ○ stove
- ○ toaster
- ● table
- ○ kitchen

📣 *Look at the words for question S1. They are stove, toaster, table, and kitchen. Fill in the bubble next to the word that is different from the other three.*

1
- ○ soda
- ● cup
- ○ juice
- ○ milk

📣 *Look at the words for question 1. They are soda, cup, juice, and milk. Fill in the bubble next to the word that is different from the other three.*

2
- ● sky
- ○ sun
- ○ cloud
- ○ moon

📣 *Look at the words for question 2. They are sky, sun, cloud, and moon. Fill in the bubble next to the word that is different from the other three.*

3
- ○ top
- ● box
- ○ side
- ○ bottom

📣 *Look at the words for question 3. They are top, box, side, and bottom. Fill in the bubble next to the word that is different from the other three.*

SPELLING

S1
- ○ that
- ○ right
- ● waye

📣 *Find the words for question S1. That is the right way. Which of the words is spelled wrong?*

1
- ● jumpd
- ○ on
- ○ pillow

📣 *Find the words for question 1. I jumped on the pillow. Which of the words is spelled wrong?*

2
- ○ shirt
- ○ lost
- ● buton

📣 *Find the words for question 2. My shirt lost a button. Which of the words is spelled wrong?*

3
- ● berd
- ○ nesting
- ○ window

📣 *Find the words for question 3. A bird is nesting outside my window. Which of the words is spelled wrong?*

4
- ● summir
- ○ hot
- ○ season

📣 *Find the words for question 4. Summer is a hot season. Which of the words is spelled wrong?*

5
- ● taik
- ○ sister
- ○ movie

📣 *Find the words for question 5. I will take my sister to the movie. Which of the words is spelled wrong?*

CAPITALIZATION

📣 *Each story in questions S1 through 3 contains a mistake in capitalization.*

S1
- ○ Today was a snowy day.
- ● mr. Quimby decided to stay
- ○ home and knit a scarf for his mother.

Read each story aloud to the class. They should fill in the bubble next to the line with a mistake.

1
- ● On monday, Julia is going
- ○ to the park. She will meet her
- ○ sister at the baseball field.

2
- ○ Grandma has a doctor's
- ○ appointment. The doctor's office
- ● is at 772 chaney Street.

3
- ○ Damian is going on
- ● vacation in utah. He likes
- ○ to ski there in the winter.

📣 *Each story in questions S1 through 3 contains a mistake in punctuation. Read the stories to yourself as I read them aloud. Fill in the bubble next to the part of the story that contains a mistake.*

PUNCTUATION

S1
- ○ My favorite thing to eat
- ○ for dinner is pizza. My dad
- ● cooks it once a week

1
- ○ Stan doesn't like to arrive at
- ○ places late. He always says,
- ● Hurry up, we have to go!

2
- ● Wait You forgot to take
- ○ your umbrella with you. It's
- ○ raining outside today.

3
- ○ Do you know how to
- ● get to Sandy's house I think
- ○ we are going the wrong way.

USAGE

S1
- ● My favoritest animal is the
- ○ lion. I want to go to the zoo
- ○ tomorrow to see the lion show.

1
- ○ We were glad the roads
- ● was empty. It made our
- ○ drive home go quickly.

2
- ○ I had a great time when
- ○ we went on the hike, but I
- ● felled on the way down the hill.

3
- ● The pile of leafs in our
- ○ backyard is huge. Mom and
- ○ I will play in it tomorrow.

4
- ○ Tara took the small horse.
- ○ with the black tail. That horse
- ● walked the most slowest.

5
- ○ I gave my bag to Jordan
- ○ because I thought he might
- ● like it more than me do.

6
- ● Yesterday Shana is going to
- ○ visit her best friend. He
- ○ is home with the flu.

7
- ● That isn't not never the right time
- ○ for the game to start. I would
- ○ come back in an hour.

📣 *Do the sample question with the class, then read each story from the Pupil Edition page aloud, pausing between questions for students to mark their answers. Each story in questions S1 through 7 contains a mistake in the way a word or words is used. Read the stories to yourself as I read them aloud to you. For each story, fill in the bubble next to the part of the story that contains a mistake. Let's look at question S1.*

GO ON ➡

WORD ANALYSIS

S1
- ○ slant
- ● sting
- ○ send

> Look at the words for question S1. Fill in the bubble next to the word with the same beginning sound as start . . . start.

1
- ● crack
- ○ cake
- ○ close

> Look at the words for question 1. Fill in the bubble next to the word with the same beginning sound as the word crane . . . crane.

2
- ○ each
- ● elbow
- ○ eleven

> Look at the words for question 2. Fill in the bubble next to the word with the same beginning sound as the word enter . . . enter.

3
- ○ anger
- ○ apple
- ● allow

> Look at the words for question 3. Fill in the bubble next to the word with the same beginning sound as the word about . . . about.

S1

> For question S1, the word in the shaded box is wall. Fill in the bubble under the picture of the new word you

 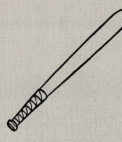 

● ○ ○

1 tree

> For question 1, the word in the shaded box is tree. Fill in the bubble under the picture of the new word you get when you take away the tr and put a b in its place.

○ ● ○

2 tar

> For question 2, the word in the shaded box is tar. Fill in the bubble under the picture of the new word you get when you take away the t and put a j in its place.

○ ○ ●

🔊 Look at the question S1. The word in the shaded box is moon. Fill in the bubble under the picture of the new word you get when you take away the m, and put an sp in its place.

S1 moon

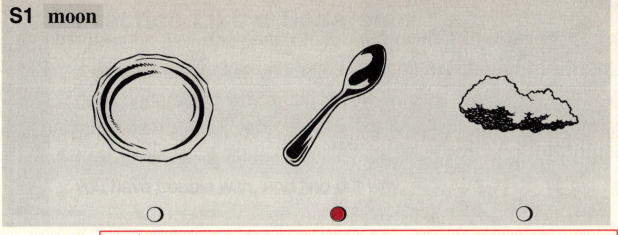

1 ramp

🔊 For question 1, the word in the shaded box is ramp. Fill in the bubble under the picture of the new word you get when you take away the r and put an st in its place.

2 think

🔊 For question 2, the word in the shaded box is think. Fill in the bubble under the picture of the new word you get when you take away the th at and put an s in its place.

GO ON ➡

S1

🔊 *Look at question S1. Listen carefully as I read a story to you: Peter took his coat off the table. He went outside to rake the leaves in the yard. Now look at the three pictures. Fill in the bubble next to the picture that shows what Peter will use to rake the leaves. The last picture, the rake, shows what Peter will use.*

1

🔊 *Look at question 1. Jane sat down at the kitchen table. There were flowers in the middle and a fork at every plate. She picked up her corn and began to eat it. Fill in the bubble below what Jane ate.*

2

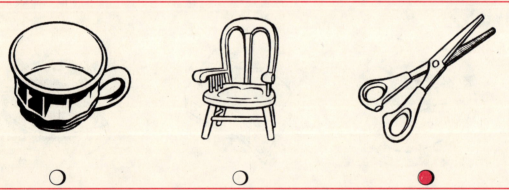

🔊 *Look at question 2. I sat in a chair. My mom poured water on my head from a cup and brushed my hair. Then she cut my hair. Fill in the bubble below what my mom used to cut my hair.*

3

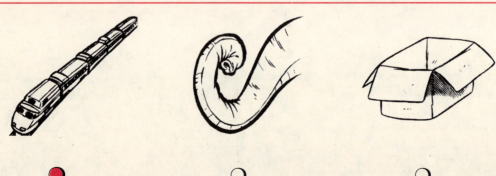

🔊 *Look at question 3. Max packed his boxes and brought them to the train station. When he was there, he saw an elephant riding on a train car. Max thought the elephant was huge. Fill in the bubble below what the elephant was riding on.*

S1 ○ job ○ grow ● grew

Look at question S1. Fill in the bubble next to the word that has the same vowel sound as true...true.

1 ● load ○ foot ○ new

Look at question 1. Fill in the bubble next to the word that has the same vowel sound as the word close...close.

2 ● voice ○ tour ○ night

Look at question 2. Fill in the bubble next to the word that has the same vowel sound as the word moist...moist.

3 ○ chair ● teach ○ crab

Look at question 3. Fill in the bubble next to the word that has the same vowel sound as the word seen...seen.

S1

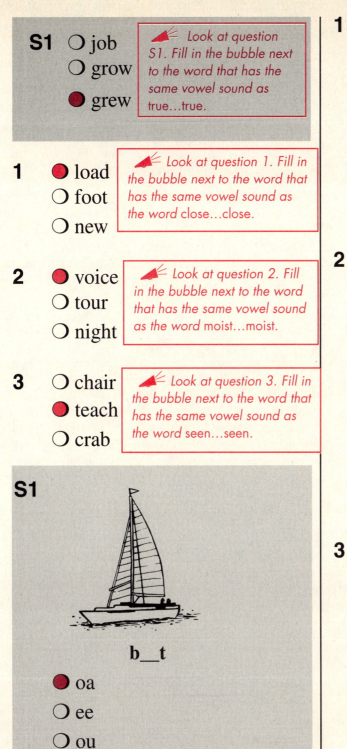

b__t

● oa ○ ee ○ ou

Now look at the picture of a boat in question S1. Fill in the bubble next to the letters that complete the word boat. The first choice, oa, shows the letters that complete the word boat.

1

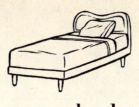

b__d

○ i ● e ○ a

Now look at the picture of a bed in question 1. Fill in the bubble next to the letter that completes the word bed.

2

d__r

○ oa ● oo ○ ea

Now look at the picture of a door in question 2. Fill in the bubble next to the letters that complete the word door.

3

sh__rt

○ e ● i ○ u

Now look at the picture of a shirt in question 3. Fill in the bubble next to the letter that completes the word shirt.

GO ON

Practice Test • Preparation and Practice for the ITBS, SAT-9, and TerraNova • Grade 2

S1
- ● wrap
- ○ wilts
- ○ worst

1
- ○ torn
- ● comb
- ○ trend

2
- ○ kings
- ○ kept
- ● knew

> 📣 Look at the three words in the example question. One of the words has a silent letter in it. For the questions in this section, you must choose which of the three words has a silent letter in it and fill in the bubble next to that word. For this question, fill in the bubble next to the first word, wrap, because the w is silent.

> 📣 For questions 1 and 2, fill in the bubble next to the word that contains a silent letter.

S1 tall
- ○ es
- ● er
- ○ en

1 quick
- ● ly
- ○ ous
- ○ ate

2 life
- ○ ed
- ○ ous
- ● less

> 📣 Look at the word in the shaded box and the three word endings in question S1. For this question, you must choose which word ending can be added to the shaded word to make a new word. Fill in the bubble under the ending -er, because adding that ending to the word tall makes a new word.

> 📣 Look at question 1. The word in the shaded box is quick. Fill in the bubble next to the ending that can be added to quick to make it a new word.

> 📣 Look at question 2. The word in the shaded box is life. Fill in the bubble next to the ending that can be added to life to make it a new word.

On Your Mark, Get Set, Go! Review

REVIEW

The following pages offer a list of the skills that students should be familiar with after completing the exercises in this book.

Punctuation

Student should know:

- Periods are used at the end of a statement
- Periods are used at the end of a command
- Question marks are used at the end of a question
- Exclamation points are used at the end of a statement of excitement
- Commas always separate the month and day from the year
- Quotation marks come before and after a person's exact words
- A period follows an abbreviation
- A period is placed between two capital letters in an abbreviation

Spelling

Students should know:

- How to form plurals by adding -s, -es, -ies, or changing -f to -v (e.g., *calf—calves*)
- What nouns change their spellings in plural form (*men, feet*)
- How to add suffixes such as -er, -less, -ly, -ful, -ous, and -en
- How to add suffixes such as -ed, -ing, -s, and -ly
- How to recognize and spell words with silent letters

Sounds

Students should know:

- The difference between the sounds of long and short vowels
- How vowel sounds change when followed by the letter *r*
- The different spellings for the short /e/ and long /e/ sound
- The difference between the sound of a soft /c/ and a hard /c/
- The difference between the sound of a soft /g/ and a hard /g/
- The sounds that result from *ph, ch,* and *tch*

Verbs

Students should know:

- The difference between a subject and a verb
- The difference between a singular and a plural subject or verb
- How to make subjects and verbs agree
- How to recognize a past, present, and future tense verb
- How to form irregular verbs in the past tense

Capitalization

Students should know:

- A capital letter always begins a sentence
- Names of people and pets should be capitalized
- Days of the week and months of the year should be capitalized
- Specific names of places should be capitalized
- Terms of respect (*Mr., Dr.*) should be capitalized
- The first letter of an abbreviation is always capitalized
- If an abbreviation is for more than one word, each letter must be capitalized

Adjectives

Students should know:

- Adjectives are words that describe nouns
- How to form comparative and superlative adjectives
- Which adjectives take *more* or *most* rather than adding a suffix

Pronouns

Students should know:

- A pronoun is used to replace a noun
- A subject pronoun takes the place of a noun in a subject
- *I, you, she, he, it, we,* and *they* are subject pronouns
- An object pronoun takes the place of a noun after a verb
- *Me, you, him, her, it, us,* and *them* are object pronouns
- The pronoun *I* always goes last when there is more than one subject

DRAWING CONCLUSIONS

Students should know:

- What it means to draw a conclusion
- The difference between a fact and a conclusion
- How to draw a conclusion by listening to a story and looking at pictures

Classifying Words

Students should know:

- What it means to classify words
- Words that have something in common belong in the same group
- How to tell if a word is different from other words in a group

Proper Language

Students should know:

- What makes up a double negative
- Never to use double negatives in a sentence
- Never to use *this, that, these,* or *those* with *there* or *here*

SAT-9

TEACHER INTRODUCTION

WHY *PREPARATION AND PRACTICE FOR THE SAT-9* IS THE BEST PREPARATION FOR STUDENTS

Welcome to the Teacher Edition of *Preparation and Practice for the SAT-9* for grade 2!

By completing each section of this book, students will:

- Increase their knowledge and understanding of language arts skills
- Become familiar with the types of questions that will be asked on the test
- Become aware of and experience first-hand the amount of time they will have to complete the test
- Become accustomed to the style of the test
- Become better writers and speakers
- Learn test-taking techniques and tips that are specifically designed to help students do their best on the SAT-9
- Feel comfortable on the day of the exam

Parts of This Book

There are eight sections of this Teacher Edition:

Teacher Introduction

The Teacher Introduction familiarizes you with the purpose and format of *Preparation and Practice for the SAT-9*. It also describes the SAT-9 sections and questions that pertain to language arts skills.

Student and Class Diagnostic Charts

This section consists of two charts. A student and a class diagnostic chart are included for the Warm-Up Test. You may use these charts to gauge student performance and to determine the skills with which students will need the most practice as you help them prepare for the SAT-9.

Student's Introduction

This section contains some tips and explanations for students as they begin their preparation for the SAT-9. Extra annotations are included for teachers to help you further explain what is expected of students and to encourage them as you begin to prepare them for the test.

Warm-Up Test

This diagnostic test reveals students' strengths and weaknesses so that you may customize your test preparation accordingly. The skill tested in each question of the Warm-Up Test directly correlates to a skill reviewed in one of the thirty On Your Mark! Get Set! Go! practice exercises.

On Your Mark! Get Set! Go!

This section consists of 30 practice exercises. Each exercise focuses on a specific language arts skill or test-taking strategy. On Your Mark! introduces and explains the skill. Get Set! provides an example question that tests the skill. (You should go over this question as a class. Get Set! is designed to bridge the gap between On Your Mark! and the test-like questions in Go!) Go! contains questions—similar to SAT-9 questions—that test the skills introduced in the exercise. Have students complete these questions on their own.

Practice Test

The Practice Test is a shortened version of the actual SAT-9. The Practice Test only contains a portion of the questions that will appear on the actual test so that students are not tapped of energy on the day of the actual SAT-9. The Practice Test includes questions from each section: word study skills, language, and spelling. The test provides students with a simulated test-taking experience. Make sure you tell students that the actual SAT-9 will be longer.

On Your Mark! Get Set! Go! Review

This section is *not* included in the Pupil Edition. This review section is an overview of the skills contained in On Your Mark! Get Set! Go! Similar skills are grouped together.

Index

The index is a brief listing of where you can look to find exercises about specific skills.

How to Use This Book

This book has been designed so that you may customize your SAT-9 test preparation according to your class's needs and time frame. However, we recommend that you begin your test preparation as early in the school year as possible. This book will yield your students' best SAT-9 scores if you diagnose your students' strengths and weaknesses early and work toward helping them achieve their best performance. Please note that preparing students for a test such as the SAT-9 is a process. As much of their preparation as possible should take place in the classroom and be discussed as a class.

Warm-Up Test

Have students complete the Warm-Up Test in class. It should be administered as early in the school year as possible. By doing so, students will gain familiarity with the types of questions and the specific skills tested on the SAT-9 *before* they begin working through the skill-specific exercises in this book. Use the student and class diagnostic charts to grade the tests. The results of the Warm-Up Test reveal students' strengths and weaknesses and allow you to focus your test preparation accordingly.

On Your Mark! Get Set! Go!

We recommend that you review an On Your Mark! Get Set! Go! exercise after completing each chapter in your McGraw-Hill language arts textbook. It is best to go through the On Your Mark! Get Set! Go! section throughout the year so that students can digest the material properly. Consider reviewing On Your Mark! and Get Set! as a class. The Go! sections may be assigned as homework or completed by students individually in class. Having students complete Go! individually will provide the best simulated preparation for the SAT-9. After students have completed the Go! exercises, go over the correct answers as a class. The Princeton Review's research and experience shows this in-class work to be an essential element in effective test preparation.

Practice Test

The Practice Test should be administered in the weeks prior to the actual exam. Testing conditions should be simulated. For example, no two desks should be placed directly next to each other, students should have two pencils at their disposal, the room should be quiet, and so on.

On Your Mark! Get Set! Go! Review

Use this review in the few days leading up to the actual exam. Its purpose is to solidify the On Your Mark! Get Set! Go! skills students have learned throughout the school year. Because this section is in the Teacher Edition only, you may want to photocopy it and review the skills as a class. Or, you may simply want to keep the information to yourself and make sure students are prepared to answer questions based on the material. If students need additional review, consult the On Your Mark! Get Set! Go! exercises that correlate to the skills. You will find the practice exercise-skill correlation information in the index.

About the Teacher Pages

Each page of the Pupil Edition is reproduced in this Teacher Edition, either reduced or full-size. Each reduced Pupil Edition page has teacher wrap. Teacher wrap consists of a **column** and a **box**.

- The column serves as a guide for you as you present the material on the Pupil Edition page in an interactive way. Guiding prompts and notes are included to ensure that information pivotal to the exercise is covered.

- The box includes teaching tips and extra activities. The extra activities are often fun, game-like activities for your class. These activities give students the opportunity to learn or apply SAT-9-related skills in a variety of ways.

Teacher wrap pages are punctuated with six icon types that help guide you through the Pupil Edition.

 This icon correlates the teacher wrap to the information in the On Your Mark! section of the Pupil Edition page.

 This icon reminds you to go over the example question in the Get Set! section of the Pupil Edition page.

 This icon reminds you to go over each question on the Go! pages of the Pupil Edition page.

 This icon provides a point of emphasis for you to make concerning the exercise on the Pupil Edition page.

 This icon identifies an extra activity.

 This icon reminds you to read any text that follows to the students.

About the Annotated Pages

Some pages in the Teacher Edition include full-size Pupil Edition pages. These occur in the Student Introduction, the Warm-Up Test section, and in the Practice Test section.

All of these full-size reproductions are highlighted with teacher annotations. These annotations, which appear in magenta ink, provide the following:

- **Teacher Script**

  A small magenta megaphone will appear directly before the script you need to read aloud.

- **Correct Answers**

  The correct answer to each question is circled in magenta ink.

- **Question Analyses**

  Sometimes an annotation offers further explanation of a specific question.

- **Extra Tips**

  Certain annotations provide you with extra teaching tips specific to the skill tested on the Pupil Edition page.

- **Hints**

  Some annotations offer hints that you can give to your students when they are working through the questions in the exercise or test sections.

Introduction to the SAT-9

SAT stands for Stanford Achievement Test. It is a standardized test administered every year by students throughout the country. Talk to your school's test administrator to get the exact testing date for this school year.

The SAT-9 is a multiple-choice test that assesses students' skills in reading, language arts, mathematics, social science, and science. This book covers the language arts section of the SAT-9, which consists of three parts:

- **Word Study Skills**
- **Language**
- **Spelling**

The specific number of questions for each skill discussed above and the time allotted for each is broken down as follows on the actual SAT-9:

Skill	Word Study Skills	Language	Spelling
Number of Items	48	30	30
Timing	25 minutes	27 minutes	25 minutes

How Language Arts Skills Are Tested

Word Study Skills

The word study skills section of the SAT-9 consists of two parts: structural analysis and phonetic analysis.

- **Structural Analysis:** These questions test students' ability to recognize compound words, words containing inflectional endings, words containing suffixes and prefixes, and contractions.

EXAMPLE:

You will say: *Fill in the bubble next to the word that has two words in it.*

○ banana

○ shopping

○ horseshoe

- **Phonetic Analysis:** These questions test students' ability to recognize relationships between letters and sounds.

EXAMPLE:

You will say: *Fill in the bubble next to the word that has the same sound as the underlined letter in* close.

cl<u>o</u>se

○ know

○ lose

○ stool

Language

The language section of the SAT-9 is divided into three sections:

- **Mechanics:** This section includes questions about capitalization, punctuation, and usage. Students are required to correct errors in the underlined parts of sentences by choosing the answer choice that contains the correct way to write the underlined section.
- **Expression in Sentences:** This section tests students' ability to recognize and correct run-on sentences, fragments, and awkward constructions.
- **Expression in Paragraphs:** Students are given short paragraphs and must demonstrate an ability to recognize extraneous information, combine sentences, and use descriptive language. Often students are asked to choose the sentence that would go best at the beginning or end of a paragraph.

Spelling

The spelling section of the SAT-9 tests students' ability to recognize misspelled words. Each question contains four answer choices. Each answer choice is a sentence with one underlined word. Students must choose the sentence that contains a misspelled word.

EXAMPLE:

Say: *Fill in the bubble next to the sentence that contains a misspelled word.*

- ○ She drives a bus.
- ○ The nife is sharp.
- ○ Bob took the ball.
- ○ This candy is sweet.

STUDENT AND CLASS DIAGNOSTIC CHARTS

How to Use the Student Diagnostic Chart

The Student Diagnostic Chart on page T39 should be used to score the Warm-Up Test in this book. The chart is designed to help you and your individual students determine the areas in which the most need practice as they begin their preparation for the SAT-9. You will need to make enough copies of the chart for each of your students.

There are two ways to use the Student Diagnostic Chart:

- You can collect the finished Warm-Up Tests from each student and fill out one chart for each student as you grade the tests.
- You can give one copy of the Student Diagnostic Chart to each student and have students grade their own tests as you read aloud the correct answer choices.

Note: Correct answer choices are marked in the Warm-Up Test of this Teacher Edition.

How to Fill Out the Student Diagnostic Chart

For each question number, there is a blank column labeled "Right or Wrong." An "R" or a "W" should be placed in that column for each question on the Warm-Up Test. By looking at the chart upon completion, students will understand which questions they answered incorrectly and to which skills these incorrect answers corresponded. The exercise from the On Your Mark! Get Set! Go! section that teaches the skill is also noted. You should encourage students to spend extra time going over the corresponding exercises covering the skills with which they had the most trouble. The charts will also help you determine which students need the most practice and what skills gave the majority of the students trouble. This way, you can plan your students' SAT-9 preparation schedule accordingly.

How to Use the Class Diagnostic Chart

The Class Diagnostic Chart on page T40 should be used to record your class's performance on the Warm-Up Test in this book. The chart is designed to help you determine what areas your class needs to practice most as you begin the preparation for the SAT-9. The Class Diagnostic Chart is strictly for your own use. You should not share it with students.

How to Fill Out the Class Diagnostic Chart

Under the "Name" column, you should write the names of each of your students. Then you should use the completed Student Diagnostic Charts to help you fill out the Class Diagnostic Chart. Fill out one row for each student.

For each question on the Warm-Up Test, there is a corresponding row in the Class Diagnostic Chart. The row is labeled with the question number and the exercise number of the correlating On Your Mark! Get Set! Go! exercise. If a student gets a question wrong, you should mark an "X" in the box underneath that question number. After completing a column for one student, add up all of the "Xs" and put a total for that student in the "Total" row on the top of the page. When you have filled out a column for each student, you should total up the "Xs" for each question. Put the totals in the "Total" column on the right-hand side of the page. Assessing both "Total" columns will help you determine two things: 1) which students are having the most trouble individually, and 2) which questions are giving the class as a whole the most trouble.

You should use the information gathered in the Class Diagnostic Chart to determine which skills to spend the most time reviewing and what students need the most individual practice and guidance.

Introduction • Preparation and Practice for the ITBS, SAT-9, and TerraNova • Grade 2

Student Diagnostic Chart

Question #	Correct Answer	Right or Wrong	Exercise #	Skill
1	2nd		1	Sentences
2	3rd		2	End Marks
3	3rd		3	Compound Words
4	3rd		4	Capitalizing Proper Nouns
5	2nd		5	Vowels
6	1st		7	Verbs
7	3rd		8	Capital Letters in Titles
8	1st		9	Helping Verbs
9	2nd		10	Commas in Dates
10	3rd		11	Verb Tenses
11	1st		12	Irregular Verbs
12	2nd		13	Vowel Sounds with R
13	1st		15	Contractions
14	2nd		16	Alphabetical Order
15	3rd		18	Paragraphs
16	3rd		17	Main Idea
17	2nd		19	Writing with a Purpose
18	3rd		22	Spelling Words with Confusing Sounds
19	4th		24	Tricky Words
20	3rd		24	Tricky Words
21	4th		24	Tricky Words
22	3rd		26	Terms of Respect
23	1st		25	Long /E/ and Short /E/ Sound
24	2nd		27	/C/ and /G/ Sounds
25	1st		29	/Ph/, /ch/, and /tch/ Sounds

Class Diagnostic Chart

Name	Q1-Ex. 1	Q2-Ex. 2	Q3-Ex. 3	Q4-Ex. 4	Q5-Ex. 5	Q6-Ex. 7	Q7-Ex. 8	Q8-Ex. 9	Q9-Ex. 10	Q10-Ex. 11	Q11-Ex. 12	Q12-Ex. 13	Q13-Ex. 15	Q14-Ex. 16	Q15-Ex. 18	Q16-Ex. 17	Q17-Ex. 19	Q18-Ex. 22	Q19-Ex. 24	Q20-Ex. 24	Q21-Ex. 24	Q22-Ex. 26	Q23-Ex. 25	Q24-Ex. 27	Q25-Ex. 29	Total

STUDENT INTRODUCTION

What is the SAT-9?

The Stanford 9, also called the SAT-9, is a multiple-choice test that helps you and your teacher find out how much you have learned in school so far. Now's your chance to show off what you know about reading and writing!

This may be the first time students are preparing to take a standardized test. Explain to them that test-taking does not have to be a stressful experience. Instead, it is an opportunity for them to demonstrate what they have learned in reading and writing. Emphasize to students that this workbook will allow them to practice these skills so that each of them will do his or her best on the SAT-9.

Instilling a positive attitude about test-taking in students from the beginning will help them get more out of the practice exercises and—most importantly—will help them approach the SAT-9 with confidence.

Introduction • Preparation and Practice for the ITBS, SAT-9, and TerraNova • Grade 2

Does the SAT-9 measure how smart I am?

No, definitely not. The SAT-9 tests how well you can use the skills you've learned in class.

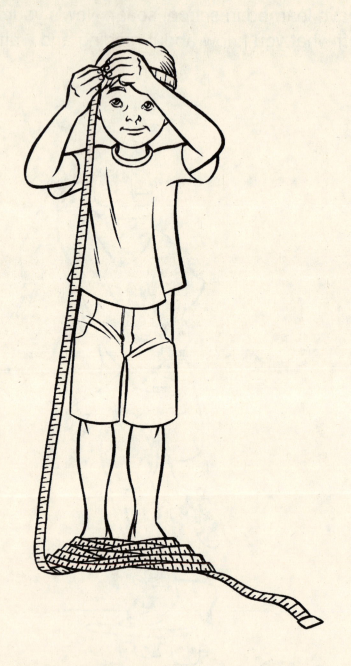

> Ease test-taking anxiety by assuring students that the SAT-9 *does not* measure their intelligence. Instead, it measures their ability to use the skills that they have learned in school.

Can I study for the SAT-9?

You can answer practice questions. You can also learn some tips that will help you do your best.

Just like riding a bike or playing the violin, studying for the SAT-9 takes practice. The more you practice, the better you will do!

> Remind students that the SAT-9 measures what they have been learning in school. Instead of studying for this standardized test, students need to review the concepts that they have learned in school and learn some test-taking tips. The exercises and activities in the workbook are designed to provide such practice. To emphasize this point, have students discuss how practicing leads to improvement. For example, ask students to name several activities (e.g., sports, music, art) in which they participate. Then, ask them to discuss how they practice for these activities. Has practice helped them improve their skills? How?

Here's how you will practice for the SAT-9:

✓ You'll take a Warm-Up Test

✓ You'll brush up on your reading and writing skills in On Your Mark! Get Set! Go!

✓ You'll take a Mini-Practice Test. After all of your practicing, you'll know exactly what to expect when you take the real SAT-9.

> So that they do not feel overwhelmed, let students know that they'll be completing these exercises over an extended period of time.

Practice Like a Superstar

Ask questions. Ask your teacher if you don't understand why an answer is wrong.

Learn from your mistakes. Notice the things you have trouble with, and find out why.

Read as much as you can. Read everything and anything you can get your hands on. Read signs as you pass by them. Read stories aloud. Listen to others read stories aloud to you.

Answering questions incorrectly can be as valuable as answering questions correctly in preparing for a standardized test. Make sure students understand that it is okay to make mistakes. The important thing is to learn from their mistakes.

As students work through the tests and exercises in this book, provide them with positive feedback and encourage them with congratulations as they improve their skills. Allowing students to celebrate their progress will help them approach the SAT-9 with confidence and a positive attitude.

Pay Attention to the Directions

The directions tell you how to answer the question. Sometimes you will read directions on your own. Other times, the teacher will read them to you. Always make sure you understand the directions.

Reinforce to students the importance of listening to all directions carefully. The directions will often provide important information about how to answer the questions.

Read Questions and Answer Choices Slowly and Carefully

Always read all the words in the questions and all the words in the answer choices carefully. Read every answer choice, even if you think you have already found the correct answer!

Let students in on a little secret: Standardized tests often contain answer choices that are designed to distract the students from the correct answer. Therefore, students need to read and compare all of the answer choices in order to figure out which is the best choice.

Get Rid of the Wrong Answer Choices First

✓ Every time you answer a question, read each answer choice, one by one.

✓ After you read each answer choice, decide whether you think the answer choice is right or wrong.

✓ Get rid of as many wrong answer choices as you can. If you still have more than one answer choice left over, guess! Try not to leave any questions blank.

Process of elimination is one of the most important strategies students can use to increase their success on standardized tests. You may want to illustrate this concept by playing some sort of guessing game with students. For example, write down four things (e.g., days of the week, types of animals, flavors of ice cream) on index cards. Share the items with students, and then have one student choose one card. Ask the rest of the class to guess the chosen card. Keep track of the number of guesses. Repeat the game with three cards, two cards, and finally, one card. This should illustrate to students how the chances of guessing correctly increase as the number of choices decreases.

Watch Yourself

Don't spend too much time on one question.

Going too slow is no good—you'll leave more questions blank than you need to.

Don't rush through the test.

Going too fast is no good, either—you'll only make silly mistakes, like misunderstanding the directions.

The SAT-9 is a timed test. Therefore, it is important to reinforce to students the importance of working carefully and efficiently. They should try to answer each question. However, they shouldn't spend too much time answering a question that is difficult for them. This might prevent them from reaching questions that they can answer correctly.

Mark Your Answers Correctly

When you find the answer to a question, fill in the bubble that goes with the answer choice you have found.

Always make sure you fill in the answer bubbles completely!

 Do NOT fill in half of the bubble. This is wrong.

 Do NOT place a checkmark over the bubble. This is wrong.

 Do NOT scribble inside the bubble. This is wrong.

 DO fill in the bubble completely. This is correct!

Now you try filling in the bubble correctly.

On the test, how should you fill in the bubble?

○ You should fill in half of the bubble.

○ You should scribble inside the bubble.

○ You should completely fill in the bubble.

Explain to students that it is important to fill in the bubbles correctly so that they get credit for their correct answer choices. Because a machine scores the test, it cannot read bubbles that are only partially filled in.

Warm-Up Test

1. I tore my pants. When I climbed over the fence.

○ I tore my pants when I climbing over the fence.
● I tore my pants when I climbed over the fence.
○ The way it is

2. My sister will let us use **her bike today.**

○ her bike today?
○ her bike. Today?
● The way it is

3.
○ envelopes
○ smiling
● placemat

For question 1, choose the answer that contains a complete sentence. If the example sentence is correct, fill in the bubble for The way it is.

For question 2, choose the answer that shows how the underlined part should be written. If it is written correctly in the example, fill in the bubble for The way it is.

For question 3, choose the word that is made of up two words.

4. The last **Sunday in April** is a holiday.

○ Sunday in april
○ sunday in april
● The way it is

5. cr**o**ss

○ cow
● soft
○ grow

6. Did you **will have** a good time last night?

● have
○ had
○ The way it is

For question 4, choose the answer that shows how the underlined part should be written. If it is written correctly in the example, fill in the bubble for The way it is.

For question 5, choose the answer that contains the same sound as the underlined letter in the word cross.

For question 6, choose the answer that shows how the underlined part should be written. If it is written correctly in the example, fill in the bubble for The way it is.

Warm-Up Test • Preparation and Practice for the ITBS, SAT-9, and TerraNova • Grade 2

> For questions 7 through 11, choose the answer that shows how the underlined part should be written. If it is written correctly in the example, fill in the bubble for The way it is.

7 Don't read the story "**Harry's Pet Worm.**"
- ○ "Harry's pet worm."
- ○ Harry's Pet Worm.
- ● The way it is

8 The shopkeeper is happy when the store **are** filling up with people.
- ● is
- ○ will
- ○ The way it is

9 The story was finished on **September 28 1999.**
- ○ september 28 1999.
- ● September 28, 1999.
- ○ The way it is

10 We **watered** the garden last Tuesday.
- ○ will water
- ○ water
- ● The way it is

11 **I never rided** a horse before today.
- ● I never rode
- ○ I never ridded
- ○ The way it is

12 st**a**r
- ○ dare
- ● park
- ○ door

> For question 12, choose the answer that contains the same sound as the underlined letter in the word star.

13 Do not worry, **hel'l** be back.
- ● he'll
- ○ hell
- ○ The way it is

> For question 13, choose the answer that shows how the underlined part should be written. If it is written correctly in the example, fill in the bubble for The way it is.

14
- ○ front
- ● fair
- ○ fast

> For question 14, choose the answer that comes first in alphabetical order.

Read the story and the question aloud to students.

Story A

Beth and her mother made a book of photographs they took on their trip. They picked the pictures of Beth standing in front of famous buildings and glued them into the album. Beth will take it to school and share it with her friends and teachers.

15 Which sentence would go <u>best</u> after the last sentence?

○ They traveled by airplane.

○ Her best friend Molly went to Spain.

● She titled her album, "Beth and Buildings."

The story is about the book Beth and her mother are making, so the sentence should be about the book.

Read the story and the question aloud to students.

Story B

Karen's new bike was red. She took it out for a ride around the block. While she was riding, she saw her neighbor Mr. Moore. He waved and called out to her, "Nice bike!"

16 **Which of these would not go with the story?**

○ Mr. Moore lived down the street.

○ It was her first ride.

● Her bike was blue.

The story says that the bike was red, not blue, so the last sentence could not go with the story.

Read the story and the question aloud to students.

Story C

Chocolate chip cookies were Toby's favorite. If one of his friends brought chocolate chip cookies in their lunch, Toby would try to trade his fruit for them. One time, he traded an orange for 2 cookies, but there were nuts inside the cookies. Toby didn't like nuts!

17 Why was this story written?

○ To tell about Toby's lunch.

● To tell about one of Toby's lunchtime trades.

○ To tell about what Toby does not like to eat.

Two out of the three answer choices are not about Toby's trades, which is the main purpose of this paragraph.

Warm-Up Test • Preparation and Practice for the ITBS, SAT-9, and TerraNova • Grade 2

> For questions 18 through 21, choose the answer that contains a misspelled word.

18
- ○ Jorge is <u>four</u> years old.
- ○ Did Tom <u>skip</u> lunch?
- ● He said <u>mabe</u> we could go.
- ○ I feel <u>pretty</u> today.

19
- ○ Who is ready to <u>draw</u>?
- ○ That picture is <u>funny</u>.
- ○ The <u>farmer</u> planted crops.
- ● Put the food in the <u>kart</u>.

20
- ○ Who won the <u>prize</u>?
- ○ We can <u>add</u> them up.
- ● Can I have a <u>doubble</u> scoop of ice cream?
- ○ Have you seen my new <u>doll</u>?

21
- ○ <u>Every</u> night we read.
- ○ He will change his <u>mind</u>.
- ○ We don't know the <u>name</u> of the road.
- ● Sew a <u>stich</u> here.

22 Will you tell <u>Mrs. Benison</u> I will be late?
- ○ mrs. Benison,
- ○ Mrs. benison
- ● The way it is

> For question 22, choose the answer that shows how the underlined part should be written. If it is written correctly in the example, fill in the bubble for The way it is.

23 gr<u>ee</u>n
- ● l<u>ea</u>f
- ○ p<u>a</u>l
- ○ s<u>i</u>ll

> For question 23, choose the answer that contains the same sound as the underlined letters in the word green.

24 <u>j</u>eans
- ○ <u>g</u>ive
- ● <u>g</u>rudge
- ○ <u>f</u>og

> For question 24, choose the answer that contains the same sound as the underlined letter in the word jeans.

25 bran<u>ch</u>
- ● <u>ch</u>ain
- ○ bla<u>ck</u>
- ○ <u>c</u>rop

> For question 25, choose the answer that contains the same sound as the underlined letter in the word branch.

On Your Mark, Get Set, Go!

Exercise 1
SENTENCES

 Discuss the difference between a complete sentence and a sentence fragment.

On the board, write a complete sentence. Discuss the fact that it contains a complete thought. It tells *who* or *what* the sentence is about, and it also tells *what happened*. Some sentences you might use are:

- *Kara played at the park.*
- *The dog ran away.*
- *Mother gave me a cookie.*
- *The boy kicked the ball.*

Now, write some sentence fragments on the board. Ask students to explain the reason why the examples are not considered complete sentences. Here are some fragments you can use:

- *Eating lunch*
- *Jacob and David*
- *Playing on the playground*

Discuss what needs to be added to each of the fragments in order to form a complete sentence. Answer any questions students have.

 Go over the example question as a class.

Exercise 1
 ## ON YOUR MARK!
Sentences

A **sentence** is a group of words that tells a complete thought.
  Maria walked up the hill.

A group of words that does not tell a complete thought is a **fragment**.
  Up the hill.

A sentence names the person or thing you are talking about. It also tells what happened.
  Maria walked up the hill.
    Who? *Maria*
    What happened? *walked up the hill.*

 ## GET SET!
Let's look at an example.
What is the best way to write the sentence below?

> Laura can't swim until after lunch.

○ Laura can't swim. Until after lunch.
○ Until after lunch Laura can't be swimming.
● Correct as it is

(1st) is **wrong**. The second sentence is not complete. It tells us *when*, but it doesn't tell us *who* or *what*.

(2nd) is **wrong**. Is this how people normally talk? No, it isn't. This sentence is hard to understand.

(3rd) is **correct!** The sentence tells us *who* and *what* in a way that is easy to understand.

 ### EXTRA ACTIVITY

As an extra class activity, divide the class into groups. Give each group a worksheet containing complete sentences and fragments. Students must decide which ones are complete sentences and which are fragments. For extra credit, students can turn the fragments into complete sentences.

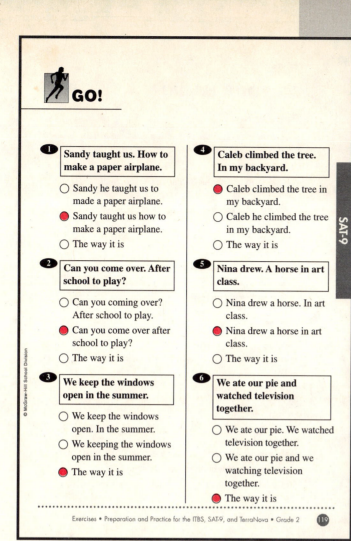

 Go over each question on this page as a class.

Find the sentence in each group that is written correctly. Fill in the bubble next to the correctly written sentence. If the example sentence is written correctly, fill in the bubble next to The way it is.

Questions 1, 2, 4, and 5

The sentences in each box contain fragments.

Question 6

The first answer choice is made up of two complete sentences, but because the directions said to find *the sentence* that is written correctly, the last answer choice is correct. The sentence in the box is already complete.

Exercise 2
END MARKS

 Go over each type of end mark with students.

On the board, write several sentences and ask students to choose the end mark for each. Some sentences you might use are:

- *The boy went home(.)*
- *Sit in your seat(.)*
- *Where are you going(?)*
- *There is a snake(!)*

Discuss with students how they decided on the end marks. For example, how did they know where to put a question mark? Answer any questions students have.

 Go over the example question as a class.

 Exercise 2

ON YOUR MARK!

End Marks

A **statement** is a sentence that tells something. It ends with a period.
> *I have to go home.*

A **command** is a sentence that tells someone to do something. It also ends with a period.
> *Please shut the door.*

A **question** is a sentence that asks something. It ends with a question mark.
> *What time is it?*

An **exclamation** is a sentence that shows strong feeling. It ends with an exclamation mark.
> *What a great time I had!*

 GET SET!

Let's look at an example.
What is the best way to write the underlined part of this sentence?

Can Timmy play <u>today!</u>
- ○ today.
- ○ today?
- ○ The way it is

(1st) is **wrong.** A question should end with a question mark.
(2nd) is **correct!** A question ends with a question mark.
(3rd) is **wrong.** This is a question. It should end with a question mark.

 EXTRA ACTIVITY

Play the punctuation game. Divide the class into two or three teams.

Have one player from each team go to the board at the same time. Read a sentence and tell each player to write the correct punctuation mark on the board. The first player (or players) to respond correctly earns a point. They also must tell why they chose that punctuation mark. (Example: I chose a question mark because the sentence asked *where* the dog was.) As a follow-up, create a worksheet containing statements, commands, questions, and exclamations, but leave out the end marks. Students must fill in the correct punctuation mark.

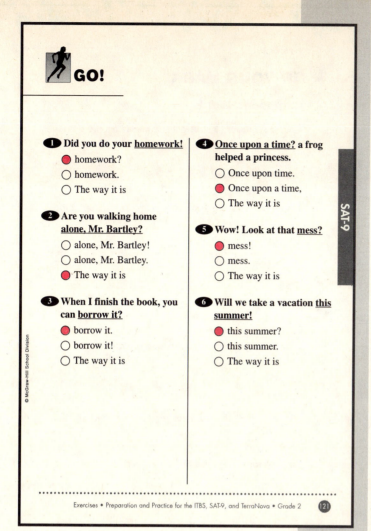

 Go over each question on this page as a class.

Read each sentence in questions 1 through 6. Look carefully at the underlined part of the sentence and the punctuation mark that follows. Fill in the bubble next to the choice that has the underlined part written correctly. If the sentence is already written correctly, fill in the bubble next to the choice The way it is.

Question 1
Question Mark—Question

Question 3
Period—Statement

Question 4
Comma—Introductory Phrase

This question requires that students understand that commas go after introductory phrases. Give students extra examples of this type of question.

Question 5
Exclamation Mark—Exclamation

Question 6
Question Mark—Question

Exercise 3
COMPOUND WORDS

 Discuss the meaning of a compound word with students.

On the board, write several compound words and ask students to find the two small words each is made from. Some compound words you might use are:

- *cowboy*
- *cupcake*
- *jellyfish*
- *sunset*

Discuss with students how they decided on the two small words. The new word made by combining the two words now has a new meaning. Ask if the small words give a clue to the meaning of the compound word. Answer any questions students have.

 Go over the example question as a class.

Exercise 3

 ON YOUR MARK!

Compound Words

A **compound word** is a word that is made from two smaller words.

fire + man = fireman
base + ball = baseball
suit + case = suitcase

Knowing the meaning and spelling of the two smaller words can help you figure out the meaning and spelling of the compound word.

> **TIP:** Never drop any letters when you combine two words to make a compound word.

 GET SET!

Let's look at an example.

Which of these words is a compound word?
○ rainbow
○ pencil
○ blanket

(1st) is **correct!** The two words *rain* and *bow* make this a compound word.

(2nd) is **wrong**. *Pen* is a word, but *cil* is not.

(3rd) is **wrong**. *Blank* is a word, but *et* is not.

 EXTRA ACTIVITY

As an extra activity, choose fifteen compound words. Write the first half of each compound word on one index card and the second half on another card. Pass the cards out to students. Give them one minute to find the partner who holds the card that will complete their compound word.

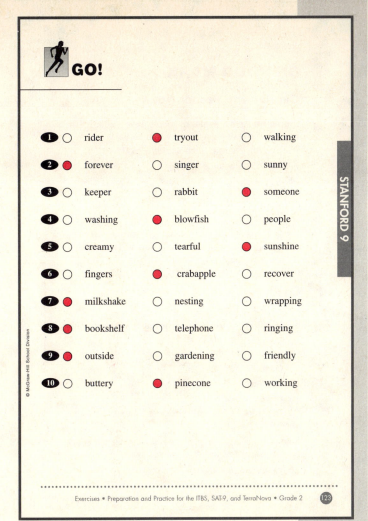

 Go over each question on this page as a class.

📣 *For questions 1 through 10, fill in the bubble next to the word that is made up of two words.*

Explain to students that there are never any letters left out of either small word when forming a compound word.

Question 1

try/out

Question 2

for/ever

Question 3

some/one

Question 4

blow/fish

Question 5

sun/shine

Question 6

crab/apple

Question 7

milk/shake

Question 8

book/shelf

Question 9

out/side

Question 10

pine/cone

Exercise 4
CAPITALIZING PROPER NOUNS

 Go over the meaning of a proper noun with students.

Point out that all proper nouns begin with capital letters.

On the board, write several sentences that contain proper nouns that have not been capitalized. Ask students to identify the proper nouns and change the lower case letter to a capital letter. Some sentences you might use are:

- *My friend's name is sarah roberts.* (Sarah Roberts)
- *I will feed my goldfish, speedy.* (Speedy)
- *I would like to visit hawaii.* (Hawaii)
- *Today is monday, october 15.* (Monday, October)

Discuss with students how they decided which words needed capital letters. Why did they consider the word to be a proper noun? Was it a name of a special person, pet, or place, or was it the name of a day or a month? Answer any questions students have.

 Go over the example question as a class.

 Exercise 4
ON YOUR MARK!
Capitalizing Proper Nouns

Proper nouns are names of people, pets, places, days, and months. A proper noun begins with a capital letter.
People: Andy Jones, Renu Shukla, Erin Ripley
Pets: My kitten's name is Felix.
Places: Mount Everest, London Bridge, France, Chicago
Days: Monday, Tuesday, Wednesday
Months: June, July, August

> **TIP:** If a proper noun is more than one word, all of the important words are capitalized. For example, Lincoln Park and Hudson River.

 # GET SET!
Let's look at an example.
What is the best way to write the underlined part of the sentence below?

I was sick on monday.
○ On monday.
○ on Monday.
○ Correct as it is

(1st) is **wrong.** *On* is not a proper noun, so it should not be capitalized.

(2nd) is **correct!** All days of the week are capitalized. *On* is not capitalized because it is not a proper noun.

(3rd) is **wrong.** *Monday* should be capitalized.

  ## EXTRA ACTIVITY

Make a worksheet that contains several different sentences. In each sentence include a proper noun that has not been capitalized. Include names of people, pets, places, days, and months. Have students capitalize the proper nouns.

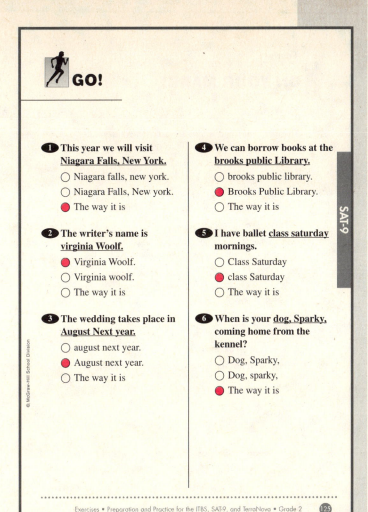

 Go over each question on this page as a class.

📣 *Read each sentence in questions 1 through 8. Look carefully at the underlined part. Find the choice that has the underlined part written correctly. If the sentence is already written correctly, fill in the bubble next to* The way it is.

Question 2

The first letter of both names should be capitalized.

Question 3

The word *next* is a common noun, not a proper noun.

Question 4

All words in the name of a place should be capitalized.

Question 5

The word *class* is a common noun. Days of the week should be capitalized.

Exercise 5
VOWELS

 Go over the difference between long vowels and short vowels with students.

Explain that vowels are considered "long" or "short" on the basis of their sound.

Look at the list in the middle of the Pupil Edition page that compares short and long vowel sounds. Have one student say *cat* out loud. Then have another student say *cave*. Discuss how the two /a/ sounds are different, even though they contain the same vowel. Follow this routine for the rest of the words listed.

Make sure students understand that a silent /e/ often comes at the end of a word with a long vowel sound.

 Go over the example question as a class.

Exercise 5

 ON YOUR MARK!

Vowels

The letters *a, e, i, o,* and *u* are called **vowels**. We call vowels *long* or *short* depending on how we say them.

Long vowels sound like we say them in the alphabet.

c*a*ve, w*e*, d*i*ve, n*o*te, fl*u*te

Look at the words above again. Notice how many words with long vowels in them end with an *e* that is silent.

cav*e*, div*e*, not*e*, flute

Short vowels do not sound like we say them in the alphabet. Compare the word pairs below to hear the difference.

Short:	c*a*t	w*e*t	b*i*t	m*o*p	p*u*ppy
Long:	c*a*ve	w*e*	d*i*ve	n*o*te	fl*u*te

 GET SET!

Let's look at an example.

Which word has the same vowel sound as the word below?

game
○ hat
○ fame
○ man

(1st) is **wrong**. *Game* has a long *a*, and *hat* has a short *a*.
(2nd) is **correct!** *Game* and *fame* both have a long *a* sounds.
(3rd) is **wrong**. *Game* has a long *a*, and *man* has a short *a*.

 Exercises • Preparation and Practice for the ITBS, SAT-9, and TerraNova • Grade 2

 TEACHING TIP

Here are some more words you can write on the board to demonstrate the difference between long and short vowel sounds. Have students read the words aloud.

- *bit   bite*
- *rat   rate*
- *met   me*
- *rod   rode*
- *mad   made*

GO!

1. **a**ge
   - ○ egg
   - ● cake
   - ○ park

2. r**o**be
   - ○ move
   - ● nose
   - ○ ton

3. t**a**n
   - ○ cape
   - ○ plane
   - ● man

4. m**u**st
   - ○ some
   - ● under
   - ○ uniform

5. sk**a**te
   - ○ and
   - ○ kite
   - ● freight

6. l**o**se
   - ○ cook
   - ○ over
   - ● rule

SAT-9

Go over each question on this page as a class.

Question 1
📢 For question 1, fill in the bubble next to the word that has the same sound as the underlined letter in the word age.

Question 2
📢 For question 2, fill in the bubble next to the word that has the same sound as the underlined letter in the word robe.

Question 3
📢 For question 3, fill in the bubble next to the word that has the same sound as the underlined letter in the word tan.

Question 4
📢 For question 4, fill in the bubble next to the word that has the same sound as the underlined letter in the word must.

Question 5
📢 For question 5, fill in the bubble next to the word that has the same sound as the underlined letter in the word skate.

Question 6
📢 For question 6, fill in the bubble next to the word that has the same sound as the underlined letter in the word lose.

Exercise 6
GETTING RID OF THE WRONG ANSWER CHOICES

 Explain to students that ruling out wrong answer choices is an important test-taking skill.

Have students read the top section of the Pupil Edition page or read it aloud to them. Point out that ruling out wrong answer choices will help them:

- Move through the test more quickly
- Increase their chances of finding the correct answer
- Score higher on the test

By getting rid of wrong answer choices, students will feel more confident that the answer they choose is the best answer.

 Go over the example question as a class. Have students raise their hands and explain why each answer choice is correct or incorrect.

Exercise 6

 ON YOUR MARK!

Getting Rid of the Wrong Answer Choices

Sometimes you might not know the answer to a question. When this happens, try to get rid of as many WRONG answer choices as you can. Ruling out just one or two wrong answer choices makes it easier for you to find the right answer. Try to answer this question:

What is Janet's favorite sport?
○ sleeping
○ eating
○ baseball

- Look at the 1st answer choice. Is *sleeping* a sport? No! Get rid of this answer.
- Look at the 2nd answer choice. Is *eating* a sport? No! Get rid of this answer.
- Look at the last choice. Is *baseball* a sport? Yes, it is!

 GET SET!

Let's look at another example. What is the best way to write the sentences below? Try to get rid of the wrong answer choices first.

| Grandma bakes cookies. In the kitchen. |

○ Grandma in the kitchen. Bakes cookies.
○ Grandma bakes cookies in the kitchen.
○ Correct as it is

(1st) is **wrong.** Both sentences are incomplete. *What does Grandma do in the kitchen? Who bakes cookies?*
(2nd) is **correct!** It tells us *who* and *what happened.*
(3rd) is **wrong.** The second sentence is not complete. *Who is in the kitchen?*

  EXTRA ACTIVITY

Play *Twenty Questions* with students to help them understand the importance of ruling out wrong answers. Have one student choose a "mystery student" in the class, but don't tell who it is. Have the other students raise their hands and ask "yes" or "no" questions about the student until they find the correct answer. By doing so, students will begin to understand how ruling out wrong answers leads them closer to the correct answer. For example, if a student asks: "Is it a boy?" and the answer is "no," then the next student will know not to guess a boy in the class. They are one step closer to determining the correct answer.

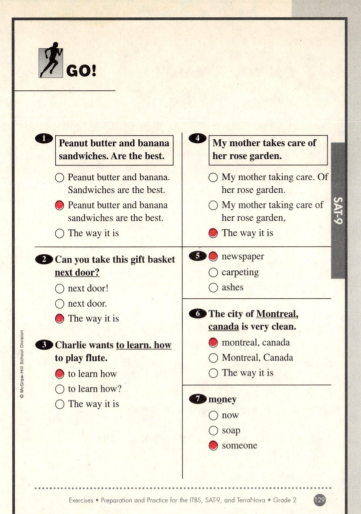

 Go over each question on this page as a class.

This page tests skills that students learned in Exercises 1 through 6. Students should try to get rid of wrong answer choices as they work through questions 1 through 7.

📣 *For questions 1 through 7, fill in the bubble next to the answer you choose.*

Question 1

📣 *For question 1, find the sentence that is written correctly. If the example sentence is written correctly, fill in the bubble next to The way it is.*

Questions 2 and 3

📣 *For questions 2 and 3, find the correct way to write the underlined part of the sentence. If the example sentence is written correctly, fill in the bubble next to The way it is.*

Question 4

📣 *For question 4, find the sentence that is written correctly. If the example sentence is written correctly, fill in the bubble next to The way it is.*

Question 5

📣 *For question 5, fill in the bubble next to the word that is made up of two words.*

Question 6

📣 *For question 6, find the correct way to write the underlined part of the sentence. If the example sentence is written correctly, fill in the bubble next to The way it is.*

Question 7

📣 *For question 7, fill in the bubble next to the word with the same sound as the underlined letter in the word money.*

Exercise 7
SUBJECTS AND VERBS

 Go over the difference between subjects and verbs.

Discuss how subjects and verbs in a sentence must agree.

Explain that a sentence must have a subject that tells *who* or *what* the sentence is about, and it must have a predicate that tells *what the subject is doing*. Write the following sentences on the board and have the students identify the subject and the predicate.

- *The dog barks loudly.*
- *Three boys play on the playground.*
- *Amanda runs around the park.*
- *Many children love to read.*

Point out that if the subject of the sentence is singular (one person or thing), the present tense verb must have an *-s* or *-es* added to the end. If the subject is plural (more than one person or thing), point out that students should not add any ending to the present tense verb. Go over each sentence again and discuss the subject and verb agreement.

 Go over the example question as a class.

 Exercise 7
ON YOUR MARK!
Subjects and Verbs

The **subject** of a sentence tells who or what does something.
  Ryan asks a question.
An **action verb** tells what someone or something is doing.
  Ryan **asks** a question.
The subject and the verb in a sentence must agree.
Add *-s* or *-es* to a present tense verb that tells about one person or thing.
  She **listens** to him.
Do not add anything to a present tense verb that tells about one person or thing.
  The kids **listen** to him.

 ## GET SET!

Let's look at an example.

Find the best way to write the underlined verb.

The children <u>watch</u> the film.
○ watches
○ watching
○ The way it is

(1st) is **wrong**. The subject *children* is more than one person, so you do not add *-es* to *watch*.

(2nd) is **wrong**. In order for *watching* to be correct, the helping verb *are* must come before it.

(3rd) is **correct!** The subject *children* is more than one, so *watch* is correct.

130 Exercises • Preparation and Practice for the ITBS, SAT-9, and TerraNova • Grade 2

 ## EXTRA ACTIVITY

Divide the class into four groups. Give each group two worksheets. On one sheet write subjects, and on the other write verbs. Have each group form complete sentences by matching the subjects and verbs. Have students check to make sure each subject and verb agrees. Have each group share their sentences with the class.

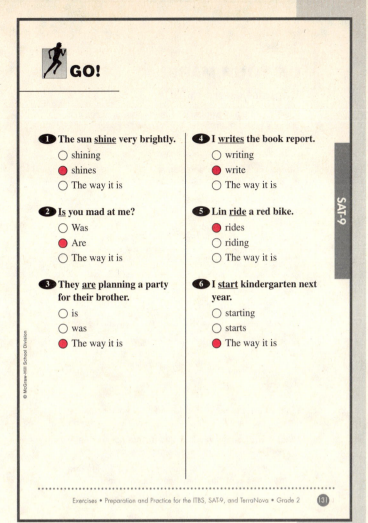

 Go over each question on this page as a class.

For questions 1 through 6, look carefully at the underlined verb. Fill in the bubble next to the choice that will make the sentence correct. If the example sentence is written correctly, fill in the bubble next to the choice The way it is.

A discussion of the verbs *is* and *are* will be helpful to students since these are not covered on Pupil's Edition page 130.

Question 1
The helping verb *is* would be needed if *shining* were correct.

Question 2
Is and *you* are never used together.

Question 4
Although *I* is singular, it often agrees with the plural form of a verb. Make sure students understand this exception.

Question 5
Lin is singular. *Ride* is plural.

Exercise 8
CAPITALIZING LETTERS IN TITLES

 Go over the different kinds of titles discussed on the Pupil Edition page.

Discuss how the first word and all other important words in titles are capitalized.

Explain that a title can be the name of a book, poem, song, short story, film, or newspaper. Discuss that all words in a title are capitalized except unimportant words such as *a, an, and, the, to, for,* and *as.* Remind students that the only time any of these words is capitalized in a title is when it is the first word. Put some titles on the board and discuss the capitalization with students. Here are some titles you might use.

- *A Chair for My Mother* (book)
- *The Wheels of the Bus* (song)
- *Keep a Poem in Your Pocket* (poem)
- *The Chicago Tribune* (newspaper)
- *The Dinosaur Movie* (film)

 Go over the example question as a class.

Exercise 8
 ON YOUR MARK!

Capital Letters in Titles

Capitalize the first word and all the important words in the title of a book, poem, song, short story, film, and newspaper.

Here are some examples of different kinds of titles:
Book: *The House at Pooh Corner*
Song: "Three Blind Mice"
Newspaper: *The New York Times*

> **TIP:** Unimportant words like *a, an, and, the, to, for,* and *as* are not capitalized unless they are the first word in a title.

 GET SET!

Let's look at an example.

Find the answer choice with the correct capital letters.

I read a book called *The wind in the willows*.
○ The Wind in the Willows
○ The Wind In The Willows
○ The way it is

(1st) is **correct!** The first word and all the other important words have capital letters.

(2nd) is **wrong.** The words *in* and *the* are not important words. They should not have capital letters.

(3rd) is **wrong.** The words *wind* and *willows* are important words in this book title. They need capital letters.

 EXTRA ACTIVITY

Make a worksheet with several sentences containing titles. Leave out the correct capitalization in some titles. Students should rewrite the sentences correctly.

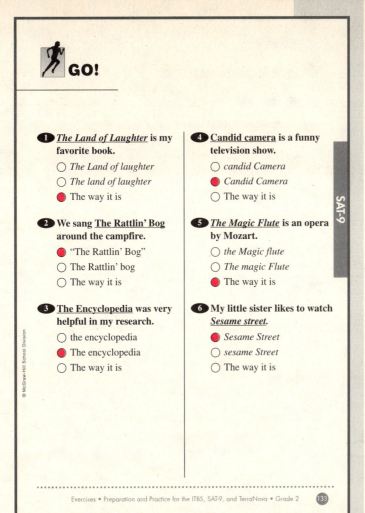

 Go over each question on this page as a class.

For questions 1 through 6, fill in the bubble next to the answer that uses correct capitalization. If the title is written correctly in the example sentence, fill in the bubble next to The way it is.

Underlining book titles and putting song titles in quotation marks was not discussed on the Pupil Edition Page.

Discuss these concepts with the students before they begin working through the questions on this page.

Question 2

All of the important words in the title of a song must be capitalized. The title must be put in quotation marks.

Question 3

An encyclopedia is a type of book, not a book title. Therefore, it is not capitalized.

Questions 4 and 6

All of the important words in the title of a television show must be capitalized. The title must be italicized.

Exercise 9
HELPING VERBS

 Go over each type of helping verb with students.

On the board, write several sentences containing helping verbs. Have students read the sentences and identify the helping verbs. Some sentences you might use are:

- *Mother is cooking dinner.* (is)
- *I am helping her cook.* (am)
- *My sisters are helping, too.* (are)
- *The dog has chased the cat.* (has)
- *I have put the cat in the house.* (have)

Discuss with students the tense of the verbs. Help them conclude that the forms of *to be* tell about things happening now, and the forms of *to have* tell about things that have already happened.

 Go over the example question as a class.

 Exercise 9

ON YOUR MARK!
Helping Verbs

A **helping verb** helps another verb show an action.
The verbs *be* and *have* can be helping verbs.
Use forms of *to be* to tell about things that are happening now.
   He **is** running.
   I **am** running.
   They **are** running.
Use forms of *to have* to tell about things that have already happened.
   He **has** eaten.
   I **have** eaten.

 # GET SET!
Let's look at an example.
What is the best way to write the underlined verb?
I is going to school.
○ are
○ am
○ They way it is

(1st) is **wrong.** *Are* is used to talk about more than one person.
(2nd) is **correct!** *Am* is the correct helping verb to use after *I*.
(3rd) is **wrong.** Only use *is* when you're talking about one person other than *I*.

EXTRA ACTIVITY

Create a worksheet that has sentences with helping verbs left out. Have students write correct helping verbs in the blanks.

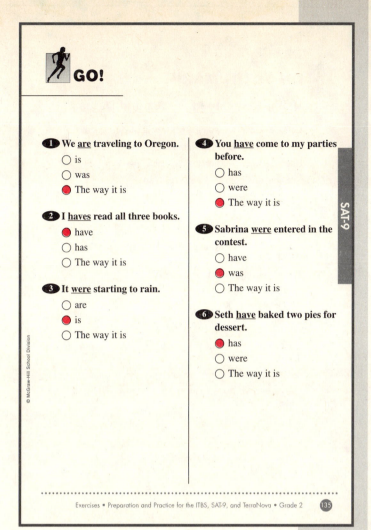

 Go over each question on this page as a class.

For questions 1 through 6, find the answer choice that corrects the underlined part of the sentence. Fill in the bubble next to the word you choose. If the example sentence is written correctly, fill in the bubble next to The way it is.

Question 2

Haves is not a word.

Questions 3 and 5

Discuss with students that *was* and *were* are also helping verbs that tell about something that has already happened.

Question 6

Have is a plural helping verb. *Seth* is singular and needs a singular helping verb.

Exercise 10
USING COMMAS IN PLACES AND DATES

 Go over the placement of commas in places and dates with students.

Put some sentences containing places and dates on the board and discuss where the commas should be placed. Here are some examples you might use:

- *Houston Texas is a big city.*

  (Houston, Texas)

- *The new school will open on September 4 2001.*

  (September 4, 2001)

- *I will be nine years old on May 16 2002.*

  (May 16, 2002)

- *It is cold in Denver Colorado.*

  (Denver, Colorado)

Answer any questions students might have.

 Go over the example question as a class.

Exercise 10

 ON YOUR MARK!

Using Commas in Places and Dates

Use a **comma** between the name of a city and a state.
   Ben is from **Saint Johnsbury, Vermont**.

Use a **comma** between the day and a year in a date.
   Eddie was born on **March 12, 1993**.

 GET SET!

Let's look at an example.

What is the best way to write the underlined part of the sentence?

We are moving on <u>October, 8 2000</u>.

○ October 8, 2000
○ October 8 2000
○ The way it is

(1st) is **correct!** A comma correctly separates the day from the year.

(2nd) is **wrong.** It is missing a comma after the day.

(3rd) is **wrong.** The comma should be between the date and the year.

 TEACHING TIP

As a daily activity, place the date on the board and emphasize that the comma goes between the day and the year.

Also, put the name of the city and state where your school is located and have students take turns putting the comma in the correct place.

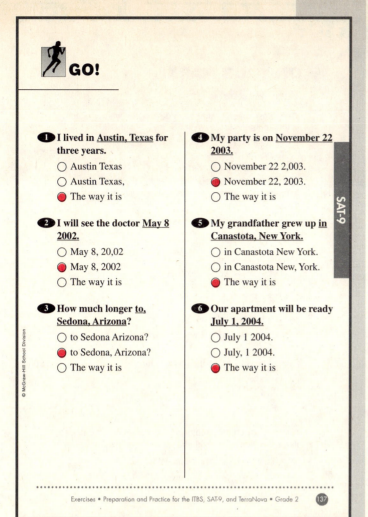

 Go over each question on this page as a class.

For questions 1 through 6, find the correct way to write the underlined part of the sentence. Fill in the bubble next to the answer you choose. If the example sentence is already written correctly, fill in the bubble next to The way it is.

Questions 2 and 4

The only comma in a date goes between the day and the year.

Question 3

A comma must go between the city and the state in an address, not before the city.

Question 5

A comma must go between the city and the state in an address. In a state with two names such as *New York*, a comma is not needed in between the two names.

Exercise 11
VERB TENSES

 Go over the different verb tenses with students.

Read the top part of the Pupil Edition page aloud to students. Discuss present and past tense verbs as you read the example sentences. Write some other sentences on the board. Have students identify and decide whether the verb is present or past tense. Here are some sentences you might use:

- *Monica ran to the playground yesterday.*

  (ran: past tense)

- *The wind is blowing very hard.*

  (is blowing: present tense)

- *Jacob writes his name very neatly.*

  (writes: present tense)

- *Dad cooked pancakes last Saturday.*

  (cooked: past tense)

Discuss with students the clue they used in each sentence to help them figure out the verb tense. Answer any questions the students might have.

 Go over the example question as a class.

 Exercise 11

ON YOUR MARK!
Verb Tenses

Verbs have different **tenses** depending on when the action in the sentence takes place.

Present tense verbs tell about something that is happening now.
  He **paints** the house.
  He **is painting** the house.

Past tense verbs tell about something that already happened. You add *-ed* to the end of most verbs to make them past tense.
  He **painted** the house.

> **TIP:** Look for clues that tell when the action took place.
> It rained *last night*.
> I like to eat *after I do my homework*.

 GET SET!

Let's look at an example.

What is the best way to write the underlined part of this sentence?

Sandra already <u>knocking</u> on the door.
  ○ knocked
  ○ knocks
  ○ The way it is

(1st) is **correct!** This sentence is past tense because it says that the action happened *already*.
(2nd) is **wrong.** *Knocks* is present tense.
(3rd) is **wrong.** *Knocking* is also present tense.

EXTRA ACTIVITY

Give each student two index cards or small pieces of paper. Have them write the words *present tense* on one, and *past tense* on the other. Read a sentence to the class that contains either a present or past tense verb. Ask students to listen carefully and decide whether the verb is a present or past tense verb. Have students respond by holding up the card with the answer he or she feels is correct.

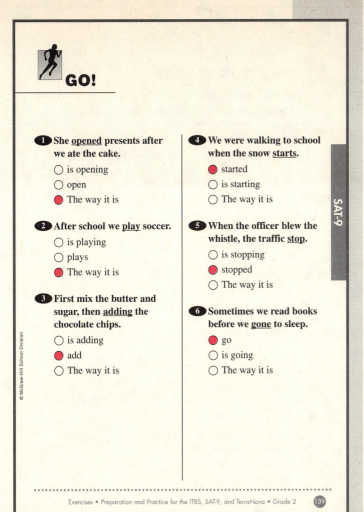

 Go over each question on this page as a class.

For questions 1 through 6, find the correct way to write the underlined part of the sentence. Fill in the bubble next to the answer you choose. If the example sentence is already written correctly, fill in the bubble next to The way it is.

Tell students to look for time indicators in the sentences. This will help them determine the correct verb tense.

Question 1

Time indicator: *after we ate*

Question 2

Time indicator: *After school*

Question 3

Time indicator: *First, then*

Question 4

Time indicator: *We were walking*

Question 5

Time indicator: *When, blew*

Question 6

Time indicator: *Sometimes*

Exercise 12
IRREGULAR VERBS

 Explain to students that all past tense verbs are not formed by adding the *-ed* ending.

Some past tense verbs change entirely when in the past tense form. These are called irregular verbs.

Look at the list in the middle of the Pupil Edition page that shows present tense verbs and their corresponding past tense irregular verbs. Ask students to think of sentences that can include the present tense verbs. Then have them change each sentence to past tense by changing the verb. For example:

- *I go to class at eight o'clock each day.*

- *Yesterday, I went to class at eight o'clock.*

Discuss with students how these verbs would sound if you *did* put *-ed* at the end. The incorrect past tense verb makes the sentence sound wrong when it is read. (*Yesterday, I goed to class at eight o'clock.*)

 Go over the example question as a class.

Exercise 12
 ON YOUR MARK!
Irregular Verbs

You cannot always add *-ed* to verbs to make them past tense. Some verbs change entirely. These are called **irregular verbs**.

Present Tense	Past Tense
go	went
do	did
say	said
see	saw
run	ran
come	came
give	gave
sing	sang
grow	grew
throw	threw

 GET SET!
Let's look at an example.
What is the best way to write the underlined word in the sentence?

Jill <u>blowed</u> on her hot soup.
○ blow
○ blew
○ Correct as it is

(1st) is **wrong.** *Blow* must end in *s* if it follows a singular person in the present tense.
(2nd) is **correct!** *Blew* is the correct past tense form of *blow*.
(3rd) is **wrong.** *Blowed* is not a word.

★ EXTRA ACTIVITY

Make a worksheet with several sentences. Leave a blank where the past tense verb should be. At the end of each sentence, give students two choices, the verb adding *-ed*, and the irregular past tense verb. Have students write the correct answer in the blank. This can be used as homework or as a classroom activity.

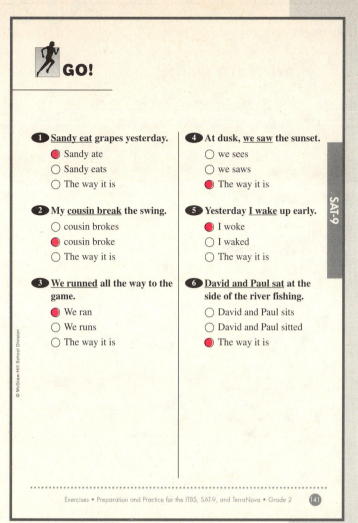

 Go over each question on this page as a class.

📣 *For questions 1 through 6, find the correct way to write the underlined part of the sentence. Fill in the bubble next to the answer you choose. If the example sentence is already written correctly, fill in the bubble next to The way it is.*

Remind students to read the whole sentence using each choice to decide which choice makes the sentence sound the best.

Exercise 13

VOWEL SOUNDS WITH THE LETTER *R*

 Explain to students that when a word has a vowel followed by an *-r,* the vowel has a new sound.

Explain that a vowel followed by an *-r* is not a long or short sound, but a different sound.

Read and discuss the examples at the top of the Pupil Edition page. Have students say the words out loud. Discuss the vowel sound they hear when they say each word. Write some more words on the board. Have students pronounce the words and discuss the vowel sound in each. Here are some words you might use.

- *first*
- *party*
- *short*
- *hammer*
- *turn*

 Go over the example question as a class.

Exercise 13

 ON YOUR MARK!

Vowel Sounds with the Letter *R*

Sometimes groups of letters that look the same make different sounds in different words.

wo<u>r</u>k   fo<u>r</u>k
hea<u>r</u>   lea<u>r</u>n   bea<u>r</u>

Sometimes different groups of letters make the same sound.

<u>for</u>   <u>tor</u>e   <u>soar</u>
l<u>earn</u> b<u>urn</u>   st<u>ern</u>   d<u>irt</u>

 GET SET!

Let's look at an example.

Which word shares the same vowel sound as the word below?

h<u>ear</u>

○ heart
○ deer
○ wear

(1st) is **wrong.** *Hear* has a long *e* sound, and *heart* has an *a* sound as in *cart*.

(2nd) is **correct!** The *ear* and *eer* in these words both make the same sound.

(3rd) is **wrong.** *Hear* makes a long *e* sound, and *wear* makes a long *a* sound.

 EXTRA ACTIVITY

Divide your class into groups. Give each group a set of word cards containing long vowels, short vowels, and vowels followed by the letter *-r.* Have students pronounce each word and sort the cards into stacks according to vowel sound.

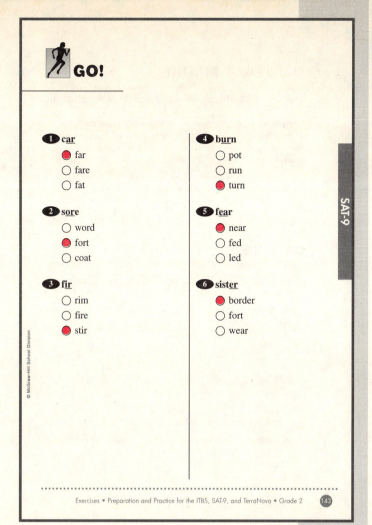

 Go over each question on this page as a class.

Question 1

📣 *For question 1, fill in the bubble next to the word with the same sound as the underlined letters in the word car.*

Question 2

📣 *For question 2, fill in the bubble next to the word with the same sound as the underlined letters in the word sore.*

Question 3

📣 *For question 3, fill in the bubble next to the word with the same sound as the underlined letters in the word fir.*

Question 4

📣 *For question 4, fill in the bubble next to the word with the same sound as the underlined letters in the word burn.*

Question 5

📣 *For question 5, fill in the bubble next to the word with the same sound as the underlined letters in the word fear.*

Question 6

📣 *For question 6, fill in the bubble next to the word with the same sound as the underlined letters in the word sister.*

Exercise 14

BE SURE TO READ ALL OF THE ANSWER CHOICES

 Explain to students that reading all of the answer choices is an important test-taking skill for the SAT-9.

Have students read the top section of the Pupil Edition page or read it aloud to them. Point out that reading all of the answer choices will give them the opportunity to choose the *best* answer possible.

 Go over the example question as a class.

Exercise 14

 ## ON YOUR MARK!

Be Sure to Read All of the Answer Choices

Sometimes when you read a question, you might think the first answer choice you read is correct. Always read *all* of the answer choices before you decide. Otherwise, you might miss a better answer that comes later.

> **TIP:** Always get rid of the wrong answer choices first. Put a finger over the wrong answer choices as you rule out each wrong answer choice.

 ## GET SET!
Let's look at an example.

What is the best way to write the underlined part of this sentence?

Henry <u>dug</u> a big hole in the sand yesterday.
○ digged
○ dig
○ The way it is

(1st) is **wrong.** *Dig* is an irregular verb, so its past tense form does not end in *-ed*.

(2nd) is **wrong.** The action happened yesterday, but *dig* is in present tense. Also, *dig* does not agree with the subject, *Henry.*

(3rd) is **correct!** *Dig* is an irregular verb. *Dug* is the correct past-tense form of *dig.*

 ### EXTRA ACTIVITY

Create a worksheet. The first sentence should say: "Read each direction before completing this page." Direction 1 might tell the student to write their name at the top of the page. Other directions might be to write the alphabet, to write numbers from 1 to 100, etc. The last direction should say: "Complete only question 1 and turn in your paper to the teacher." This will point out the importance of reading each choice before deciding which is the best.

 Go over each question on this page as a class.

This page tests skills that students learned in previous exercises. Students should be sure to read all of the answer choices carefully and get rid of wrong ones as they work through questions 1 through 6.

📣 *For questions 1 through 6, find the correct way to write the underlined part of the sentence. Fill in the bubble next to the answer you choose. If the example sentence is already written correctly, fill in the bubble next to The way it is.*

Question 1
Helping verb question

Question 2
Capitalizing titles question

Question 3
Helping verb question

Question 4
Capitalizing places question

Question 5
Verb tense question

Question 6
Subject-verb agreement question

Exercise 15
CONTRACTIONS

 Go over the meaning of a contraction.

Explain that an *apostrophe* takes the place of the letters that are left out when two words are joined.

Look at the contractions in the middle of the Pupil Edition page. Discuss the two words each contraction stands for. Make sure students notice the letter or letters that are left out and replaced by an apostrophe.

Write two words on the board. Write the contraction below it. Have students look carefully and find the letters that are the same. Circle the letter or letters that are left out and replaced by an apostrophe. Some of the contractions you might use are:

- are not   aren't
- she will   she'll
- we have   we've
- that is   that's

After discussing each contraction, have students make a sentence using each one.

 Go over the example question as a class.

 Exercise 15
ON YOUR MARK!
Contractions

A **contraction** is a short form of two words.
An **apostrophe** (') takes the place of the letters that are left out when two words are joined.
Some contractions are words that are combined with *not*.

did not ⟶ didn't
is not ⟶ isn't
have not ⟶ haven't

Other contractions are words that are combined with forms of *be* and *have*.

they have ⟶ they've
she is ⟶ she's
I am ⟶ I'm
we are ⟶ we're

 GET SET!

Let's look at an example.
What is the best way to write the underlined word?

<u>Its'</u> cold outside today.
○ It's
○ I'ts
○ The way it is

(1st) is **correct!** The apostrophe replaces the letter *i* in *is*.
(2nd) is **wrong.** The apostrophe is dividing the word *it*, not replacing a letter.
(3rd) is **wrong.** The apostrophe does not replace a letter.

146 Exercises • Preparation and Practice for the ITBS, SAT-9, and TerraNova • Grade 2

EXTRA ACTIVITY

Divide the class into three or four teams. One student from each team will come to the board.

You will say two words. Each team member will write the contraction for the two words. The first team or teams to write the contraction correctly will earn a point for his or her team. The team with the most points wins.

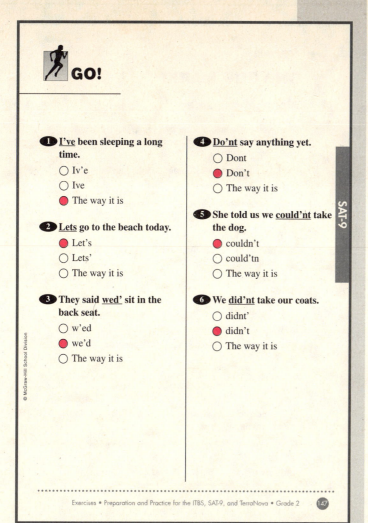

 Go over each question on this page as a class.

For questions 1 through 6, read each sentence. Look carefully at the underlined contraction and the answer choices. Fill in the bubble next to the correct way to write the underlined contraction. If the contraction is written correctly in the example sentence, fill in the bubble next to The way it is.

Remind students of the following:

- Every contraction has an apostrophe.
- The apostrophe goes in place of the missing letters.

Exercise 16

ALPHABETICAL ORDER

 Go over the meaning of alphabetical order with students.

On the board, write several words beginning with different letters. Have students decide the correct order.

Some words you might use are:

- fan   (ant)
- deck   (band)
- ant   (deck)
- lock   (fan)
- band   (lock)

Put some examples on the board of words that begin with the same first letter or first two letters and have students put the words in alphabetical order. Some words you might use are:

- pin   (patch)
- pencil   (pencil)
- patch   (pin)
- pot   (pot)
- drum   (drag)
- drip   (dress)
- drag   (drip)
- dress   (drum)

Discuss with students how they decided the order in which to put the words.

 Go over the example question as a class.

Exercise 16

 ON YOUR MARK!

Alphabetical Order

When you put words in order by their spelling, it is called **alphabetical order**, or **ABC order**. The words defined in a dictionary are listed in ABC order.

You can put words in ABC order by their first letter.

   able   give   sat

When words begin with the same letter, use the second letter to put them in ABC order.

   cat   cent   corn

When words begin with the same two letters, use the third letter to put them in ABC order.

   crash   crook   crumb

 GET SET!

Let's look at an example.

Which word should come first in ABC order?

○ door
○ dump
○ drip

(1st) is **correct!** The letter *o* in *door* comes before the *u* in *dump* and the *r* in *drip*.

(2nd) is **wrong**. The *u* in *dump* comes after the *o* in *door* and the *r* in *drip*.

(3rd) is **wrong**. The *r* in *drip* comes after the *o* in *door*.

 EXTRA ACTIVITY

Have students put themselves in a line using alphabetical order. The student with the last name that is highest in the alphabet, for example, *Abramson*, should stand up first. Then the student with the last name that comes next in alphabetical order should stand up, and so on. Help students as they complete this activity.

GO!

1. ○ won
   ○ with
   ● want

2. ○ best
   ● beach
   ○ bend

3. ○ card
   ● candy
   ○ chart

4. ○ nose
   ● nest
   ○ road

5. ○ door
   ● dirt
   ○ draft

6. ● open
   ○ oval
   ○ pear

SAT-9

Go over each question on this page as a class.

For questions 1 through 6, find the word that would come first in alphabetical order. Fill in the bubble next to the word you choose.

Exercise 17
TOPIC SENTENCE

 Go over the meaning of topic sentences with the class.

Have students read the top part of the Pupil Edition page or read it aloud to the class. To help students understand the concept of topic sentences, write the following paragraph on the board.

Fridays are fun at my school. First, our class reads with book buddies. Then, we get to play computer games. The math game is hard. Finally, we get to eat pizza for lunch.

Have students read the paragraph. Ask the class which sentence did not belong in that paragraph. Discuss the reason that *The math game is hard* does not belong in the paragraph.

 Go over the example question as a class.

Exercise 17

 ON YOUR MARK!

Topic Sentence

A **topic sentence** is the first sentence in a paragraph. It tells the main idea of the paragraph.

If a sentence does not talk about the main idea in a paragraph, it does not belong.

My mom didn't have to work today, so she took me to the zoo. Mom works in an office. We saw monkeys, tigers, and huge elephants. It was a really fun day.

The underlined sentence in the paragraph above tells details about things other than the main idea. It does not belong.

 GET SET!

Let's look at an example.

Read the paragraph below. Then find the sentence does not belong in the paragraph.

One day I found a baby bird lying on the ground. I took the bird home. I cared for the bird until it was old enough to fly. Then I set it free.

○ The bird's mother was nowhere to be found.
○ The bird had fallen out of its nest.
○ My cat didn't like the bird.

(1st) is **wrong**. This sentence belongs in the paragraph. It tells why the writer cared for the bird.
(2nd) is **wrong**. This sentence tells why it was on the ground.
(3rd) is **correct!** This sentence does not belong in the story. It talks about the writer's cat. It does not tell more about how the writer took care of the bird.

 EXTRA ACTIVITY

Put a topic sentence on the board. Ask students to write the topic sentence and two more sentences that tell details about the topic sentence. When completed, share the paragraphs with the class.

GO!

Story 1
Sasha waters her sister's plants while she is away at camp. Once a week she fills the watering can with water. Then she pours a little bit of water into each pot. She likes the fern the best.

1 Find the sentence that does <u>not</u> go with this paragraph.
- ● Her sister learned to swim at camp.
- ○ Sasha liked to take care of plants.
- ○ Her sister had many different kinds of plants.

Story 2
On Saturday mornings, Jimmy and his father went to soccer practice together. His father was the coach. He was a good coach. Jimmy was proud of him.

2 Find the sentence that does <u>not</u> go with this paragraph.
- ○ Jimmy helped his father carry the soccer balls.
- ○ His father encouraged the players to play fairly.
- ● Jimmy took the bus to the soccer field.

 Go over each question on this page as a class.

Read the stories and the questions aloud to students.

Question 1
The paragraph is about Sasha and her sister's plants. It is not about Sasha's sister and what she did at camp.

Question 2
The paragraph is about how Jimmy's father coached Jimmy's soccer team. It is not about how Jimmy got to soccer practice

Exercise 18

SHARING YOUR IDEAS IN PARAGRAPHS

 Explain to students that a paragraph is a group of sentences telling about one idea.

On the board, write a short paragraph. Read the paragraph aloud and underline the first sentence. Explain that usually the first sentence tells the main idea of the paragraph, and all the other sentences must tell details about the main idea. A paragraph you might want to use is:

Dogs are good pets. They love to be petted. Taking them for walks is fun. Playing ball with my puppy makes me happy.

All the sentences in the paragraph tell about the main idea sentence, *"Dogs are good pets."* Ask students if they can think of other sentences that would go in this paragraph. Answer any questions they might have.

 Go over the example question as a class.

Exercise 18

 ON YOUR MARK!

Sharing Your Ideas in Paragraphs

A **paragraph** is a group of sentences.

The sentences in a paragraph tell about one idea. This is called the **main idea**.

The main idea is usually in the first sentence of the paragraph.

All sentences in a paragraph *must* be about the main idea.

 GET SET!

Let's look at an example.

Choose the sentence that would best follow the last sentence in this paragraph.

My mom and dad just gave me a big surprise. They handed me a box with holes in it, and told me to look inside. When I opened it, I found a little puppy.

○ My new job is to feed the puppy.
○ It was the best present I ever got.
○ I have to keep the puppy on a leash.

(1st) is **wrong**. The paragraph is about a *big surprise* and not about the writer's chores.

(2nd) is **correct!** This sentence tells more about the *big surprise*.

(3rd) is **wrong**. The paragraph is not about how the writer will take care of the puppy.

 EXTRA ACTIVITY

Create a worksheet containing two or three paragraphs. Students must underline the main idea sentence and choose from three additional sentences the one that would best fit at the end of that paragraph.

GO!

Story 1
Pedro was planning a party for his mother's birthday. He invited his cousins, aunts, and uncles. Some of them would bring presents and food. Pedro was going to bake the cake.

1 Find the sentence that would go <u>best</u> at the end of this story.
- 🔴 He planned to make a chocolate cake with vanilla frosting.
- ○ Uncle Edwin can't eat sugar.
- ○ Last year Pedro didn't have a birthday party.

Story 2
Sarah had never ridden on a horse before. She was nervous at first, but her brother told her to calm the horse by whispering in its ear. Her brother led the horse around the pen while she balanced herself on its back.

2 Find the sentence that would go <u>best</u> at the end of this story.
- ○ The horse's stall needed to be cleaned.
- 🔴 She decided she liked it and would do it again soon!
- ○ He didn't have a lot of homework to do later.

 Go over each question on this page as a class.

Read the stories and the questions aloud to students.

Question 1
The sentence in the first choice discusses the cake mentioned in the paragraph. The paragraph does not mention Uncle Edwin or Pedro's birthday.

Question 2
Only the sentence in the second choice talks about Sarah riding the horse—the main idea of the paragraph.

Exercise 19

WRITING WITH A PURPOSE

 Explain to students that there are different purposes for writing.

Read the top part of the Pupil Edition page to the class. Discuss each reason for writing. Have students think of subjects to go with each type of writing. Examples might be:

- *special event*   *birthday*
- *description*   *the playground*
- *how to*   *make a kite*

Have students offer extra examples and write their suggestions on the board.

 Go over the example question as a class.

Exercise 19

 ON YOUR MARK!

Writing with a Purpose

A **main purpose** is the reason why something is written. Sentences in a story give details about the main purpose.

You will understand a story better if you can tell why it was written. Ask yourself these questions when you read a story:

Does it describe a special event?

Does it describe a person, place, or thing?

Does it explain how to do something?

 GET SET

Let's look at an example. Read the story below.

> I was a little scared on my first day of school. I was the new kid in class, and I didn't know anyone. My new teacher told the class my name and where I am from. During recess, two girls asked me to play with them. I think I'm going to like my new school!

This story was written to—

 Describe a student's first day at a new school

 Tell what happened at recess

○ Tell about a new teacher

(1st) is **correct!** Every sentence in the story tells something about this main purpose.

(2nd) is **wrong.** This is only a small part of the story.

(3rd) is **wrong.** This is only a small part of the story.

⭐ EXTRA ACTIVITY

Assign the students a main purpose for writing. Have them write a main idea sentence and three detail sentences. Let them share their stories with a partner.

GO!

Story 1
Jake had chores every Saturday. His job was to gather together all of the recycling and take it to edge of the street. Sometimes he forgot to do it. Then the bottles and cans would pile high until the next week.

1 This story was written to tell about—
- 🔴 Jake's chores on Saturday
- ○ The things Jake recycled
- ○ What Jake did on Saturdays

Story 2
A family of ducks lives on the shore of the creek behind Judy's house. They spend the days in the water, paddling around and fishing for food. They spend the nights on the shore curled up in soft nests made of leaves and feathers.

2 This story was written to tell about—
- ○ What the ducks' nest is made of
- 🔴 The ducks that live behind Judy's house
- ○ What the ducks like to eat in the summer

 Go over each question on this page as a class.

Read the stories and the questions aloud to students.

Question 1

1st choice: Correct

2nd choice: The objects Jake recycles are not discussed.

3rd choice: The paragraph only discusses the chores Jake does on Saturday. It does not discuss everything Jake does on Saturday.

Question 2

1st choice: The materials used to make the ducks' nest is not discussed.

2nd choice: Correct

3rd choice: The ducks diet is not discussed.

Exercise 20

READING SLOWLY AND CAREFULLY

 Explain to students that reading slowly and carefully is an important test-taking skill for the SAT-9.

Have students read the top section of the Pupil Edition page or read it aloud to them. Point out that reading slowly and carefully will help them know exactly what the questions ask and will keep them from making silly mistakes.

Remind students that sometimes the questions ask them to find something that is *not* included. If they read too fast, they might skip over the word *not* and choose the wrong answer to the question.

 Go over the example question as a class. Have students explain why each answer choice is correct or incorrect.

Exercise 20

 ## ON YOUR MARK!

Reading Slowly and Carefully

When you take the SAT-9, read *slowly and carefully*. If you read too quickly, you might miss important words and get the question wrong. Look at this question:

Find the sentence that does not belong in the paragraph.

If you had read the question above too quickly, you might have missed the word *not*, and chosen the wrong answer.

Read slowly and carefully so you don't make silly mistakes!

 ## GET SET!

Look at this example. Practice reading it slowly and carefully.

> When I grow up, I want to draw my own comic strip. My comic strip will be in all the newspapers. It will make thousands of people laugh every day.

Find the sentence that does not belong in the paragraph.
○ My friends think that I am very funny.
○ I will draw a comic strip about a dog.
○ I will be proud to make so many people happy.

(1st) is **correct!** The story is about what the writer wants to be when he or she grows up. It is *not* about what the writer's friends think.

(2nd) is **wrong.** It adds an important detail about the comic strip.

(3rd) is **wrong.** It tells more about how the writer will feel about drawing the comic strip.

 ## EXTRA ACTIVITY

Give students a paragraph to read. The paragraph should include several mistakes in spelling, capitalization, grammar, and so on. Tell the students to circle all the errors. Remind them that they might miss errors if they do not read slowly and carefully.

GO!

Story 1

Janet got chicken pox from her sister. Her parents kept them both home from school for a week. They were well enough to play together, but Janet was sad because she would miss the class Valentine's Day party.

1 Find the sentence that would go **best** at the end of this story.
- ● Her teacher promised to drop off her Valentine's cards.
- ○ Almost all of Janet's classmates had chicken pox that year.
- ○ Her father drove them home from school.

2 Find the sentence does **not** go with this story.
- ○ Janet and her sister played Go Fish and War.
- ○ Her sister got chicken pox from her friend.
- ● Janet and her sister share a bicycle.

3 This story was written to tell about—
- ● Janet getting chicken pox
- ○ the Valentines' Day party at school
- ○ who gave Janet chicken pox

4 I'm in trouble now.
- ○ Im
- ○ Im'
- ● The way it is

 Go over each question on this page as a class.

This page tests skills that students learned in the previous exercises. Students should read slowly and carefully as they work through questions 1 through 4.

For questions 1 through 3, read the story and the questions aloud to students.

Question 1

Only the sentence in the first choice is connected to the mention of Valentine's Day in the last sentence of the paragraph.

Question 2

The paragraph is about what happened when Janet and her sister both got the chicken pox. It is not about what they share.

Question 3

1st choice: Correct

2nd choice: The party is mentioned, but the paragraph doesn't tell anything about the party.

3rd choice: The paragraph doesn't say who gave Janet chicken pox.

Question 4

 For question 4, fill in the bubble next to the best way to write the contraction. If the contraction is written correctly in the example sentence, fill in the bubble next to The way it is.

Exercise 21
WORDS WITH SILENT LETTERS

 Explain to students that there are some words that contain silent letters.

Have students read the top section of the Pupil Edition page or read it aloud to the class. Go over each example word containing a silent letter. Explain to students that even though they do not hear the letter when they pronounce the word, it must be included for the word to be spelled correctly. Put some other words containing silent letters on the board. Some words you might want to use are:

- *lamb*
- *bridge*
- *knew*
- *eight*

Go over the words with students. Point out the silent letters in each. Ask students to offer more examples of words with silent letters. Write their suggestions on the board.

 Go over the example question as a class.

Exercise 21
ON YOUR MARK!

Words with Silent Letters

Silent Letters

Sometimes a word is spelled with a letter that you cannot hear when you say the word. These words have **silent letters**.

walk	clim**b**	**k**now
write	**g**naw	nigh**t**

> **TIP:** When you spell words, try changing the way you say them to yourself. Sound out *all* of the letters in your head, even the silent ones. For example, to remember that the word *knot* begins with a *k*, say **/ke not/** to yourself.

 ## GET SET!

Let's look at an example.

Which sentence has an underlined word that is spelled wrong?
- ○ I like to <u>clim</u> trees.
- ○ My two sisters always <u>fight</u>.
- ○ <u>Have</u> you read this book?
- ○ My answer was <u>wrong</u>.

(1st) is **correct!** There should be a silent *b* at the end of *climb*.
(2nd) is **wrong.** This word is spelled correctly with a silent *gh*.
(3rd) is **wrong.** This word is spelled correctly with a silent *e*.
(4th) is **wrong.** This word is spelled correctly with a silent *w*.

 ## TEACHING TIP

Explain to students when words contain letters that are not heard, they must try to remember how the word looks. Students should make a picture in their mind of the way the word looks when it is spelled correctly.

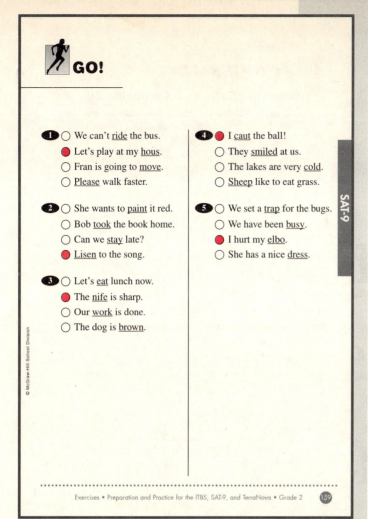

 Go over each question on this page as a class.

For questions 1 through 5, fill in the bubble next to the sentence that contains a misspelled word.

Question 1
House should have a silent /e/.

Question 2
Listen should have a silent /t/.

Question 3
Knife should have a silent /k/.

Question 4
Caught should have a silent /gh/.

Question 5
The *w* in *elbow* is technically not a silent letter even though the /w/ is not pronounced. The *ow* results in a long /o/, making the *w* seem silent.

Exercise 22

SPELLING WORDS WITH CONFUSING SOUNDS

 Explain to students that different vowels can often sound very much alike. This can sometimes be confusing.

Have students read the top section of the Pupil Edition page or read it aloud to the class. Go over the examples of confusing words. Go over the tip box on the Pupil Edition page. Explain to students that for words with confusing sounds, they should try to visualize the way it looks when it is spelled correctly. If it doesn't look right, it is probably spelled wrong.

 Go over the example question as a class.

Exercise 22

 ON YOUR MARK!

Spelling Words with Confusing Sounds

Sometimes it is easy to confuse vowel sounds. Here are some examples of vowel sounds that may be confusing.

Wrong	Correct
pinny	→ penny
agen	→ again
halp	→ help
werd	→ word

TIP: If a word looks funny to you, look at each letter. Then try to think of other words that rhyme with that word. How is the rhyming word spelled? Most rhyming words are spelled alike.

 GET SET!

Let's look at an example.

Find the underlined word that is spelled wrong.
○ Vincent's <u>face</u> is dirty.
○ Gina asked to borrow a <u>pencil</u>.
○ I always <u>forgit</u> my umbrella.
○ Fredo is my best <u>friend</u>.

(1st) is **wrong.** The *s* sound in *face* is correctly spelled with a *ce*.
(2nd) is **wrong.** The *s* sound in *pencil* is correctly spelled with a *c*.
(3rd) is **correct!** This word is spelled wrong. The *i* should be an *e*.
(4th) is **wrong.** The short *e* sound is correctly spelled with an *ie*.

  EXTRA ACTIVITY

Each student will work with a partner. One student will call out words to his or her partner. The second student will write the word on individual chalkboards or paper. Then the students will check together to see if the words are spelled correctly and correct any mistakes. They will trade places and the other student will call out the words. The students will get practice in both roles.

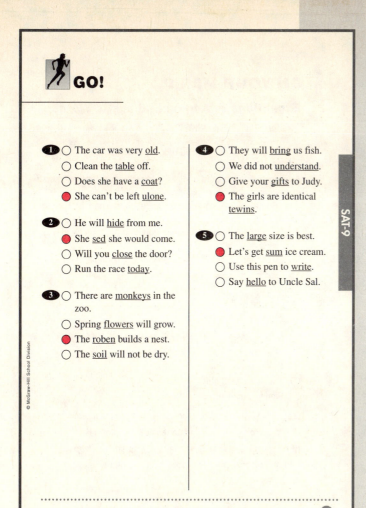

 Go over each question on this page as a class.

📣 *For questions 1 through 5, fill in the bubble next to the sentence that contains a misspelled word.*

Question 1

Correct spelling—*alone*

Question 2

Correct spelling—*said*

Question 3

Correct spelling—*robin*

Question 4

Correct spelling—*twins*

Question 5

Correct spelling—*some*

In question 5, *sum* is a homophone. Go over homophones with the class. Provide them with extra examples and explain why the meaning of a word is important when determining whether it is spelled correctly. Some examples you might use include:

- *hair   hare*
- *there   their*
- *read   red*
- *past   passed*

Exercises • Preparation and Practice for the ITBS, SAT-9, and TerraNova • Grade 2

Exercise 23

EXCEPTIONS TO ADDING ENDINGS TO WORDS

 Explain to students that there are certain exceptions in adding endings to words.

Have students read the top section of the Pupil Edition page or read it aloud to the class. Go over each exception mentioned on the Pupil Edition page. Put a list of words on the board. Work through the list with students pointing out what must be done to correctly add the ending. Some words you might use are:

- dress   dresses
- ride   riding
- penny   pennies
- bury   buried
- put   putting
- fox   foxes
- catch   catches

Review the words and their endings with students.

 Go over the example question as a class.

Exercise 23

 ON YOUR MARK!

Exceptions to Adding Endings to Words

Adding -s: If a word ends in *x, z, s, sh,* or *ch,* you add *-es.*
  buzz ⟶ buzzes
If a word ends in *y,* you drop the *y* and add *-ies.*
  fly ⟶ flies

Adding -ed: If the word ends in *y,* you drop the *y* and add *-ied.*
  carry ⟶ carried
Sometimes you need to double the consonant at the end.
  hop ⟶ hopped

Adding -ing: If a word ends in *e,* you drop the *e* and add *-ing.*
  hide ⟶ hiding
Sometimes you need to double the consonant at the end.
  sit ⟶ sitting

 GET SET!

Let's look at an example.

Find the underlined word that is NOT spelled correctly.
○ I <u>kicked</u> the ball.
○ Howie <u>makes</u> funny faces.
○ The baby is <u>sleeping</u>.
○ I am <u>giveing</u> a present to Linda.

(1st) is **wrong.** It is spelled correctly. Add *-ed* to *kicked.*
(2nd) is **wrong.** It is spelled correctly. Add *-s* to *make.*
(3rd) is **wrong.** It is spelled correctly. Add *-ing* to *sleep.*
(4th) is **correct!** The *e* in *give* should dropped when you add *-ing.*

 EXTRA ACTIVITY

Create a worksheet of sentences, each containing a blank. At the end of each sentence, write the root word that needs an ending added. The students must add the ending correctly and write it in the blank.

For example: I like to eat _____ on my cereal. (berry)

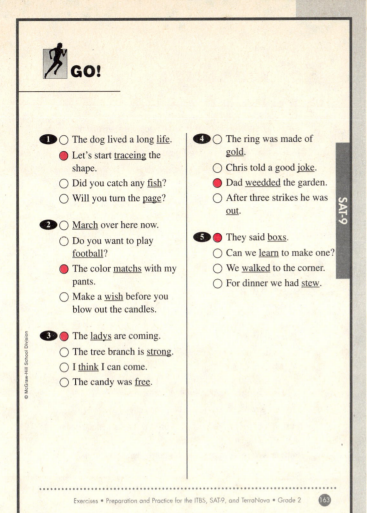

 Go over each question on this page as a class.

📢 *For questions 1 through 5, fill in the bubble next to the sentence that contains a misspelled word.*

Question 1

tracing—e should be dropped before adding -*ing*

Question 2

matches—word ends with *ch* so ending is -*es*

Question 3

ladies—y needs to be changed to *i* before adding -*es*

Question 4

weeded—d does not need to be doubled before adding -*ed*

Question 5

boxes—word ends with *x* so ending is -*es*

Exercise 24
TRICKY WORDS

 Explain to students that some words are not spelled like they sound and are tricky to spell.

Have students read the top section of the Pupil Edition page or read it aloud to the class. Together, discuss each word listed and look carefully at the underlined "tricky" part. Remind students that with "tricky" words, they must make a "picture in their mind" of the way the word looks when it is spelled correctly. Ask students to think of other "tricky" words. List and discuss the words they suggest. Answer any questions the students might have.

 Go over the example question as a class. Have students explain why each answer choice is correct or incorrect.

Exercise 24

 ON YOUR MARK!

Tricky Words

Some words can be hard to spell because they are not spelled like they sound. Read the list of tricky words below. Notice how each underlined group of letters is unusual.

| w<u>ould</u> | <u>r</u>ight | s<u>ai</u>d | pe<u>o</u>ple | th<u>ere</u> | w<u>ere</u> |
| b<u>ow</u>l | c<u>oa</u>t | <u>on</u>ce | b<u>e</u>cause | th<u>ei</u>r | pat<u>ch</u> |

There are not always rules to follow when spelling tricky words. The best way to learn spelling is to read as much as you can. The more you read, the easier it will be for you to notice when words are spelled wrong.

 GET SET!

Let's look at an example.

Find the underlined word that is NOT spelled correctly.
○ I wish I <u>could</u> go with you.
○ Here we go <u>again</u>.
○ I am <u>owt</u> of paper.
○ My pants need a <u>patch</u>.

(1st) is **wrong.** *Could* is spelled correctly.
(2nd) is **wrong.** *Again* is spelled correctly.
(3rd) is **correct!** The *w* should be a *u*. The correct spelling is *out*.
(4th) is **wrong.** *Patch* is spelled correctly.

EXTRA ACTIVITY

Play *Spelling Hangman* with the students. Divide the class into two teams. Choose one of the "tricky" words, count the letters, and put one blank on the board for each letter in the word. Let one student from the first team guess a letter. If the letter is in the word, the next person on the same team gets to guess another letter. This goes on until that team either misses a letter or spells the word correctly. If the first team misses a letter, it is the second team's turn to guess. The team that correctly spells the word earns a point. Continue with more "tricky" words.

GO!

1. ● Stoar the cake in the box.
   ○ The playground was warm and sunny.
   ○ We have a new student in class.
   ○ If you blink you will miss it.

2. ○ Ride up the hill.
   ○ The story he told was true.
   ○ Together they made a quilt.
   ● Coud we go to the movie?

3. ○ We were so hungry we ate early.
   ○ Cover him with this blanket.
   ○ Can you stay late?
   ● It would seme true.

4. ● She was not very tird.
   ○ Next month is her party.
   ○ Can you chop the wood?
   ○ I hope she will win.

5. ○ She spoke to me about it.
   ○ I belong to that group.
   ● Hold tight to the roap.
   ○ They will never give up.

Go over each question on this page as a class.

For questions 1 through 5, fill in the bubble next to the sentence that contains a misspelled word.

Question 1
The correct spelling is *store*.

Question 2
The correct spelling is *could*.

Question 3
The correct spelling is *seem*.

Question 4
The correct spelling is *tired*.

Question 5
The correct spelling is *rope*.

Exercise 26

LONG E AND SHORT E SOUNDS

 Explain to students that there are several ways to spell /e/ sounds.

Go over the short sound of /e/ and the long sound of /e/ and have students note the difference. Go over the examples of different ways to spell each /e/ sound noted on the Pupil Edition page. Make a chart on the board with a column for each /e/ sound. Write a word on the board that contains an /e/ sound and have the students decide which column it would fit in. Some words you might use are:

- ever   short
- mean   long
- monkey   long
- happy   long
- meet   long
- whether   short
- mend   short

Discuss each sound and the letter pattern that made the sound. Have students offer extra examples and write their suggestions on the board.

 Go over the example question as a class. Have the students explain why each example is correct or incorrect.

 Exercise 25

ON YOUR MARK!

Long *e* and Short *e* Sounds

There are several different ways to spell the *e* sounds. Below are some examples.

Short *e* Sound
Just with e: best
With ea: feather

Long *e* Sound
With y: busy
With ey: key
With ee: seen
With ie: thief
With ea: bean

 GET SET!

Let's look at an example.

Find the word that has the same vowel sound as the word below.

lean

 chief
○ met
○ weather

(1st) is **correct!** The *ea* in *lean* and the *ie* in *chief* both make long *e* sounds.

(2nd) is **wrong.** The *e* in *met* makes a short *e* sound.

(3rd) is **wrong.** The *ea* in *weather* makes a short *e* sound.

EXTRA ACTIVITY

Create a worksheet. Write a sentence leaving an /e/ word out. Give three choices of spelling at the end of the sentence. The students must choose the /e/ word that is spelled correctly and write it in the blank. This can be used as a homework activity to give students extra practice spelling /e/ words.

James was in the (lead, leed, lied) at the beginning of the race.

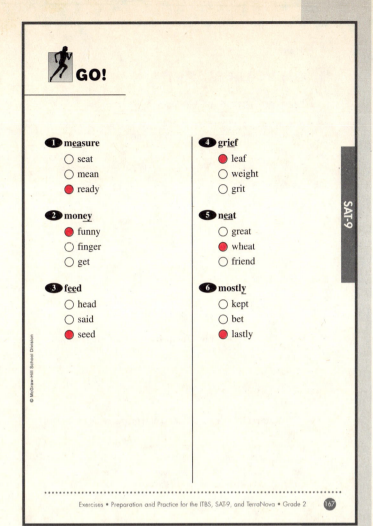

 Go over each question on this page as a class.

Question 1

For question 1, fill in the bubble next to the word that has the same sound as the underlined letters in the word measure.

Question 2

For question 2, fill in the bubble next to the word that has the same sound as the underlined letters in the word money.

Question 3

For question 3, fill in the bubble next to the word that has the same sound as the underlined letters in the word feed.

Question 4

For question 4, fill in the bubble next to the word that has the same sound as the underlined letters in the word grief.

Question 5

For question 5, fill in the bubble next to the word that has the same sound as the underlined letters in the word neat.

Question 6

For question 6, fill in the bubble next to the word that has the same sound as the underlined letter in the word mostly.

Exercise 26
WRITING TERMS OF RESPECT AND LETTER GREETINGS AND CLOSINGS

 Go over the capitalization rules discussed on the Pupil Edition page.

Discuss with students that terms of respect or titles before a person's name are always capitalized. Ask students to list all the titles they can think of. Make a list on the board. These should include:

- *Mr. Jones*
- *Mrs. Smith*
- *Miss Brown*
- *Ms. Green*
- *Dr. Martin*

Explain greetings and closings to students. Write some examples of greetings and closings on the board. You might include:

- *Dear Sally*
- *Dear Mr. Andrews*
- *Yours truly*
- *Sincerely yours*

Explain to students why some words are capitalized and some aren't. Have students offer extra examples and write their suggestions on the board.

 Go over the example question as a class. Have students explain why each answer choice is correct or incorrect.

Exercise 26

 ON YOUR MARK!

Writing Terms of Respect

A **term of respect** is a person's title. Always capitalize the title that comes before a person's name.
*I went to see **Doctor** Diaz.*
*My teacher is **Mr.** Jones.*

Writing Letter Greetings and Closings

A **letter greeting** says the name of the person you are writing to. The first word always begins with a capital letter.
Dear Larry,

A **letter closing** tells that the letter is ending. The first word always begins with a capital letter.
Yours truly,

 GET SET!

Let's look at an example.
Which is the correct way to write the letter greeting below?

<u>dear Willy,</u>
○ Dear Willy,
○ Dear willy,
○ The way it is

(1st) is **correct!** Both the first word and proper noun have capital letters.
(2nd) is **wrong.** *Willy* is a person's name, so it must begin with a capital letter.
(3rd) is **wrong.** The word *dear* is the first word in a letter greeting. It must begin with a capital letter.

 EXTRA ACTIVITY

Have students write a letter to someone they admire. They should include a greeting and a closing in their letters. Check their letters for correct use of capitalization.

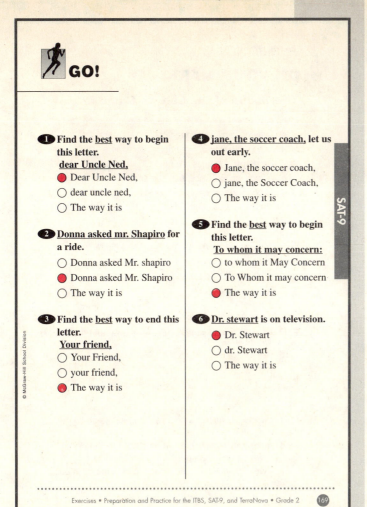

 Go over each question on this page as a class.

For questions 1 through 6, fill in the bubble next to the answer that has the underlined part written correctly. If the underlined part is written correctly in the example sentence, fill in the bubble next to The way it is.

Question 1

The first word and any proper nouns in a letter greeting must be capitalized.

Question 2

A term of respect and any proper noun that follows it must be capitalized.

Question 3

Only the first word of a letter closing is capitalized.

Question 4

Jane is a proper noun. *Soccer coach* is a common noun.

Question 5

The first word in a letter greeting must be capitalized.

Question 6

A term of respect and any proper noun that follows it must be capitalized.

Exercise 27

THE SOUND OF THE LETTERS C AND G

 Explain to students that the letters /c/ and /g/ have two different sounds.

Read the top section of the Pupil Edition page to students. Go over the examples of the hard and soft /c/ and /g/. Have students say the words orally and notice the difference in the sounds they hear. Stress the rule that if a *c* or *g* is followed by an *i*, *e*, or *y*, it will have the soft sound. Write a list of words on the board, have students sort the words under the headings of *soft /c/*, *hard /c/*, *soft /g/*, and *hard /g/*. Some words you might use are:

- candle   (hard)
- game   (hard)
- change   (soft)
- race   (soft)
- frog   (hard)
- pencil   (soft)
- cage   (soft)
- attic   (hard)

Have students come up with extra examples on their own. Write their suggestions under the correct headings on the board.

 Go over the example question as a class.

Exercise 27

 ON YOUR MARK!

The Sound of the Letters *C* and *G*

Hard *c* and **hard *g*** sounds are heard in words such as

c → **c**at, **c**ar, **c**lip, **c**rayon
g → **g**as, **g**row, ba**g**, bi**g**, fro**g**,

Soft *c* and **soft *g*** sounds are heard in words such as:

c → ra**c**e, spa**c**e, tra**c**e, pla**c**e, gra**c**e
g → pa**g**e, sta**g**e, ca**g**e, a**g**e, ra**g**e

When the *s* sound is spelled with a *c*, the *c* is always followed by *e*, *i*, or *y*.
    fa**ce**   la**cy**   **ci**ty

When the *j* sound is spelled with a *g*, the *g* is always followed by *e*, *i*, or *y*.
    ju**dge**   **gi**ant   **gy**m

 GET SET!

Let's look at an example.

Find the word that has the same consonant sound underlined in the word below.

ge**m**
○ game
○ badge
○ egg

(1st) is **wrong.** *Gem* has a soft *g* sound, and *game* has a hard *g* sound.
(2nd) is **correct!** *Gem* has a soft *g* sound, and the *dge* in *badge* makes a soft *g* sound.
(3rd) is **wrong.** *Gem* has a soft *g* sound, and the *gg* in *egg* makes a hard *g* sound.

 TEACHING TIP

Give students a list of words containing the soft /c/ and /g/ sounds. Have them keep the list in their desks and add to it each time they come across a new word with either of the sounds.

GO!

1. gr<u>a</u>pe
   - ○ giant
   - ● guide
   - ○ judge

2. <u>g</u>as
   - ● get
   - ○ gentle
   - ○ jot

3. pa<u>c</u>e
   - ○ fuse
   - ○ neck
   - ● mice

4. ri<u>c</u>e
   - ○ his
   - ● fuss
   - ○ buzz

5. <u>e</u>ngine
   - ○ golf
   - ● just
   - ○ grid

6. <u>j</u>ewel
   - ● gentleman
   - ○ gum
   - ○ give

 Go over each question on this page as a class.

Question 1
📣 For question 1, find the word that has the same sound as the underlined letter in the word grape.

Question 2
📣 For question 2, find the word that has the same sound as the underlined letter in the word gas.

Question 3
📣 For question 3, find the word that has the same sound as the underlined letter in the word pace.

Question 4
📣 For question 4, find the word that has the same sound as the underlined letter in the word rice.

Question 5
📣 For question 5, find the word that has the same sound as the underlined letter in the word engine.

Question 6
📣 For question 6, find the word that has the same sound as the underlined letter in the word jewel.

Exercise 28

USING RHYMING WORDS TO HELP YOU SPELL

 Explain to students that rhyming words can often help with spelling.

Read the top part of the Pupil Edition page to students. Discuss rhyming words: how they *sound* and how they *look*. Explain to students that when trying to spell a word that they are not sure of, it is sometimes helpful to think of a rhyming word. Put some examples on the board and discuss this concept. Some words you might use are:

- boat　　coat　　float
- bike　　alike　　hike
- hook　　brook　　took
- light　　bright　　flight
- keep　　sheep　　weep

Ask students to come up with extra examples of rhyming words. Write their suggestions on the board.

 Go over the example question as a class.

Exercise 28

 ON YOUR MARK!

Using Rhyming Words to Help You Spell

When you are not sure if a word is misspelled, think of a word that rhymes with it that you do know how to spell. Look at this word: *bake*

Do you think *bake* is spelled correctly? If you're not sure, think of another word with the same ending. It might be a rhyming word, like this one: *take*

Compare the letters in the two words. You will find that they both end with an *ake*. This is a clue that *bake* is spelled correctly.

 GET SET!

Let's look at an example.

Find the underlined word that is spelled wrong.
○ My dog likes to <u>growl</u>.
○ Don't you feel <u>wel</u>?
○ I feel just <u>fine</u>.
○ Mikey dug a hole in the <u>soil</u>.

(1st) is **wrong.** If you think of the word *owl*, you will find that this word is spelled correctly.

(2nd) is **correct!** *Well* is misspelled. If you think of the word *sell*, you will find that there should be a second *l* at the end of *wel*.

(3rd) is **wrong.** If you think of the word *mine*, you will find that this word is spelled correctly.

(4th) is **wrong.** If you think of the word *boil*, you will find that this word is spelled correctly.

 EXTRA ACTIVITY

Create a worksheet with several sentences. Leave a blank in each sentence and have students find a word that would make sense in the sentence and rhyme with the word in parentheses at the end of the sentence. For example: *I love to eat _____ for lunch. (shapes)* *grapes

GO!

1
- ○ Take this to the <u>class</u>.
- ○ Are you <u>happy</u> to go?
- ○ That <u>boy</u> is new this year.
- ● Can you <u>anser</u> the question?

2
- ○ Do you <u>own</u> your bike?
- ○ <u>Follow</u> us to the park.
- ○ We like your new <u>clothes</u>.
- ○ <u>Cach</u> me if you can!

3
- ○ The sun is <u>bright</u>.
- ○ He <u>askes</u> a lot of questions.
- ○ Be careful, don't <u>crash</u>!
- ○ <u>Push</u> the cart over here.

4
- ○ I will go <u>down</u> the road.
- ○ Did you <u>clene</u> your room?
- ○ He <u>stood</u> in the dark.
- ○ The <u>cat</u> lay back in the grass.

5
- ○ He <u>shook</u> himself to dry his hair.
- ○ I took a <u>bight</u>.
- ○ Then he ran into the <u>bushes</u>.
- ○ Your <u>brother</u> can come with us.

Go over each question on this page as a class.

Tell students to try to think of words that rhyme with the underlined words on this page. Sometimes this will help them determine whether or not the word is spelled correctly.

For questions 1 through 5, fill in the bubble next to the sentence that contains a misspelled word.

Question 1
Missing silent /w/

Question 2
Rhyming words: hatch, batch

Question 3
Rhyming words: tasks, masks

Question 4
Rhyming words: mean, jean

Question 5
Long /i/ spelled i-e

Exercises • Preparation and Practice for the ITBS, SAT-9, and TerraNova • Grade 2

Exercise 29

PH, CH, AND TCH SOUNDS

 Explain to students that certain letter combinations make different sounds than the letters make when they are alone.

Have students read the top of the Pupil Edition page or read it aloud to the class. Discuss the letter combinations *ph, ch,* and *tch*. Have students think of examples for each letter combination. Words you might use are:

ph	ch	tch
photograph	march	patch
paragraph	chip	matches
geography	much	latch

Have students offer extra examples of words with these spellings and sounds. Write their suggestions on the board.

 Go over the example question as a class.

Exercise 29

 ON YOUR MARK!

Ph, ch, and **tch** Sounds

Certain letters sound different when they are next to each other than when they are apart. For example, the *ch* sound in *choice* sounds different than the *c* sound in *cape* or the *h* sound in *Henry*.

When the letters *p* and *h* are together, they make an *f* sound.
 phone
 alphabet

When the letters *c* and *h* are together, they make a *ch* sound.
 chore
 which

When the letters *t, c,* and *h* are together, they make a *ch* sound.
 watch
 itch

 GET SET!

Let's look at an example.
Which word makes an *f* sound?
○ photo
○ pail
○ tap

(1st) is **correct!** The word *photo* starts with an *f* sound.
(2nd) is **wrong.** The word *pail* starts with a *p* sound.
(3rd) is **wrong.** The word *tap* ends with a *p* sound.

 EXTRA ACTIVITY

Have students try to write one sentence that contains words with all three letter combinations. Encourage them to have fun with it, and allow them to write silly sentences.

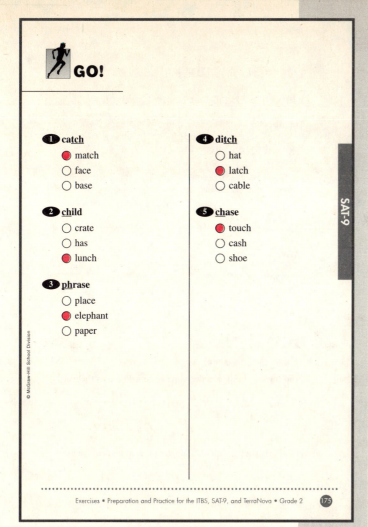

 Go over each question on this page as a class.

Question 1

📢 *For question 1, find the word that has the same sound as the underlined letters in the word catch.*

Question 2

📢 *For question 2, find the word that has the same sound as the underlined letters in the word child.*

Question 3

📢 *For question 3, find the word that has the same sound as the underlined letters in the word phrase.*

Question 4

📢 *For question 4, find the word that has the same sound as the underlined letters in the word ditch.*

Question 5

📢 *For question 5, find the word that has the same sound as the underlined letters in the word chase.*

Exercise 30

LISTEN TO THE DIRECTIONS CAREFULLY

 Explain to students that listening to directions carefully is an important test-taking skill for the SAT-9.

Have students read the top section of the Pupil Edition page or read it aloud to the class. Point out that listening carefully can make a difference between answering a question correctly and getting it wrong. There are many ways to answer questions and students must be sure that they are answering the question that is asked.

 Go over the example question as a class.

Exercise 30

 ## ON YOUR MARK!

Listen to the Directions Carefully

The directions explain how to answer the questions on the test. When your teacher reads the test directions to you, always listen very closely. There are many different kinds of directions:

- Sometimes the directions tell you to find the word that is made up of two smaller words.
- Sometimes the directions tell you to find the words that have the same ending.
- Sometimes the directions tell you to find the words that have the same sound.
- Every time you work on a question that has new directions, your teacher will read the directions to you slowly and clearly.
- Then you will answer a sample question using those new directions. **A sample question** is a question that is only practice.

 ### GET SET!

Let's look at an example.

Find the word that has the same ending sound as the word *catch*.

○ fetch
○ face
○ cat

(1st) is **correct!** The letters *tch* in the word *fetch* make the same sound as the letters *tch* in the word *catch*.

 ### EXTRA ACTIVITY

Give students a sheet of paper and ask them to get crayons on their desk. Read a set of directions aloud, reading each direction only one time. Give students time to complete the activity but do not repeat the direction.

This activity will impress on the students the importance of listening carefully. An example of the directions you might use are:

- *Draw a blue bubble in the top right corner of your paper.*
- *Make a black dot in the center of your paper.*
- *Write the number 5 under the black dot.*

Continue with ten or so directions.

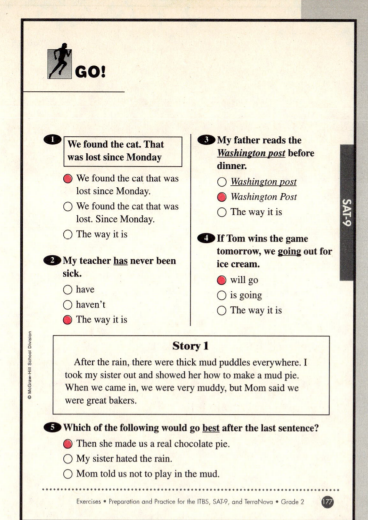

Go over each question on this page as a class.

This page tests skills students have learned in the previous exercises. Students should listen very carefully to directions as they work through questions 1 through 5.

Question 1

For question 1, fill in the bubble next to the sentence that is written correctly. If the example sentence is correct, fill in the bubble next to The way it is.

Questions 2, 3, and 4

For questions 2, 3, and 4, fill in the bubble next to the answer that has the underlined part written correctly. If the example sentence is written correctly, fill in the bubble next to The way it is.

Question 5

For question 5, read the story and the question aloud to students.

Practice Test

Language

> For Samples A and B and questions 1 through 5, choose the answer that shows how the underlined part should be written. If it is written correctly in the example, fill in the bubble for The way it is.

SAMPLE A

Has anyone seen my **book**?
- ○ book.
- ○ book!
- ● The way it is

Make sure students know the questions Sample A and Sample B are for practice only. They will not be scored.

SAMPLE B

That movie **were** very good.
- ○ am
- ● was
- ○ The way it is

1. In **june I won't** go on vacation.
- ○ june, I won't
- ● June I won't
- ○ The way it is

2. Our parents' anniversary is in **september**.
- ● September.
- ○ September?
- ○ The way it is

A month of the year is always capitalized.

3. You have **growed** so much since last year!
- ● grown
- ○ grewed
- ○ The way it is

4. The steps are steep, so watch **out!**
- ○ out,
- ○ out?
- ● The way it is

5. How should you begin this letter?
dear mom,
- ○ Dear mom,
- ● Dear Mom,
- ○ The way it is

The first letter of a greeting of a letter is always capitalized.

SAMPLE C

Rory takes her dog, for a walk.

- ● Rory takes her dog for a walk.
- ○ Rory taking her dog for a walk.
- ○ The way it is

SAMPLE D

He put the book. On the shelf.

- ● He put the book on the shelf.
- ○ He putting the book on the shelf.
- ○ The way it is

6

Parker baked the cake and then let it cool.

- ○ Parker baked the cake. And then let it cool.
- ○ Parker baking the cake and letting it cool.
- ● The way it is

7

At the library. We got many books.

- ● At the library we got many books.
- ○ At the library we getting many books.
- ○ The way it is

8

Before we play cards, we need to do homework.

- ○ Before, we play cards we need to do homework.
- ○ Before we play, cards we need to do homework.
- ● The way it is

For Samples C and D and questions 6 through 8, choose the answer that contains a complete sentence. If the example sentence is correct, fill in the bubble for The way it is.

Read the stories and questions aloud to students.

Story A

Many houseplants such as ivy need to be watered two to three times a week. Plants that come from warmer climates, however, don't need as much water. A cactus plant, for example, grows very well if you water it only once a month.

S1 This story was probably written to—
- ○ Tell people how much sun plants need.
- ● Tell about the different watering needs of plants.
- ○ Describe forest plants.

S2 Which sentence would go best after the last sentence?
- ○ Did you know that plants need to be watered?
- ○ Forests provide shade for the plants.
- ● They are able to store the moisture in their stems.

Story 1

At our picnic, we had many different things to eat. We could eat tuna fish, egg salad, or a turkey sandwich. There were also different kinds of fruit, such as apples, strawberries, and peaches. The best part was dessert. I chose a chocolate chip cookie instead of a fig bar.

9 Find the sentence that does not go with the story.
- ○ Dessert is my favorite!
- ○ After the picnic, we read books and played a game of hide and seek.
- ● The best chocolate comes from France.

10 Which sentence would go best at the end of the story?
- ○ At lunch I have different things to eat.
- ● Chocolate chip cookies have always been my favorite cookies.
- ○ March is a risky time to have a picnic.

STANFORD 9

GO ON

Practice Test • Preparation and Practice for the ITBS, SAT-9, and TerraNova • Grade 2

Read the story and questions aloud to students.

Story 2

Peter had to write a paper about monkeys. He went to the library to find books about them. The librarian helped him find several good books. He took them to his desk and began to read about the many different types of monkeys. He decided he would write about chimpanzees, since he had seen them before at the zoo and already knew a lot about them.

11 This paragraph was written to describe—

○ The library just being built
○ Monkeys as interesting animals
● Peter finding a topic for his paper

12 Find the sentence that would go <u>best</u> at the end of the paragraph.

● Peter got right to work.
○ They have lived in the zoo all their lives.
○ The library was full of books.

13 Find the sentence that does <u>not</u> go with this story.

● Books about monkeys are very hard to find.
○ He could use his encyclopedias at home for information, too.
○ Peter began to get excited to start writing!

The sentence in the first choice would not go with the story because the story stated that the library had several books on monkeys.

Spelling

For the sample question and questions 1 through 7, choose the answer that contains a misspelled word.

SAMPLE
- ○ The bird is <u>blue</u>.
- ● <u>Wat</u> does she want?
- ○ <u>Start</u> the clock.
- ○ The sun <u>rises</u>.

1
- ● Do <u>citys</u> have parks?
- ○ They took the bus <u>themselves</u>.
- ○ It <u>printed</u> our work.
- ○ I have all my baby <u>teeth</u>.

2
- ○ She <u>drives</u> a bus.
- ● The <u>nife</u> is sharp.
- ○ Bob <u>took</u> the ball.
- ○ This candy is <u>sweet</u>.

3
- ● There are clowns at the <u>curcus</u>.
- ○ Do you like <u>cornbread</u>?
- ○ Don't <u>stare</u> at the sun.
- ○ She sure can run <u>fast</u>!

Questions 2 and 6 are both missing silent letters.

4
- ○ We can <u>soak</u> up the dirt.
- ○ Hang up your <u>coat</u>.
- ● Please <u>cary</u> my books.
- ○ I have a <u>part</u> in the play.

5
- ○ He <u>read</u> a book to me.
- ○ Take the mail to the post <u>office</u>.
- ● We can have ice cream <u>efter</u> dinner.
- ○ The snow covered the park in <u>white</u>.

6
- ○ She walks <u>every</u> day.
- ○ There are <u>buds</u> on the tree.
- ○ The dancer did not <u>speak</u>.
- ● We <u>coud</u> take the train.

7
- ● Ride the bike <u>dowen</u> the hill.
- ○ I was <u>born</u> on the 4th of July.
- ○ He was <u>very</u> late.
- ○ We <u>must</u> get there on time.

Practice Test • Preparation and Practice for the ITBS, SAT-9, and TerraNova • Grade 2

Word Study Skills

SAMPLE A
- ○ banana
- ○ shopping
- ● horseshoe

For Sample 1 and questions 1 and 2, choose the word that is made up of two words.

SAMPLE B
- ○ walks
- ● walked
- ○ walking

For Sample B, fill in the bubble next to the word walked. We walked to the store.

1
- ○ walking
- ○ happiness
- ● lampshade

2
- ○ restful
- ○ period
- ● hangnail

3
- ○ dancer
- ○ dancing
- ● dances

For question 3, fill in the bubble next to the word dances. He dances around the living room.

4
- ○ playing
- ● player
- ○ plays

For question 4, fill in the bubble next to the word player. She is a good tennis player.

SAMPLE C
- ○ didn't
- ● isn't
- ○ can't

For Sample C, fill in the bubble next to the word that is the contraction for is not. Is not.

SAMPLE D

j<u>e</u>lly
- ○ flower
- ○ garden
- ● giant

For Sample D, choose the answer that contains the same sound as the underlined letter in the word jelly.

5
- ○ he'll
- ● he'd
- ○ he's

For question 5, fill in the bubble next to the word that is the contraction for he would. He would.

6
- ○ haven't
- ● aren't
- ○ weren't

For question 6, fill in the bubble next to the word that is the contraction for are not. Are not.

7 cl<u>o</u>se
- ● know
- ○ lose
- ○ stool

For question 7, choose the answer that contains the same sound as the underlined letter in the word close.

8 <u>a</u>rt
- ○ fancy
- ● chart
- ○ cat

For question 8, choose the answer that contains the same sound as the underlined letter in the word art.

SAT-9

9 mo<u>ti</u>on
- ○ tired
- ● shine
- ○ chance

> For question 9, choose the answer that contains the same sound as the underlined letters in the word motion.

10 <u>ch</u>ick
- ○ shark
- ○ school
- ● chin

> For question 10, choose the answer that contains the same sound as the underlined letters in the word chick.

11 <u>sh</u>ell
- ○ such
- ○ south
- ● shoe

> For question 11, choose the answer that contains the same sound as the underlined letters in the word shell.

12 s<u>ui</u>t
- ○ built
- ○ puddle
- ● zoo

> For question 12, choose the answer that contains the same sound as the underlined letters in the word suit.

13 s<u>a</u>lt
- ● cellar
- ○ alter
- ○ crush

> For question 13, choose the answer that contains the same sound as the underlined letter in the word salt.

14 tr<u>ay</u>
- ○ tack
- ● try
- ○ part

> For question 14, choose the answer that contains the same sound as the underlined letters in the word tray.

15 t<u>oo</u>k
- ● put
- ○ open
- ○ out

For question 15, choose the answer that contains the same sound as the underlined letters in the word took.

16 b<u>u</u>tterfly
- ○ flow
- ○ pull
- ● supper

For question 16, choose the answer that contains the same sound as the underlined letter in the word butterfly.

17 <u>str</u>ange
- ○ trap
- ○ stack
- ● strike

For question 17, choose the answer that contains the same sound as the underlined letters in the word strange.

18 b<u>ri</u>ng
- ○ brag
- ● trying
- ○ negative

For question 18, choose the answer that contains the same sound as the underlined letters in the word bring.

19 wh<u>a</u>t
- ● wet
- ○ hat
- ○ stitch

For question 19, choose the answer that contains the same sound as the underlined letters in the word what.

20 tr<u>a</u>ck
- ○ take
- ○ cake
- ● cap

For question 20, choose the answer that contains the same sound as the underlined letter in the word track.

On Your Mark, Get Set, Go! Review

REVIEW

The following pages offer a list of the skills that students should be familiar with after completing the exercises in this book.

Sentences

Students should know:

- A sentence is a complete thought
- A fragment is not a complete thought
- How to tell the difference between a sentence and a fragment

Compound Words

Students should know:

- A compound word is made up of two words
- How to recognize and form a compound word

Punctuation

Students should know:

- Periods are used at the end of a statement
- Periods are used at the end of a command
- Question marks are used at the end of a question
- Exclamation marks are used at the end of a statement of excitement
- Commas always separate the month and day from the year
- A period follows an abbreviation
- Commas are used between the name of a city and state

Spelling

Students should know:

- How to form plurals by adding -s, -es, or -ies
- How to add suffixes such as -ied, -ing, -s, and -ly
- How to recognize and spell words with silent letters
- How to spell words with confusing sounds such as *penny, again, help,* and *word*
- How to spell tricky words such as *because, bowl, people, were,* and *patch*

Sounds

Students should know:

- The difference between the sounds of long and short vowels
- How vowel sounds change when followed by the letter *r*
- The different spellings for the short /e/ and long /e/ sound
- The difference between the sound of a soft /c/ and a hard /c/
- The difference between the sound of a soft /g/ and a hard /g/
- The sounds that result from *ph, ch,* and *tch*

Verbs

Students should know:

- The difference between a subject and a verb
- The difference between a singular and a plural subject or verb
- How to make subjects and verbs agree
- How to recognize a past and a present tense verb
- How to form irregular verbs in the past tense
- What a helping verb is and how it is used

Capitalization

Students should know:

- A capital letter always begins a sentence
- Names of people and pets should be capitalized
- Days of the week and months of the year should be capitalized
- Specific names of places should be capitalized
- Terms of respect (*Mr., Dr.*) should be capitalized
- The first letter of an abbreviation is always capitalized
- If an abbreviation is for more than one word, each letter must be capitalized
- The first word and all important words in a title should be capitalized
- The first word of a letter greeting or closing is capitalized

Contractions

Students should know:

- A contraction is a short form of two words
- Where to place an apostrophe in a contraction
- Contractions are words that are combined with *not, be,* and *have*

Alphabetical Order

Students should know:

- What alphabetical order means
- How to put words in alphabetical order using the first, second, or third letter

Paragraphs

Students should know:

- What a main idea is
- A topic sentence is the first sentence in a paragraph and tells the main idea
- What makes a good topic sentence
- How to recognize sentences that do or do not belong in a paragraph
- How to determine the main purpose of a paragraph

TERRANOVA

TEACHER INTRODUCTION

WHY *PREPARATION AND PRACTICE FOR THE TERRANOVA* IS THE BEST PREPARATION FOR STUDENTS

Welcome to the Teacher Edition of *Preparation and Practice for the TerraNova* for grade 2!

By completing each section of this book, students will:

- Increase their knowledge and understanding of language arts skills
- Become familiar with the types of questions that will be asked on the test
- Become aware of and experience first-hand the amount of time they will have to complete the test
- Become accustomed to the style of the test
- Become better writers and speakers
- Learn test-taking techniques and tips that are specifically designed to help students do their best on the TerraNova
- Feel comfortable on the day of the exam

Parts of This Book

There are eight sections of this Teacher Edition:

Teacher Introduction

The Teacher Introduction familiarizes you with the purpose and format of *Preparation and Practice for the TerraNova*. It also describes the TerraNova sections and questions on the test that pertain to language arts skills.

Student and Class Diagnostic Charts

A student and a class diagnostic chart are included for the Warm-Up Test. You may use these charts to gauge student performance and to determine the skills with which students will need the most practice.

Student Introduction

This section contains some tips and explanations for students as they begin their preparation for the TerraNova. Extra annotations are included for teachers to help you further explain what is expected of students and to encourage them as they begin their test preparation.

Warm-Up Test

This diagnostic test reveals students' strengths and weaknesses so that you may customize your test preparation accordingly. The skill tested in each question of the Warm-Up Test directly correlates to a skill reviewed in one of the 30 practice exercises.

On Your Mark! Get Set! Go!

This section consists of 30 practice exercises. Each exercise focuses on a specific language arts skill or test-taking strategy. On Your Mark! introduces and explains the skill. Get Set! provides an example question that tests the skill. (You should go over the question as a class.) Go! contains questions similar to TerraNova questions that test the skills introduced in the exercise. Have students complete these questions on their own.

Practice Test

The Practice Test only contains a portion of the questions that will appear on the actual test so that students are not tapped of energy. The Practice Test includes questions from each section to provide students with a simulated test-taking experience. Make sure you tell students that the actual TerraNova will be longer. *Note: The Practice Test contains reading comprehension passages and questions in addition to language arts questions. These were included because the actual TerraNova combines these two sections. To give your students a realistic test-taking experience, administer the test in its entirety.*

On Your Mark! Get Set! Go! Review

This section is *not* included in the Pupil Edition. It is an overview of the skills contained in On Your Mark! Get Set! Go!

Index

The index is a brief listing of where you can look to find exercises about specific skills.

How to Use This Book

This book has been designed so that you may customize your TerraNova test preparation according to your class's needs and time frame. However, we recommend that you begin your test preparation as early in the school year as possible. This book will yield your students' best TerraNova scores if you diagnose your students' strengths and weaknesses early and work toward helping them achieve their best performance. Please note that preparing students for a test such as the TerraNova is a process. As much of their preparation as possible should take place in the classroom and be discussed as a class.

Warm-Up Test

Have students complete the Warm-Up Test in class. It should be administered as early in the school year as possible. By doing so, students will gain familiarity with the types of questions and the specific skills tested on the TerraNova *before* they begin working through the skill-specific exercises in this book. Use the student and class diagnostic charts to grade the tests. The results of the Warm-Up Test reveal students' strengths and weaknesses and allow you to focus your test preparation accordingly.

On Your Mark! Get Set! Go!

We recommend that you review an On Your Mark! Get Set! Go! exercise after completing each chapter in your McGraw-Hill language arts textbook. It is best to go through the On Your Mark! Get Set! Go! section throughout the year so that students can digest the material properly. Consider reviewing On Your Mark! and Get Set! as a class. The Go! sections may be assigned as homework or completed by students individually in class. Having students complete Go! individually will provide the best simulated preparation for the TerraNova. After students have completed the Go! exercises, go over the correct answers as a class. The Princeton Review's research and experience show this in-class work to be an essential element in effective test preparation.

Practice Test

The Practice Test should be administered in the weeks prior to the actual exam. Testing conditions should be simulated. For example, no two desks should be placed directly next to each other, students should have two pencils at their disposal, the room should be quiet, and so on.

On Your Mark! Get Set! Go! Review

Use this review in the few days leading up to the actual exam. Its purpose is to solidify the On Your Mark! Get Set! Go! skills students have learned throughout the school year. Because this section is in the Teacher Edition only, you may want to photocopy it and review the skills as a class. Or, you may simply want to keep the information to yourself and make sure students are prepared to answer questions based on the material. If students need additional review, consult the On Your Mark! Get Set! Go! exercises that correlate to the skills. You will find the practice exercise-skill correlation information in the index.

About the Teacher Pages

Each page of the Pupil Edition is reproduced in this Teacher Edition, either reduced or full-size. Each reduced Pupil Edition page has teacher wrap. Teacher wrap consists of a **column** and a **box**.

- The column serves as a guide for you as you present the material on the Pupil Edition page in an interactive way. Guiding prompts and notes are included to ensure that information pivotal to the exercise is covered.

- The box includes teaching tips and extra activities. The extra activities are often fun, game-like activities for your class. These activities give students the opportunity to learn or apply TerraNova-related skills in a variety of ways.

 This icon correlates the teacher wrap to the information in the On Your Mark! section of the Pupil Edition page.

 This icon reminds you to go over the example question in the Get Set! section of the Pupil Edition page.

 This icon reminds you to go over each question on the Go! pages of the Pupil Edition.

 This icon provides a point of emphasis for you to make concerning the exercise on the Pupil Edition page.

 This icon identifies an extra activity.

 This icon reminds you to read the text that follows aloud to students.

About the Annotated Pages

Some pages in the Teacher Edition include full-size Pupil Edition pages. These occur in the Student Introduction, the Warm-Up Test section, and the Practice Test section.

All of these full-size reproductions are highlighted with teacher annotations. These annotations, which appear in magenta ink, provide the following:

- **Teacher Script**

A small magenta megaphone will appear directly before the script you need to read aloud.

- **Correct Answers**

The correct answer to each question is circled in magenta ink.

- **Question Analyses**

Sometimes an annotation offers further explanation of a specific question.

- **Extra Tips**

Certain annotations provide you with extra teaching tips specific to the skill tested on the Pupil Edition page.

- **Hints**

Some annotations offer hints that you can give to your students when they are working through the questions in the exercise or test sections.

Introduction to the TerraNova

The TerraNova is a standardized test taken every year by students throughout the country. Talk to your school's test administrator to get the exact testing date for this school year.

The TerraNova is a multiple-choice test that assesses students' skills in reading, language arts, mathematics, science, and social studies. This book covers the language arts section of the TerraNova. There are three sections of the TerraNova that incorporate language arts skills:

- **Reading and Language Arts**
- **Language Mechanics**
- **Spelling**

The specific number of questions for each section discussed above and the time allotted fot it is broken down as follows on the actual TerraNova:

Skill	Reading and Language Arts	Language Mechanics	Spelling
Number of Items	60	20	20
Time	75 minutes	15 minutes	15 minutes

How Language Arts Skills Are Tested

The reading and language arts section of the TerraNova includes *both* reading comprehension questions and language skills questions. For the purposes of this book, you should only be concerned with the language skills questions.

There are several different types of language arts skills questions on the TerraNova.

- **Word Usage:** Students are asked to pick the pronoun or form of a verb, adjective, or noun that best fits into the provided sentence.

- **Compound Words:** Students are asked to choose the compound word from three word choices.

- **Sentence Structure:** Students are asked to determine which sentence is complete.

- **Punctuation:** Students must choose the correctly punctuated sentence, address, or date to replace an incorrect or blank section of a sentence or a paragraph.

- **Capitalization:** Students are asked to pick the sentence that has correct capitalization.

- **Supporting Sentences:** Students are asked to determine which sentence does or does not belong with the theme of a paragraph.

- **Sounds:** Students are asked to choose words that contain the same vowel sound or the same middle sound as a given word.

- **Contractions:** Students are asked to choose the correct spelling of a contraction.

- **Root Words:** Students are asked to pick the root word of an underlined word.

Language Mechanics

In this section, students are asked to identify a wide variety of punctuation and capitalization errors.

EXAMPLE

Students must choose the sentence with the correct punctuation.

- ○ I will be back later.
- ○ I think mr. martin's class is fun.
- ○ My brother and i do not like meatloaf.

This question tests students' ability to pick out the correct capitalization. Other language mechanics questions will address punctuation and capitalization rules for quotations, exclamations, proper nouns, and letter greetings and closings. There will also be questions about correct punctuation usage for addresses, dates, and times.

Spelling

For this section, students are tested on their ability to recognize whether a word is misspelled. Students are required to choose the correct spelling of the word.

EXAMPLE

Students must choose the sentence with the correctly spelled word.

I like to _____ my grandpa.

- ○ visit
- ○ viset
- ○ visut

For this question, students must choose the correctly spelled form of the word. Other spelling questions contain sentences with several words underlined. Students much choose which of the underlined words, if any, is spelled incorrectly.

Introduction • Preparation and Practice for the ITBS, SAT-9, and TerraNova • Grade 2

STUDENT AND CLASS DIAGNOSTIC CHARTS

How to Use the Student Diagnostic Chart

The Student Diagnostic Chart on page T61 should be used to score the Warm-Up Test in this book. The chart is designed to help you and your individual students determine the areas in which they need the most practice as they begin their preparation for the TerraNova. You will need to make enough copies of the chart for each of your students.

There are two ways to use the Student Diagnostic Chart:
- You can collect the finished Warm-Up Tests from each student and fill out one chart for each student as you grade the tests.
- You can give one copy of the Student Diagnostic Chart to each student and have students grade their own tests as you read aloud the correct answer choices.

Note: Correct answer choices are marked in the Warm-Up Test of this Teacher Edition.

How to Fill Out the Student Diagnostic Chart

For each question number, there is a blank column labeled "Right or Wrong." An "R" or a "W" should be placed in that column for each question on the Warm-Up Test. By looking at the chart upon completion, students will understand which questions they answered incorrectly and to which skills these incorrect answers correspond. The exercise from the On Your Mark! Get Set! Go! section that teaches the skill is also noted. You should encourage students to spend extra time going over the corresponding exercises covering the skills with which they had the most trouble. The charts will also help you determine which students need the most practice and what skills gave the majority of the students trouble. This way, you can plan your students' TerraNova preparation schedule accordingly.

How to Use the Class Diagnostic Chart

The Class Diagnostic Chart on page T62 should be used to record your class's performance on the Warm-Up Test in this book. The chart is designed to help you determine which areas your class needs to practice most as you begin the preparation for the TerraNova. The Class Diagnostic Chart is strictly for your own use. You should not share it with students.

How to Fill Out the Class Diagnostic Chart

Under the "Name" column, you should write the names of each of your students. Then you should use the completed Student Diagnostic Charts to help you fill out the Class Diagnostic Chart. Fill out one row for each student.

For each question on the Warm-Up Test, there is a corresponding row in the Class Diagnostic Chart. The row is labeled with the question number and the exercise number of the correlating On Your Mark! Get Set! Go! exercise. If a student gets a question wrong, you should mark an "X" in the box underneath that question number. After completing a column for one student, add up all of the "Xs" and put a total for that student in the "Total" row on the top of the page. When you have filled out a column for each student, you should total up the "Xs" for each question. Put the totals in the "Total" column on the right-hand side of the page. Assessing both "Total" columns will help you determine two things: 1) which students are having the most trouble individually, and 2) which questions are giving the class as a whole the most trouble.

You should use the information gathered in the Class Diagnostic Chart to determine which skills to spend the most time reviewing and which students need the most individual practice and guidance.

Student Diagnostic Chart

Question #	Correct Answer	Right or Wrong	Exercise #	Skill
1	2nd		1	End Marks
2	2nd		2	Complete and Incomplete Sentences
3	2nd		3	Capitalizing Sentences
4	2nd		4	Capitalizing Names of People
5	3rd		6	Capitalizing Names of Places
6	3rd		5	Vowels
7	3rd		8	Compound Words
8	1st		9	Letter Greetings and Closings
9	3rd		9	Letter Greetings and Closings
10	1st		10	Verbs
11	2nd		11	Vowel Sounds with R
12	1st		12	Terms of Respect
13	1st		14	Days, Months, and Holidays
14	1st		15	Topic Sentences
15	3rd		16	Detail Sentences
16	2nd		17	Contractions
17	1st		18	Pronouns
18	2nd		20	Capitalizing the Pronoun I
19	1st		21	Silent Letters
20	3rd		22	Long /e/ and Short /e/ Sound
21	1st		23	/c/ and /g/ Sounds
22	1st		24	/ph/, /ch/, and /tch/ Sounds
23	2nd		26	Tricky Words
24	2nd		29	Words with Silent /e/
25	2nd		28	Changing Y to I
26	3rd		27	Root Words

Introduction • Preparation and Practice for the ITBS, SAT-9, and TerraNova • Grade 2

Class Diagnostic Chart

Name	Q1–Ex. 1	Q2–Ex. 2	Q3–Ex. 3	Q4–Ex. 4	Q5–Ex. 5	Q6–Ex. 5	Q7–Ex. 8	Q8–Ex. 9	Q9–Ex. 9	Q10–Ex. 10	Q11–Ex. 11	Q12–Ex. 12	Q13–Ex. 14	Q14–Ex. 15	Q15–Ex. 16	Q16–Ex. 17	Q17–Ex. 18	Q18–Ex. 20	Q19–Ex. 21	Q20–Ex. 22	Q21–Ex. 23	Q22–Ex. 24	Q23–Ex. 21	Q24–Ex. 29	Q25–Ex. 28	Q26–Ex. 27	Total
Total																											

STUDENT INTRODUCTION

What is the TerraNova?

The TerraNova is a multiple-choice test that helps you and your teacher find out how much you have learned in school so far. Now's your chance to show off what you know about reading and writing!

This may be the first time students are preparing to take a standardized test. Explain to them that test-taking does not have to be a stressful experience. Instead, it is an opportunity for them to demonstrate what they have learned in reading and writing. Emphasize to students that this workbook will allow them to practice these skills so that each of them will do his or her best on the TerraNova.

Instilling a positive attitude about test-taking in your students from the beginning will help them get more out of the practice exercises—and most importantly, will help them approach the TerraNova with confidence.

Does the TerraNova measure how smart I am?

No, definitely not. The TerraNova tests how well you can use the skills you've learned in class.

> Ease test-taking anxiety by assuring students that the TerraNova does not measure their intelligence. Instead, it measures their ability to use the skills that they have learned in school.

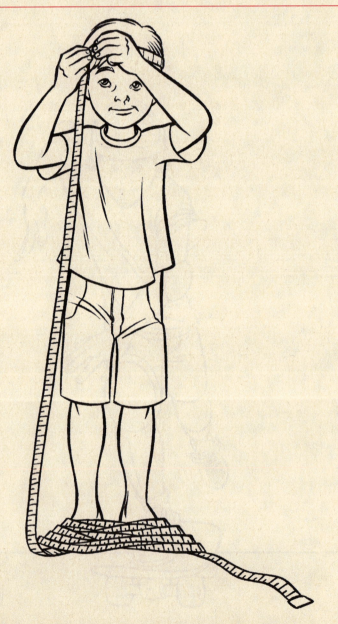

Can I study for the TerraNova?

You can answer practice questions. You can also learn some tips that will help you do your best.

Just like riding a bike or playing the violin, studying for the TerraNova takes practice. The more you practice, the better you will do!

Remind students that the TerraNova measures what they have been learning in school. Instead of studying for the TerraNova, students need to review the concepts that they have learned in school and practice some test-taking tips. The exercises and activities in the workbook are designed to accomplish this. To emphasize this point, have students discuss how practicing leads to improvement. For example, ask students to name several activities (e.g., sports, music, art) in which they participate. Then ask them to discuss how they practice for these activities. Has practice helped them improve their skills? How?

Introduction • Preparation and Practice for the ITBS, SAT-9, and TerraNova • Grade 2

Here's how you will practice for the TerraNova:

✔ You'll take a Warm-Up Test.

✔ You'll brush up on your reading and writing skills in On Your Mark! Get Set! Go!

✔ You'll take a Mini-Practice Test. After all of your practicing, you'll know exactly what to expect when you take the real TerraNova.

> Let students know that they'll be completing these exercises over an extended period of time so that they do not feel overwhelmed when you are introducing the material to them. One critical aspect of helping students do their best on the TerraNova is to make sure that the process of preparing and practicing is fun for them.

Practice Like a Superstar

Ask questions. Ask your teacher if you don't understand why an answer is wrong.

Learn from your mistakes. Notice the questions you have trouble with, and find out how to answer them correctly.

Read as much as you can. Read everything and anything you can get your hands on. Read signs as you pass by them. Read stories aloud. Listen to others read stories aloud to you.

Answering questions incorrectly can be as valuable as answering questions correctly when preparing for a standardized test. Make sure students understand that it is okay to make mistakes. The important thing is that students learn from their mistakes.

Also, remind them how important it is to practice reading. Reading is exercise for the brain, and the more they exercise their brains by reading all types of materials, the greater improvement they'll see in their overall reading and language arts comprehension.

Introduction • Preparation and Practice for the ITBS, SAT-9, and TerraNova • Grade 2

Pay Attention to the Directions

The directions tell you how to answer the questions. Sometimes you will read directions on your own. Other times, your teacher will read them to you. Always make sure that you understand the directions.

Reinforce to students the importance of reading all directions carefully. The directions will often provide important information about how to answer the questions.

Read Questions and Answer Choices Slowly and Carefully

Always read all the words in the questions and all the words in the answer choices carefully. Read every answer choice, even if you think you already found the correct answer!

Let your students in on a little secret: Standardized tests often contain answer choices that are designed to distract them from the correct answer choices. As a result, students need to read and compare all of the answer choices in order to figure out which is the best choice.

Get Rid of the Wrong Answer Choices First

✔ Every time you answer a question, read each answer choice, one by one.

✔ After you read each answer choice, decide whether you think it is right or wrong.

✔ Get rid of as many wrong answer choices as you can. If you still have more than one answer choice left over, *guess*! Try not to leave a question blank.

Process of elimination is one of the most important strategies students can use to increase their success on standardized tests. You may want to illustrate this concept by playing some sort of guessing game with your students. For example, write down four things (e.g., types of board games) on index cards. Share the items with students, and then have one student choose one card. Ask the rest of the class to guess the chosen card. Keep track of the number of guesses. Repeat the game with three cards, two cards, and finally, one card. This should illustrate to students how the chances of guessing correctly increase as the number of choices decreases.

Watch Yourself

Don't spend too much time on one question.

Going too slowly is no good—you'll leave more questions blank than you need to.

Don't rush through the test.

Going too fast is no good, either—you'll only make silly mistakes, like misunderstanding the directions.

The TerraNova is a timed test. Therefore, it is important to reinforce to students the importance of working carefully and efficiently. They should try to answer each question. However, they shouldn't spend too much time answering a question that is difficult for them. This might prevent them from reaching questions that they can answer correctly.

Mark Your Answers Correctly

When you find the answer to a question, fill in the bubble that goes with the answer choice you have found.

 Do NOT fill in half of the bubble. This is wrong.

 Do NOT place a checkmark over the bubble. This is wrong.

 Do NOT scribble inside the bubble. This is wrong.

 DO fill in the bubble completely. This is correct!

Now you try filling in the bubble correctly.

On the test, how should you fill in the bubble?
- ○ You should fill in half of the bubble.
- ○ You should scribble inside the bubble.
- ○ You should completely fill in the bubble.

Explain to students that it is important to fill in the bubbles correctly so that they get credit for their correct answer choices. Because a machine scores the test, it cannot read bubbles that are only partially filled out.

Warm-Up Test

Read along with the questions and answer choices as I read them aloud to you. Look at Number 1. (Direct students to look at each question as you move through the test. Pause between questions for students to mark their answers.)

1 Choose the sentence that uses end marks correctly.
- ○ George and I like to study together?
- ● Have you seen my jacket?
- ○ When is the last day of school.

A statement needs a period

2 Find the sentence that is complete and that is written correctly.
- ○ Going to the park.
- ● Fran ate her lunch.
- ○ He swimming.

(1st) Missing a subject and a verb
(2nd) Correct
(3rd) Missing a helping verb

Directions For Numbers 3 through 5, choose the sentence that uses capital letters

3
- ○ heather is a good soccer player.
- ● Soon school will be over.
- ○ rabbits like to eat lettuce and carrots.

Heather and rabbits should be capitalized.

4
- ○ Jannette's brother larry is in third grade.
- ● I like Kirk's painting the best.
- ○ We saw willy Jenkins at the store.

Larry and Willy should be capitalized.

5
- ○ There is a carnival in the town of hillsboro.
- ○ Mom likes to shop in cedarburg city.
- ● Dominic is from Havana, Cuba.

Hillsboro and Cedarburg should be capitalized.

6 Find the word that has the same vowel sound as <u>deal</u>.

did   fell   read
○   ○   ●

Both deal and read have a long /e/ sound.

7 Which one of these is a compound word?
- ○ washing
- ○ distance
- ● something

Only the word something can be separated into two words: some and thing.

Directions

For Numbers 8 and 9, read the letter. Then find the answer choices with the correct capital letters and end marks for each missing part.

> February 12, 2000
>
> ___(8)___
>
> I am having a great time in Texas. I can't wait to show you my new boots. See you soon!
>
> ___(9)___
>
> Cindy

8
- ● Dear Christine,
- ○ Dear christine,
- ○ Dear, Christine

> Letter greetings end with commas, and peoples' names are capitalized.

9
- ○ Your Friend!
- ○ your friend,
- ● Your friend,

> A letter closing always begins with a capital letter and ends with a comma.

10 Find the word that best fits in the blank.

Jack and Lamont _____ to school.

- ● ran
- ○ runs
- ○ running

> The subject and the verb in a sentence must agree.

11 Find word that has the same vowel sound as <u>wore</u>.

wound   tore   top

Directions

For Numbers 12 and 13, choose the sentence that uses capital letters correctly.

12
- ● Brad spoke rudely to Mrs. West.
- ○ I helped mr murphy pull weeds.
- ○ We made a get well card for miss James.

> (1st) Correct
> (2nd) Mr. Murphy should be capitalized and needs a period.
> (3rd.) The title Miss should be capitalized.

13
- ● I like to wear green on Saint Patrick's Day.
- ○ I like to wear green on saint Patrick's Day.
- ○ I like to wear green on Saint Patrick's day.

> All of the major words in a holiday should be capitalized.

14 Find the sentence that best completes the story.

_____. Whenever he finds an animal that is hurt, he brings it home. He takes care of the animal until it is better.

- ● Mark wants to be an animal doctor when he grows up.
- ○ Mark is only in the second grade.
- ○ Animals need help.

> Need a topic sentence. A topic sentence tells the main idea of the story.

15 Find the sentence that best completes the story.

Tom wanted a guitar for a long time. Every year, he asked his parents if he could have one. _____.

- ○ He also asked them for a violin.
- ○ Guitars can be very expensive.
- ● Finally, Tom's parents decided that he was old enough to have a guitar.

> Need a detail sentence. A detail sentence tells more about the main idea in the topic sentence.

16 Find the answer choice that can take the place of the underlined word.

He <u>doesn't</u> do his chores like he should.

- ○ do not
- ● does not
- ○ did not

> The contractions for *do not* and *did not* are *don't* and *didn't*.

17 Find the answer choice that can take the place of the underlined word.

The old car belongs to <u>Marc</u>.

- ● him
- ○ he
- ○ it

> Need to replace *Marc* with a singular object pronoun. *He* is a subject pronoun.

18 Choose the sentence that uses capital letters correctly.

- ○ When it got cold, i went inside.
- ● Mark thinks I am funny.
- ○ Will and i won the contest.

> The pronoun *I* is always capitalized.

19 Which underlined word is spelled correctly?

- ● apples in the <u>bowl</u>
- ○ bandage on my <u>nee</u>
- ○ <u>giv</u> me some food

> Correct spellings: *knee* and *give*

20 Which word has the same vowel sound as <u>pleasure</u>?

- ○ gave
- ○ lean
- ● steady

Pleasure and *steady* have short /e/ middle sounds. *Gave* has a long /a/ middle sound. *Lean* has a long /e/ middle sound.

21 Find the word that has the same consonant sound underlined in the word giant.

- ● gym
- ○ game
- ○ grace

Giant and *gym* both have a soft /g/ consonant sound. *Game* and *grace* have a hard /g/ consonant sound.

22 Find the underlined word that is spelled correctly.

- ● dig the <u>ditch</u>
- ○ the washing <u>matchine</u>
- ○ the big <u>elefant</u>

Correct spellings: *machine* and *elephant*

23 Find the underlined word that is spelled correctly.

- ○ <u>Poot</u> the box in the trunk.
- ● Our team came in <u>third</u>.
- ○ I am so <u>tyred</u>.

Correct spellings: *put* and *tired*

Directions

For Numbers 24 and 25, choose the word that is spelled correctly and fills in the blank.

24 Mom is _____ cookies.

- ○ bakiing
- ● baking
- ○ bakking

> When you add -ing to words that have a silent /e/, you drop the e and add -ing.

25 That building is ten _____ tall.

- ○ storyies
- ● stories
- ○ storrys

> When a word ends with a consonant and a y, change the y to i and add the ending.

26 Find the word that is the root, or base word of <u>newer</u>?

er	wer	new
○	○	●

> A root word is a word that you can add endings to in order to make another word. Only *new* is a root word.

On Your Mark, Get Set, Go!

Exercise 1
END MARKS

 Go over each type of end mark with your students.

On the board, write several sentences and ask students to choose the end mark for each. Some examples you might use are:

- The sun is shining(.)
- Listen to this song(.)
- Where is your school(?)
- This cake is yummy(!)

Discuss with students how they decided on the end marks. For example, how did they know where to put a question mark? Answer any questions students have.

 Go over the example question as a class.

Exercise 1
 ## ON YOUR MARK!
End Marks

A **statement** is a sentence that tells something. It ends with a period.
I have to go home.

A **command** is a sentence that tells someone to do something. It also ends with a period.
Please shut the door.

A **question** is a sentence that asks something. It ends with a question mark.
What time is it?

An **exclamation** is a sentence that shows strong feeling. It ends with an exclamation mark.
That skateboarding trick was amazing!

 ## GET SET!
Let's look at an example.
Which sentence uses end marks correctly?
○ That roller coaster ride was exciting?
○ Where is my pink sweater.
○ Don't forget to do your homework.

(1st) is **wrong.** This sentence is a statement, so it should have a period, not a question mark.

(2nd) is **wrong.** This sentence is a question, so it should have a question mark, not a period.

(3rd) is **correct!** This sentence is command, so it has a period.

★ EXTRA ACTIVITY

As extra practice with end marks, play "Punctuation Friends" with your class. Make fun cutouts of animals, people, or characters students have learned about. Draw punctuation marks on them. On the board, write sentences without punctuation. Make sure to include statements, commands, questions, and exclamations. Have students take turns selecting the missing punctuation mark and taping the appropriate punctuation friend after each sentence. Make sure students explain why they chose the punctuation they did.

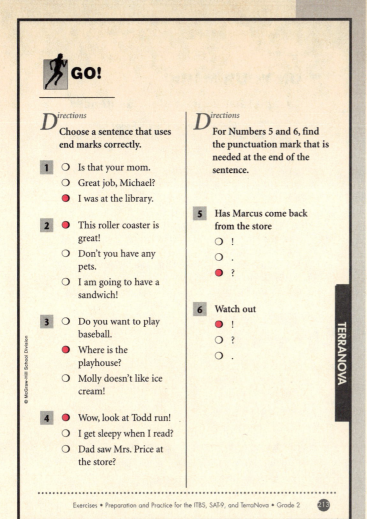

 Go over each question on this page as a class.

For Numbers 1 through 4, find the sentence that uses end marks correctly. Fill in the bubble next to the correct sentence.

Question 1
1st choice: question mark
2nd choice: exclamation point

Question 2
2nd choice: question mark
3rd choice: period

Question 3
1st choice: question mark
3rd choice: period

Question 4
2nd choice: period
3rd choice: period

For Numbers 5 and 6, find the punctuation mark that is needed at the end of the sentence. Fill in the bubble next to the correct end mark.

Question 5
This is a question.

Question 6
This is an exclamation.

Exercises • Preparation and Practice for the ITBS, SAT-9, and TerraNova • Grade 2

Exercise 2

COMPLETE AND INCOMPLETE SENTENCES

 Go over the definitions of complete and incomplete sentences with students.

Explain that a complete sentence must have a subject and a verb. Review that a subject tells *who* or *what* does or did something. The verb tells what a subject *does* or *did*.

On the board, write some complete sentences. Ask students to identify the subjects and the verbs in each. Then write some incomplete sentences. Ask students to identify what is missing in each of the examples. Some examples you might use are:

- *Draws a picture* (missing a subject)
- *The girl next door* (missing a verb)
- *Frank and Gino* (missing a verb)
- *Calls my name* (missing a subject)

 Go over the example question as a class.

Exercise 2

 ## ON YOUR MARK!

Complete and Incomplete Sentences

A **complete sentence** tells a complete thought. An **incomplete sentence** is a group of words that does not tell a complete thought. You should always write using complete sentences.

WRONG: *Plays on the swing.*
Who plays on the swing? This group of words is missing a subject.
CORRECT: *Angie plays on the swing.*
WRONG: *The man at the circus.*
The man does what at the circus? This group of words is missing a verb.
CORRECT: *The man at the circus sells balloons.*
WRONG: *Into the forest.*
Who is into the forest? What happened there? This group of words is missing a subject and a verb.
CORRECT: *A deer ran into the forest.*

 ## GET SET!

Let's look at an example.
Which group of words is a complete sentence?
○ Over the rainbow.
○ The sun is shining.
○ Swims in the lake.

(1st) is **wrong**. It's missing a subject and a verb.
(2nd) is **correct!** It has a subject and a verb.
(3rd) is **wrong**. It is missing a subject.

  ## EXTRA ACTIVITY

Create two separate piles of cards with sentence fragments on them—some should have only a subject and the rest should have only an action. Have students mix and match subject and action fragments that make logical sense together. This can be done in the form of relay races, where one team picks an action card and sticks it up on the wall, and the other team has to choose a subject card that fits. Teams can get points for the number of complete sentences they can create in a certain amount of time.

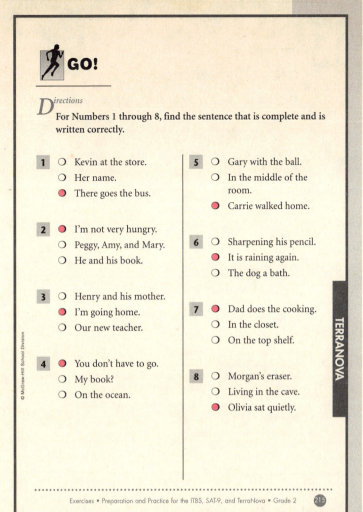

 Go over each question on this page as a class.

For Numbers 1 through 8, find the group of words that is a complete sentence. Fill in the bubble next to the complete sentence.

Question 1
Subject *the bus*, verb *goes*

Question 2
Subject *I*, verb *'m not*

Question 3
Subject *I*, verb *'m going*

Question 4
Subject *you*, verb *don't have to go*

Question 5
Subject *Carrie*, verb *walked*

Question 6
Subject *it*, verb *is raining*

Question 7
Subject *Dad*, verb *does*

Question 8
Subject *Olivia*, verb *sat*

Explain to students that, in the case of contractions, the subject and action are sometimes linked in the same word. For example, in questions 2 and 3, *I* is the subject and *am* is part of the action.

Exercise 3

CAPITALIZING THE BEGINNING OF A SENTENCE

 Go over the sentence capitalization rule with your students.

Explain that a sentence is a complete idea. On the board, write some complete sentences and some incomplete sentences. Make sure to include at least one complete statement, command, exclamation, and question. Ask students to tell you which should be capitalized. Some examples you might use are:

- *he likes baseball*
- *his favorite sport*
- *what time does the game start*
- *to the ball game*
- *buy me a hotdog*
- *what a catch*
- *on first base*

Discuss with students how they decided which sentences were complete and needed a capital letter. Answer any questions students have.

 Go over the example question as a class.

Exercise 3

 ON YOUR MARK!

Capitalizing the Beginning of a Sentence

A **sentence** is a set of words that tell a complete idea.

I walk in the park.

If words do not tell a complete idea, they do not make a sentence.

in the park

A sentence always begins with a **capital letter**. A capital letter means the start of a new idea.

*A*re you ready? *I* want to go outside. *I*t is so warm and sunny!

 GET SET!

Let's look at an example.
Which sentence uses capital letters correctly?
○ stan and Roger stayed home.
○ our family has a new car.
● Please color your pictures neatly.

(1st) is **wrong**. *Stan* must be capitalized since it is the beginning of the sentence and a person's name.
(2nd) is **wrong**. *Our* must be capitalized since it is the beginning of the sentence.
(3rd) is **correct!** *Please* is capitalized because it is the beginning of the sentence.

 TEACHING TIP

To give students more practice with capitalizing sentences, write a paragraph or two containing several sentences on the board. Include some capitalization errors at the beginning of some sentences. Have students come up to the board and circle the capitalization errors. Correct the errors and explain to students that the first letter immediately following a period, question mark, or exclamation point will always be capitalized.

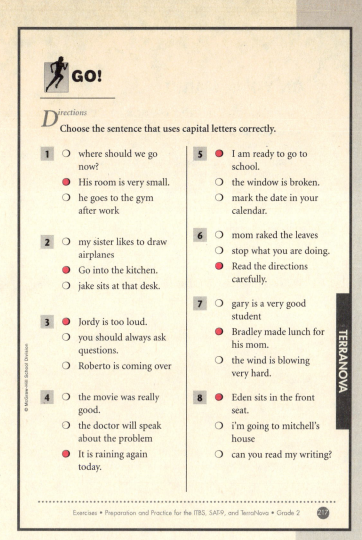

GO!

Directions
Choose the sentence that uses capital letters correctly.

1. ○ where should we go now?
   ● His room is very small.
   ○ he goes to the gym after work

2. ○ my sister likes to draw airplanes
   ● Go into the kitchen.
   ○ jake sits at that desk.

3. ● Jordy is too loud.
   ○ you should always ask questions.
   ○ Roberto is coming over

4. ○ the movie was really good.
   ○ the doctor will speak about the problem
   ● It is raining again today.

5. ● I am ready to go to school.
   ○ the window is broken.
   ○ mark the date in your calendar.

6. ○ mom raked the leaves
   ○ stop what you are doing.
   ● Read the directions carefully.

7. ○ gary is a very good student
   ● Bradley made lunch for his mom.
   ○ the wind is blowing very hard.

8. ● Eden sits in the front seat.
   ○ i'm going to mitchell's house
   ○ can you read my writing?

TERRANOVA

Exercises • Preparation and Practice for the ITBS, SAT-9, and TerraNova • Grade 2   217

 Go over each question on this page as a class.

For Numbers 1 through 8, find the sentence that uses capital letters correctly. Fill in the bubble next to the correct sentence.

On this page, the correctly capitalized sentence is always a statement or a command. Make sure you give students extra practice with capitalizing questions and exclamations. This page also does not give any examples of incomplete sentences. Make sure students understand the difference between a complete and an incomplete sentence.

Exercise 4
CAPITALIZING SPECIFIC NAMES OF PEOPLE

 Go over the difference between common and proper nouns with your students.

Discuss how these types of nouns are used when referring to people.

Explain that a common noun refers to a general person:

- *boy*
- *girl*
- *uncle*

Explain that a proper noun refers to a specific person:

- *Pedro*
- *Tamika*
- *Uncle Sebastian*

A common noun, such as *girl*, can refer to any girl, so it is not capitalized. A proper noun, on the other hand, such as *Tamika*, is capitalized because it refers to a particular girl.

 TEACHING TIP

Make sure students understand that the pronoun *I* is always capitalized.

Exercise 4

 ON YOUR MARK!

Capitalizing Specific Names of People

A **common noun** is a general name for a person, place, or thing. Common nouns are <u>not</u> capitalized.

A **proper noun** is the name of a specific person, place, or thing. Proper nouns are always capitalized.

The word *David* is the name of a specific person. It is always capitalized.

 GET SET!

Let's look at an example.

Find the sentence with the correct use of capital letters.

○ The elephant is named jumbo.
● Grandma Spadafora lives nearby.
○ I went to a birthday party for dennis.

(1st) is **wrong.** *Jumbo* is the specific name of an animal, so it must be capitalized.

(2nd) is **correct!** *Grandma Spadafora* is a specific name of a person, so it must be capitalized.

(3rd) is **wrong.** *Dennis* is the name of a specific person, so it must be capitalized.

 EXTRA ACTIVITY

Make a worksheet with a list of several "people" nouns and hand it out to your class. Do not capitalize the proper nouns. Have students write "common" or "proper" next to each noun. Then have them fix the capitalization mistakes for each proper noun.

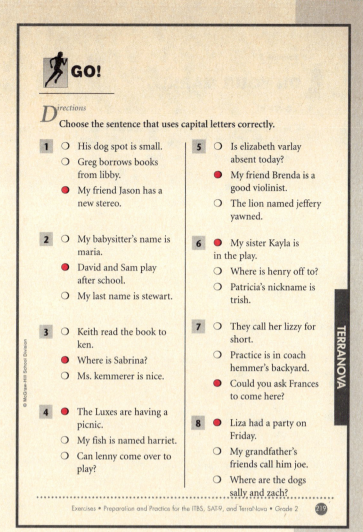

 Go over each question on this page as a class.

For Numbers 1 through 8, find the sentence that has correct capital letters. Fill in the bubble next to the correct sentence.

For extra practice with capitalizing proper nouns, have students go back through questions 1 through 8 and correct all of the capitalization errors.

Question 1

Spot

Libby

Question 2

Maria

Stewart

Question 3

Ken

Kemmerer

Question 4

Harriet

Lenny

Question 5

Elizabeth Varlay

Jeffery

Question 6

Henry

Trish

Question 7

Lizzy

Coach Hemmer's

Question 8

Joe

Sally and Zach

Point out that the word *coach* should be capitalized in question 7 because *coach* is part of a person's name. It is a title.

Exercise 5
VOWELS

 Go over the difference between long vowels and short vowels with your students.

Explain that vowels are considered "long" or "short" on the basis of their sound.

Look at the list in the middle of the Pupil Edition page that compares short and long vowel sounds. Have one student say *cat* aloud. Then have another student say *cave*. Discuss how the two sounds are different, even though they contain the same vowel. Follow this routine for the rest of the words listed.

 TEACHING TIP

Make sure students understand that a silent /e/ often comes at the end of the word with a long vowel sound.

 Go over the example question as a class.

 Exercise 5
ON YOUR MARK!
Vowels

The letters *a, e, i, o,* and *u* are called **vowels**. We call vowels *long* or *short,* depending on how we say them.

Long vowels sound like we say them in the alphabet.

c<u>a</u>ve, w<u>e</u>, d<u>i</u>ve, n<u>o</u>te, c<u>u</u>te

Look at the words above again. Notice how many words with long vowels in them end with an *e* that is silent.

cav<u>e</u>, div<u>e</u>, not<u>e</u>, cute

Short vowels do not sound like we say them in the alphabet. Compare the word pairs below to hear the difference.

Short: c<u>a</u>t   w<u>e</u>t   b<u>i</u>t   m<u>o</u>p   s<u>u</u>nk
Long: c<u>a</u>ve w<u>e</u>   d<u>i</u>ve n<u>o</u>te c<u>u</u>te

 GET SET!

Let's look at an example.
Find the word that has the same vowel sound as <u>lake</u>.
last   hard   face
 ○   ○   ○

(1st) is **wrong**. *Last* has a short *a* sound, but *lake* has a long *a* sound.

(2nd) is **wrong**. *Hard* does not have a long *a* sound.

(3rd) is **correct!** *Face* has a long *a* sound just like *lake*.

 EXTRA ACTIVITY

This is a group activity to give more practice with short and long vowel sounds. Divide students into small groups and give each group alphabet cards. Call out a spelling word. Using the cards, the groups must spell out the word. When all of the groups have finished, each group presents its spelling. Correct spellings earn the group one point. Some spelling words you might use are:

- bin   bite
- rat   rate
- met   me
- rod   rode
- bun   bite

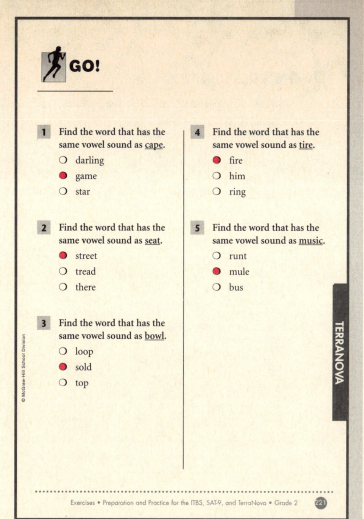

 Go over each question on this page as a class.

📣 *For Numbers 1 through 5, choose the word that shares the same vowel sound as the example word. Fill in the bubble next to your choice.*

(More work with long /e/ and short /e/ spellings can be found in Exercise 22 on Pupil Edition page 254.)

Explain to your students that there are many ways to spell long and short vowel sounds. Consider reviewing some alternative vowel spellings such as:

- Long /a/: *ai, ay* as in *rain, play*
- Long /e/: *ee, ea* as in *feet, eat*
- Long /o/: *oa, ow, oe* as in *boat, snow, toe*
- Long /i/: *igh, ie, y* as in *light, pie, my*
- Long /u/: *oo, u* as in *food, rule*

Exercise 6

CAPITALIZING NAMES OF SPECIFIC PLACES

 Go over the difference between common and proper nouns with your students.

Discuss how these types of nouns are used when referring to places.

Explain that a common noun refers to a general place and should not be capitalized. For example:

- street
- city
- country
- island
- avenue
- state

Explain that a proper noun refers to a specific place and therefore must be capitalized. For example:

- Hillside Street
- Hollywood
- France
- Ellis Island
- Park Avenue
- Florida

A common noun, such as *state*, can refer to any state so it is not capitalized. A proper noun, on the other hand, such as *Florida*, is capitalized because it refers to a particular state.

 Go over the example question as a class.

Exercise 6

 ON YOUR MARK!

Capitalizing Names of Specific Places

A **common noun** is a general name for a person, place, or thing. Common nouns are *not* capitalized.

A **proper noun** is the name of a specific person, place, or thing. Proper nouns are *always* capitalized.

Streets, cities, and countries are all proper nouns. They must start with a capital letter.

 GET SET!

Let's look at an example.

Which sentence uses capital letters correctly?
- ○ The president lives in The white house.
- ○ I live in the state of Texas.
- ○ We go to Moses dewitt elementary School.

(1st) is **wrong**. *The White House* is a specific place, so it must be capitalized.

(2nd) is **correct!** *Texas* is a specific place, so it must be capitalized.

(3rd) is **wrong**. *Moses DeWitt Elementary School* is a specific place, so all the words must be capitalized.

  TEACHING TIP

Explain to students that if a proper noun contains more than one word, then all the major words are capitalized. Write examples on the board. Some examples you might use are:

- *United States of America*
- *Dominican Republic*
- *Martin Luther King High School*

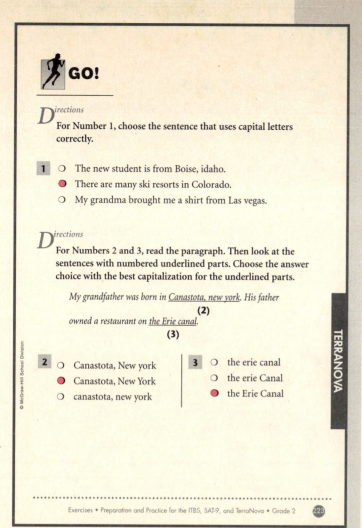

GO!

Directions
For Number 1, choose the sentence that uses capital letters correctly.

1
○ The new student is from Boise, idaho.
● There are many ski resorts in Colorado.
○ My grandma brought me a shirt from Las vegas.

Directions
For Numbers 2 and 3, read the paragraph. Then look at the sentences with numbered underlined parts. Choose the answer choice with the best capitalization for the underlined parts.

My grandfather was born in <u>Canastota, new york</u>. His father
(2)
owned a restaurant on <u>the Erie canal</u>.
(3)

2
○ Canastota, New york
● Canastota, New York
○ canastota, new york

3
○ the erie canal
○ the erie Canal
● the Erie Canal

 Go over each question on this page as a class.

Question 1

For Number 1, choose the sentence that has correct capitalization. Fill in the bubble next to the correct sentence.

Questions 2 and 3

For Numbers 2 and 3, read the paragraph. Then look at the sentences with underlined parts. Choose the answer choice with the correct capitalization for the underlined parts. Fill in the bubbles next to the correct answers.

To help students recognize proper nouns that refer to places, it might be useful to make a list of states, familiar cities, and so on, and hand it out to your class.

Exercise 7

GETTING RID OF WRONG ANSWER CHOICES

 Explain to students that ruling out wrong answer choices is an important test-taking skill.

Have students read the top section of the Pupil Edition page, or read it aloud to them. Point out that ruling out wrong answers will help them:

- Move through the test more quickly
- Increase their chances of finding the correct answer
- Score higher on the test

By getting rid of wrong answer choices, students will feel more confident that the answer they choose is the best answer.

 Go over the example question as a class. Have students raise their hands and explain why each answer choice is correct or incorrect.

Exercise 7

 ON YOUR MARK!
Getting Rid of Wrong Answer Choices

Sometimes you might not know the answer to a question. When this happens, try to get rid of as many WRONG answer choices as you can.

Which sentence has correct capitalization?
○ Our principal's name is doug Smith.
○ I played a joke on Brian and susan.
● My friend likes my dog Charlie.

Look at the 1st answer choice. The first word in the sentence is capitalized, and so is the last name *Smith*, but *Doug* is not capitalized. Get rid of it.

Look at the 2nd answer choice. The first word in the sentence is capitalized, and so is the name *Brian*, but *Susan* is not capitalized. Get rid of it.

There is only one answer left. The first word of the sentence is capitalized, and so is the dog's name, *Charlie*. This answer choice is **correct!**

 GET SET!
Let's look at an example.
Which sentence is complete and correct?
○ My best friend.
○ Sitting in the room.
○ Swimming is fun.

(3rd) has a subject, *swimming*, and a verb, *is*. All the other answer choices are not complete sentences. This one must be **correct!**

224 Exercises • Preparation and Practice for the ITBS, SAT-9, and TerraNova • Grade 2

 EXTRA ACTIVITY

Play *Twenty Questions* with your students to help them understand the importance of ruling out wrong answers. Think of a famous person that your class will know. Then have students raise their hands and ask "yes" or "no" questions about the famous person until they come up with the correct answer. By doing so, students will begin to understand how ruling out wrong answers leads them closer to the correct answer. For example, if a student asks: "Is it a boy?" and the answer is "no," then the next student will know not to guess a famous male. They are one step closer to determining the correct answer.

If time permits, repeat the game, this time allowing a student to think of a famous person and to field the "yes"/ "no" questions.

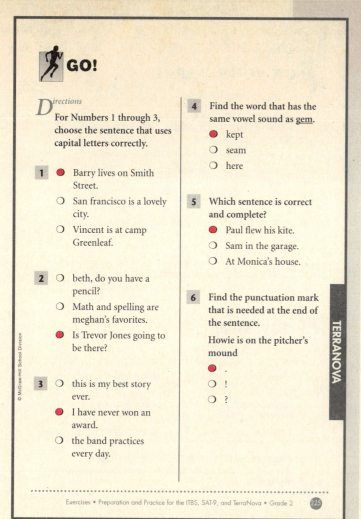

 Go over each question on this page as a class.

This page tests skills that students learned in Exercises 1 through 6. Students should try to get rid of wrong answer choices as they work through Numbers 1 through 6. To make sure that students are eliminating answer choices when they do these questions, tell them that they do not have to fill in the bubble next to the correct answer. Instead, they just have to cross out the answer choices they believe are wrong.

For Numbers 1 through 6, try to find the correct answer by getting rid of wrong answer choices first. Cross out the answer choices that you think are probably wrong.

Question 1
Both words in the name of a specific place should be capitalized.

Question 2
Names of specific people should be capitalized.

Question 3
The first word of a sentence should be capitalized.

Question 4
Short /e/ sound

Question 5
A complete sentence must contain a subject and a verb.

Question 6
A statement ends with a period.

Exercise 8
COMPOUND WORDS

 Go over the definition of compound words with students.

Explain that knowing the meaning of the two smaller words can help them figure out the meaning of the compound word.

Go over each example on the Pupil Edition page that demonstrates the components of some compound words. Then write a few more compound words on the board. Some examples you might use are:

- *grasshopper*
- *backyard*
- *scarecrow*
- *doghouse*

Ask students to tell you the two small words that make up each compound word. Then have students offer examples of more compound words to the class. Write their suggestions on the board.

 TEACHING TIP

Make sure students understand the tip in the dotted circle on the Pupil Edition page.

 Go over the example question as a class.

 Exercise 8
ON YOUR MARK!
Compound Words

A **compound word** is a word that is made from two smaller words. Knowing the meaning of the two smaller words can help you figure out the meaning of the compound word.

Two Words	Compound Word	Meaning
bed + room	bedroom	a room with a bed
sail + boat	sailboat	a boat with a sail
moon + light	moonlight	light that comes from the moon
club + house	clubhouse	a house where a club meets

TIP: Do not confuse syllables with compound words. Just because a word has more than one syllable, it does not mean that it is a compound word.

 GET SET!

Let's look at an example.
Find the compound word.

apartment   smiling   blueberry
   ○   ○   ○

(1st) is **wrong**. *Apartment* is not a compound word made of two words.

(2nd) is **wrong**. *Smiling* is not a compound word made of two words.

(3rd) is **correct!** *Blueberry* is a compound word because it is made up of two words, *blue* and *berry*. It means a berry that is blue.

  EXTRA ACTIVITY

Play *Cool Vocabulary* with your class. Give students a list of compound words from which to choose. Have each student select a compound word and create a collage poster made up of two halves. One half should include pictures that describe or show one of the smaller words in the compound word, and the second half should do the same for the second smaller word. For example, a collage poster for the compound word *doghouse* might have pictures of dogs on half of it, and pictures of houses on the other half. Either individually (on paper) or as a class (out loud), students should guess the compound word represented by each student's poster.

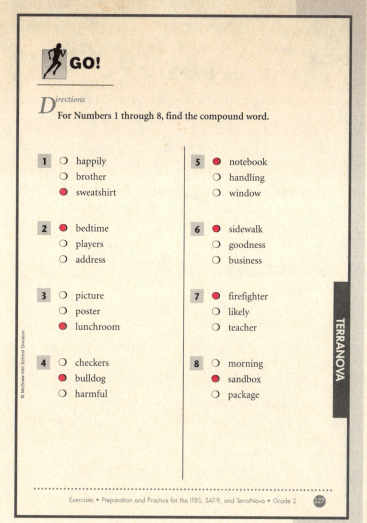

GO!

Directions
For Numbers 1 through 8, find the compound word.

1. ○ happily
   ○ brother
   ● sweatshirt

2. ● bedtime
   ○ players
   ○ address

3. ○ picture
   ○ poster
   ● lunchroom

4. ○ checkers
   ● bulldog
   ○ harmful

5. ● notebook
   ○ handling
   ○ window

6. ● sidewalk
   ○ goodness
   ○ business

7. ● firefighter
   ○ likely
   ○ teacher

8. ○ morning
   ● sandbox
   ○ package

 Go over each question on this page as a class.

For Numbers 1 through 8, find the compound word. Fill in the bubble next to your answer.

Remind students of the tip on the previous page. Not all words with multiple syllables are compound words. Point out a few examples from Numbers 1 through 8. You might use *picture*, *window*, or *morning* as examples of multi-syllabic words that are not compound words.

Question 1
sweat/shirt

Question 2
bed/time

Question 3
lunch/room

Question 4
bull/dog

Question 5
note/book

Question 6
side/walk

Question 7
fire/fighter

Question 8
sand/box

Exercise 9

WRITING LETTER GREETINGS AND CLOSINGS

 Go over letter greetings and closings with the class.

Explain the use of capitalization and commas in letter greetings and closings.

Write examples of incorrect greetings and closings on the board. Have students come up to the board and add the necessary punctuation and capitalization. Some greetings and closings you might use are:

- *dear sam*
- *dear aunt betty*
- *dear paul and carl*
- *your friend*
- *yours truly*
- *love always*

 TEACHING TIP

Remind students to always capitalize proper nouns. The nouns *Sam, Aunt Betty, Paul,* and *Carl* are proper nouns referring to specific people. Therefore, they must begin with capital letters.

 Go over the example question as a class.

Exercise 9

 ON YOUR MARK!

Writing Letter Greetings and Closings

A **letter greeting** usually starts with *Dear* and ends with the name of the person the letter is written to.

The first word begins with a capital letter. A comma comes at the end of the line.

 Dear Larry,

A **letter closing** tells that the letter is ending.

The first word always begins with a capital letter. A comma comes at the end of the line.

 Yours truly,

 GET SET!

Let's look at an example.

Which answer choice has correct capitalization and punctuation?
○ Dear Aunt Phoebe,
○ dear Aunt Phoebe,
○ Dear Aunt Phoebe

(1st) is **correct!** *Dear* is capitalized, and the greeting ends with a comma.

(2nd) is **wrong.** *Dear* is a greeting, so it must be capitalized.

(3rd) is **wrong.** *Dear* is capitalized, but the greeting does not end with a comma.

 EXTRA ACTIVITY

Have students write a letter to a friend, relative, or celebrity. Tell them to be creative, and make sure they use proper letter writing formats.

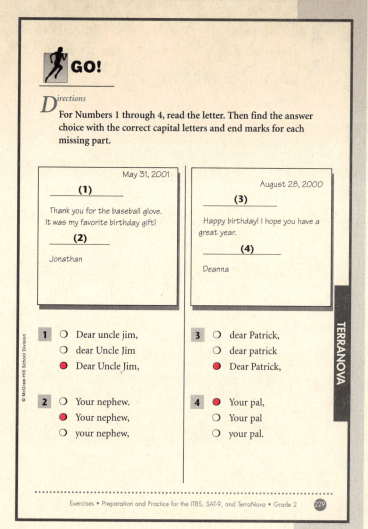

 Go over each question on this page as a class.

For Numbers 1 through 4, read the letter and find the answer choice that has correct capitalization and punctuation. Fill in the bubble next to the correct choice.

Remind students that all proper nouns need to be capitalized.

Question 1

The first word and all proper nouns in a letter greeting must be capitalized. A letter greeting must be followed by a comma.

Question 2

Remind students that *nephew* is not a proper noun and should therefore not be capitalized.

Question 3

The first word and all proper nouns in a letter greeting must be capitalized. A letter greeting must be followed by a comma.

Question 4

Only the first word in a letter closing should be capitalized. A letter closing must be followed by a comma.

Exercise 10
VERBS

 Go over the definitions of an action verb and helping verb with the class.

Explain that the subject and the verb in a sentence must agree.

Go over the list in the middle of the Pupil Edition page with your class. Explain that *am*, *is*, and *are* are all forms of the verb *be* and can work as helping verbs.

Point out that *I*, *she*, *he*, and *it* are singular subjects because they refer to only one person, place, or thing. Tell students to use *am* and *is* with singular subjects. *You*, *we*, and *they* are plural subjects because they refer to more than one person, place, or thing. Tell students to use *are* with plural subjects.

Explain to students that *am*, *is*, and *are* express present tense action. The helping verbs *was* (singular) and *were* (plural) express past tense.

 TEACHING TIP

Make sure students understand the need for helping verbs in certain sentences, especially in sentences where the verb ends in *-ing*.

 Go over the example question as a class.

Exercise 10

 ON YOUR MARK!
Verbs
An **action verb** is a word that shows action.
   Gina **dances** to the music.
A **helping verb** helps another verb show action. The verb *be* is a helping verb.
CORRECT: *I am making a sandcastle.*
If the helping verb is missing, the group of words would be an incomplete sentence.
WRONG: *I making a sandcastle.*
The **subject** and the **verb** in a sentence must agree. The verb *be* is formed differently than most verbs.

Subject	Present
I	am
she, he, it	is
you, we, they	are

 GET SET!
Let's look at an example.
Find the complete sentence.
○ My sister picking blueberries.
○ They is best friends at summer camp.
○ We are cooking hamburgers.

(1st) is **wrong**. *Picking* needs the helping verb *is*.

(2nd) is **wrong**. The singular verb *is* does not agree with the plural subject *they*. It should be *They are best friends at summer camp.*

(3rd) is **correct!** The plural subject *we* has a plural helping verb *are*.

  EXTRA ACTIVITY

Play *The Doctor Is In*. Put a few sentences with incorrect or missing helping verbs up on the board. Have students take turns dressing up like a doctor (lab coat and stethoscope) and diagnosing each sentence. If the doctor finds something wrong with the sentence, then the doctor operates to correct the problem.

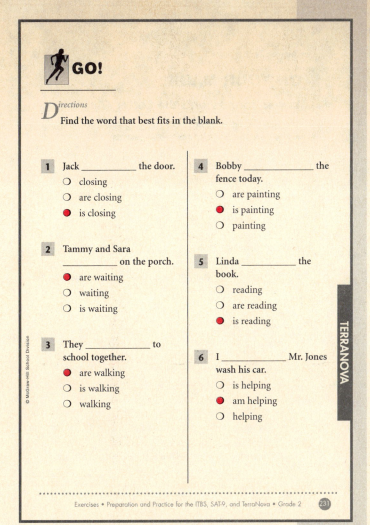

GO!

Directions Find the word that best fits in the blank.

1. Jack _____ the door.
   ○ closing
   ○ are closing
   ● is closing

2. Tammy and Sara _____ on the porch.
   ● are waiting
   ○ waiting
   ○ is waiting

3. They _____ to school together.
   ● are walking
   ○ is walking
   ○ walking

4. Bobby _____ the fence today.
   ○ are painting
   ● is painting
   ○ painting

5. Linda _____ the book.
   ○ reading
   ○ are reading
   ● is reading

6. I _____ Mr. Jones wash his car.
   ○ is helping
   ● am helping
   ○ helping

 Go over each question on this page as a class.

For Numbers 1 through 6, find the word or words that best fit in the blank. Fill in the bubble next to the correct answer.

Remind students that the subject and verb must agree.

Question 1

Jack is singular, so the helping verb must be singular.

Question 2

Tammy and Sara is plural, so the helping verb must be plural.

Question 3

They is plural, so the helping verb must be plural.

Question 4

Bobby is singular, so the helping verb must be singular.

Question 5

Linda is singular, so the helping verb must be singular.

Question 6

I is singular, so the helping verb must be singular.

Exercise 11

VOWEL SOUNDS WITH THE LETTER *R*

 With your class, go over the explanation of vowel sounds with the letter *r*.

Make sure that students say to themselves the indicated words and that they listen carefully to the list of words with the same vowel sound. Once you have read each list of words, have the students themselves read the words aloud. Write the words on the board. Then ask students to come up with other words with the same vowel sound. Some words they might think of are:

- *car*—park, star, yarn, harp, spark
- *for*—door, shore, board, floor, sport
- *stir*—girl, curl, pearl, swirl
- *near*—here, steer, clear, spear, year

 TEACHING TIP

Tell students that the vowel sounds with the letter *r* are neither long or short. These vowel sounds are special and make their own sound.

 Go over the example question as a class.

Exercise 11

 ON YOUR MARK!

Vowel Sounds with the Letter *R*

You have looked at **short vowel** and **long vowel** sounds. Now we will look at a few more vowel sounds.

Say the word *car* to yourself. *I drive my **car**.* Listen to the same vowel sounds in these words:

   far   tar   barn   arm

Say the word *for* to yourself. *The gift is **for** Donna.* Listen to the same vowel sound in these words:

   or   more   store

Say the word *stir* to yourself. *I **stir** with my spoon.* Listen to the same vowel sound in these words:

   dirt   fir   hurt   were

Say the word *near* to yourself. *I live **near** the park.* Listen to the same vowel sound in these words:

   dear   spear   fear   hear

GET SET!

Let's look at an example.

Which word has the same vowel sound as the underlined word?

  <u>star</u>   farm   came   raft
          ○   ○   ○

(1st) is **correct**! *Star* and *farm* have the same vowel sound.

(2nd) is **wrong**. *Came* has a long *a* vowel sound. It does not sound like *star*.

(3rd) is **wrong**. *Raft* has a short *a* vowel sound. It does not sound like *star*.

 EXTRA ACTIVITY

Explain to students that *rhyming* words are words that end with the same sound. Have students compose simple rhyming poems using some of the words from the lists generated on the board. Students may share their poems with the class.

GO!

1. Which word has the same vowel sound as the underlined word?
   <u>car</u>   far ●   fare ○   fat ○

2. Which word has the same vowel sound as the underlined word?
   <u>sore</u>   word ○   fort ●   coat ○

3. Which word has the same vowel sound as the underlined word?
   <u>fir</u>   rim ○   fire ○   stir ●

4. Which word has the same vowel sound as the underlined word?
   <u>burn</u>   pot ○   run ○   turn ●

5. Which word has the same vowel sound as the underlined word?
   <u>fear</u>   near ●   fed ○   led ○

6. Which word has the same vowel sound as the underlined word?
   <u>were</u>   term ●   bow ○   wear ○

7. Which word has the same vowel sound as the underlined word?
   <u>tar</u>   yard ●   take ○   tack ○

Go over each question on this page as a class.

For Numbers 1 through 7, find the word with the same vowel sound as the underlined word. Fill in the bubble below the correct answer.

Remind students that the vowel sounds in the underlined words are neither long nor short.

Exercise 12
TERMS OF RESPECT

 Go over the definition of an abbreviation and the rule for abbreviating terms of respect.

Look at the examples on the Pupil Edition page. On the board, write a few more examples of abbreviated and non-abbreviated terms of respect. Some examples you might use are:

- *Mrs. White—Mistress*
- *Dr. King—Doctor King*
- *Miss Lee—(no abbreviation)*
- *Mr. Jones—Mister*

 TEACHING TIP

Make sure students understand that Miss is a term of respect that has no abbreviated version. It still follows the same rules for capitalization, but requires no period at the end.

Write some sentences on the board that contain errors in capitalization and punctuation of terms of respect. Ask students to correct the errors. Some sentences you might use are:

- dr smith gave me a checkup.
- My teacher's name is mr ross.
- I sent a letter to miss baker.

 Go over the example question with the class.

Exercise 12

 ON YOUR MARK!

Terms of Respect

An **abbreviation** is a short form of a word.

Terms of respect are usually abbreviated. The abbreviation begins with a **capital letter** and ends with a **period**.

Abbreviated	Not Abbreviated
Mr. Harold Austin	Mister Harold Austin
Dr. Jackson	Doctor Jackson

 **GET SET!**

Let's look at an example.

Which of the following sentences uses capital letters and periods correctly?
- ○ The note is for mr. kline.
- ○ I spoke with Mrs. Goodman about my work.
- ○ We went to the movies with Ms Chan.

(1st) is **wrong**. *Mr. Kline* must be capitalized because *Mr.* is a term of respect and *Kline* is a specific person and a proper noun.

(2nd) is **correct!** *Mrs.* is capitalized and ends with a period, and *Goodman* is capitalized.

(3rd) is **wrong**. *Ms.* does not end with a period as it should.

 EXTRA ACTIVITY

Have students make up an invitation list to a big birthday party. The list should include all of their friends and family. The names on the list must be written using the appropriate term of respect. For example, Susie Smith's parents' names would be written *Mr. and Mrs. Smith*.

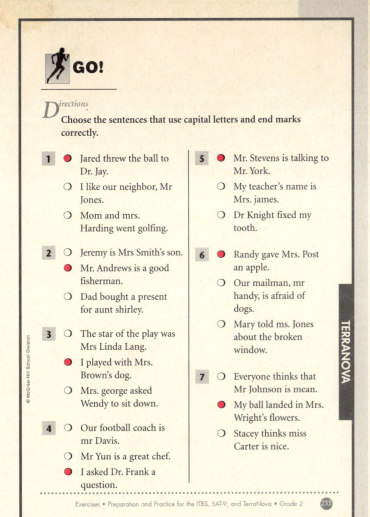

 Go over each question on this page as a class.

For Numbers 1 through 7, find the sentence that uses capital letters and periods correctly. Fill in the bubble next to the correct sentence.

Question 1

An abbreviated term of respect must be capitalized and followed by a period.

Question 2

A title such as *Aunt*, when followed by a name, should always be capitalized.

Question 3

Mrs should be followed by a period and *george* should be capitalized.

Question 4

An abbreviated term of respect must be capitalized and followed by a period.

Question 5

James should be capitalized.

Dr should be followed by a period.

Question 6

Mr, ms., and *handy* should be capitalized. *Mr* should be followed by a period.

Question 7

All terms of respect should be capitalized. An abbreviated term of respect must be followed by a period.

Exercise 13
READ THE DIRECTIONS CAREFULLY

 Go over the examples on the top of the Pupil Edition page that demonstrate different types of directions.

Explain to students that moving too quickly through the test and not reading the directions carefully can cause careless mistakes. Even if students think they know what the directions say, they should always read the directions carefully. Sometimes one or two small words can make a big difference in what the directions are saying.

TEACHING TIP

Point out to students that sometimes the teacher will read aloud the instructions to them. Remind students that they should listen just as carefully to these types of directions.

 Go over the example question as a class.

Exercise 13

ON YOUR MARK!
Read the Directions Carefully

Sometimes the directions tell you to find the correct sentence.

Directions
Choose the sentence that uses capital letters correctly.

Other times the directions tell you to find two things.

Directions
Find the sentence that is complete and is written correctly.

Directions
Choose the sentence that uses capital letters and end marks correctly.

Always read the words in the directions carefully!

GET SET!

Let's look at an example.
Choose the sentence that uses capital letters and end marks correctly.

● Mrs. Dickson teaches reading.
○ Noel and Mr Perkins went skiing.
○ Ms. peters read a story to us.

(1st) is **correct!** *Mrs. Dickson* is written correctly.
(2nd) is **wrong.** *Mr. Perkins* is capitalized correctly but it is not punctuated correctly. *Mr.* is missing a period.
(3rd) is **wrong.** *Ms.* is capitalized and punctuated correctly, but *Peters* is not capitalized correctly.

EXTRA ACTIVITY

Pair up students and have them sit back to back to play *Guided Drawing*. One student in the pair gets a drawing of a very simple shape or figure. The other student gets a blank piece of paper and a drawing utensil. The student with the drawing must give directions to the other student on how to draw the simple shape or figure. The trick is that this must be done without either student seeing the other's paper. When the drawings are completed, students can compare papers and talk about how easy or difficult the task was.

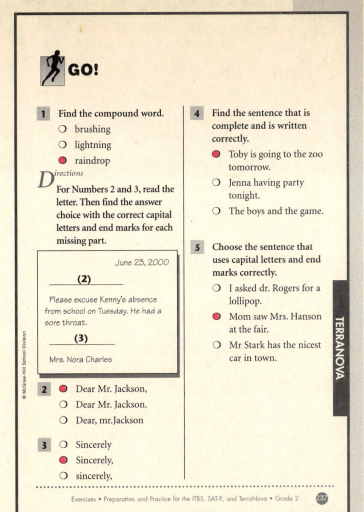

 Go over each question on this page as a class.

This page tests skills that students learned in Exercises 7 through 12. Students should make sure to read the directions carefully for Numbers 1 through 5.

For questions 1 through 5, fill in the bubble next to the answer you choose. Make sure to read the directions carefully.

Question 1
A compound word is made up of two smaller words.

Question 2
A letter greeting must end with a comma. The first word and all proper nouns must be capitalized.

Question 3
A closing must start with a capital letter and end with a comma.

Question 4
A complete sentence must have a subject and a verb.

Question 5
A term of respect must begin with a capital letter and end with a period.

Exercise 14

DAYS, MONTHS, AND HOLIDAYS

 Go over the capitalization and punctuation rules for writing days, months, and holidays.

Explain that the words *days*, *months*, and *holidays* are common nouns because they are not referring to a particular time. They do not need to be capitalized. For example:

- *I plan to go on vacation for a month. I will leave on a sunny day. I will leave on a holiday.*

Explain that a proper noun refers to a specific day, month, or holiday, and therefore must be capitalized. For example:

- *I plan to go on vacation next July. I will leave on the first Saturday. It will be Independence Day.*

Explain that a *date* is made up of a month, day, and year. A comma must always come after the day and before the year. Also, explain that a comma must always separate a day from a date, for example, *Monday, November 16.*

Ask students to correct the following sentences on the board:

- *My birthday is january 5 1986.*
- *There is no school next tuesday.*
- *thanksgiving day is on thursday november 23.*

 Go over the example question as a class.

Exercise 14

 ON YOUR MARK!

Days, Months, and Holidays

Capitalization

The **days of the week** begin with a capital letter.
Sunday, Monday, Tuesday, Wednesday, Thursday, Friday, Saturday

The **months of the year** begin with a capital letter.
January, February, March, April, May, June, July, August, September, October, November, December

Every word of a **holiday** must begin with a capital letter.
Mother's Day, Valentine's Day, Memorial Day

Punctuation

A date is a month, day, and year. A comma must always come after the day and before the year.
January 29, 2002   December 12, 2004

 GET SET!

Let's look at an example.

Which sentence has correct capitalization and punctuation?

- ● My sister was born on June 10, 1996.
- ○ Lenny's favorite holiday is independence day.
- ○ Most schools are closed on saturday and sunday.

(1st) is **correct!** There is a comma between the day and the year, and *June* is capitalized.

(2nd) is **wrong.** *Independence Day* is a holiday, so it must be capitalized.

(3rd) is **wrong.** *Saturday* and *Sunday* are days of the week, so they must be capitalized.

 EXTRA ACTIVITY

Have students write a short paragraph about their favorite day of the week, month of the year, or holiday. Check their paragraphs for capitalization mistakes.

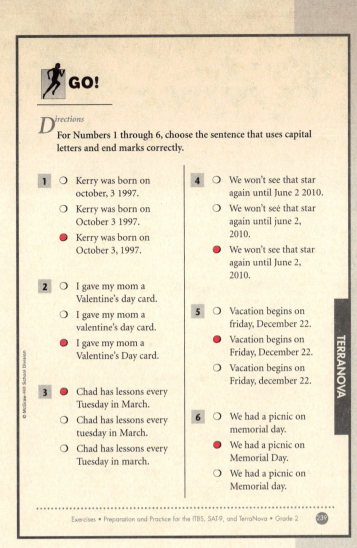

 Go over each question on this page as a class.

For Numbers 1 through 6, find the sentence with the correct capitalization and punctuation. Fill in the bubble next to the correct sentence.

Questions 1 and 4

Names of months are capitalized.

A comma goes between the day and the year.

Questions 2 and 6

Both words in the name of a holiday are capitalized.

Questions 3 and 5

Days of the week and months are capitalized.

Exercise 15
TOPIC SENTENCES

 With your class, go over the definition of a topic sentence.

Read the example paragraph aloud. Ask students to identify the topic sentence. Explain that the rest of the sentences in the paragraph are detail sentences. The detail sentences must include details about the main idea stated in the topic sentence, or else they don't belong in the paragraph. In this example, the underlined sentence tells details about things other than the main idea, so it does not belong in the paragraph.

Write the following paragraph on the board and ask students to select an appropriate topic sentence:

_____

She is not afraid of the dark. She rides her sled down big hills. She jumps into the pool from the diving board. My sister isn't afraid of anything.

◯ *My sister likes ice cream.*

◯ *My sister is very brave.**

◯ *My sister is shy.*

 Go over the example question as a class. Ask students to identify the topic sentence before they select an answer choice.

 Exercise 15

ON YOUR MARK!
Topic Sentences

A **topic sentence** is the first sentence in a paragraph. It tells the main idea of the paragraph.

My mom didn't have to work today, so she took me to the zoo. <u>Mom works in an office.</u> We saw monkeys, tigers, and huge elephants. It was a really fun day.

The underlined sentence in the paragraph above tells details about things other than the main idea. It does not belong in the paragraph.

 GET SET!

Let's look at an example.

Which sentence best completes the story?

My little brother Jack acts silly during dinner. _____. When he eats his food, he makes airplane noises while he puts the spoon into his mouth.

◯ After he's finished, mom wipes him up with a napkin.

◯ I eat dinner after soccer practice.

◯ When he drinks his milk, he blows bubbles through his straw.

(1st) is **wrong.** This sentence tells about something that happens *after* he's eaten dinner, but the sentence after the blank is about something that happens *during* dinner.

(2nd) is **wrong.** The story is about Jack, his younger brother.

(3rd) is **correct!** This sentence talks about Jack and how silly he is at the dinner table.

 TEACHING TIP

Consider presenting the idea of a topic sentence in a visual form such as a web diagram. On the board or on a handout, show the paragraph about the brave sister as a web diagram, with the topic sentence, *My sister is very brave,* in the center, and the detail sentences branching out from the topic sentence at the center.

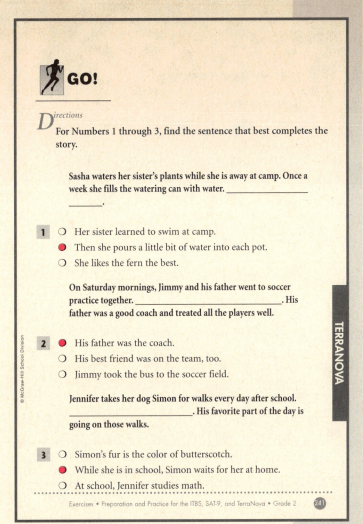

 Go over each question on this page as a class.

For Numbers 1 through 3, find the sentence that best completes the story. Make sure you underline the topic sentence before you select an answer choice. Your answer choice should tell more about the main idea in the topic sentence. Fill in the bubble next to your choice.

You might want to walk around and check to see that students are underlining the topic sentence in each paragraph.

Remind students that even though the answer choice should tell more about the main idea in the topic sentence, students will need to read all of the detail sentences in the paragraph to determine the correct answer choice.

Exercise 16
DETAIL SENTENCES

 With your class, go over the definition of details.

Explain that details are contained in detail sentences. Read the example given at the top of the page aloud. Make sure students understand how to use the clues provided in the topic sentence and in the surrounding detail sentences to find the missing detail sentence. In this case, the clues suggest that the missing sentence not only tells something about Julio's birthday party, but must also fit into a specific sequence of events.

 TEACHING TIP

Tell students that frequently the missing detail sentence will need to:

- Fit into a sequence of events (as in the previous example)

    or

- Provide the conclusion to a paragraph (as in the example in the Get Set! section on this page)

    or

- Add another detail about the main idea in the topic sentence (as in Number 2 on Pupil Edition page 243)

 Go over the example question as a class. The correct answer is the only choice that provides an appropriate conclusion to the paragraph.

Exercise 16
 ON YOUR MARK!

Detail Sentences

Every story has details. The **details** tell more about the main idea that is in the topic sentence.

TOPIC SENTENCE: Julio plans his birthday party.
DETAIL SENTENCE: _____.
DETAIL SENTENCE: Then he writes invitations.

The **topic sentence** tells you that the missing sentence should be about Julio planning his birthday party. The last **detail sentence** tells you that the missing sentence should be about something that comes before writing invitations.

WRONG: Julio wants a red bicycle for his birthday.
CORRECT: He makes a list of friends to invite.

 GET SET!

Let's look at an example.

Find the missing sentence.

Jesse wants to be a swimmer in the Olympics. He practices every day for at least two hours.
_____.

○ Jesse has no goals for the future.
○ Jesse is not a hard worker.
○ Jesse is serious about swimming.

(1st) is **wrong.** Jesse wants to be in the Olympics! That's a goal!

(2nd) is **wrong.** Jesse practices every day for at least two hours!

(3rd) is **correct!** This sentence is about swimming and working hard.

  EXTRA ACTIVITY

Write on the board the writing prompt *My favorite time of the year is...* Have students complete the topic sentence and then write two or three detail sentences about their topic sentence. Either you can check the papers, or students can swap papers and see if their partner stayed on topic and wrote appropriate detail sentences.

GO!

Directions
Find the sentence that best completes the story.

1. Timmy had a busy weekend. _____. On Sunday, Timmy wrote a book report for school.
   ○ Timmy's mom stayed home.
   ● On Saturday, he and his dad went fishing.
   ○ Timmy likes the outdoors.

2. Maria had fun at her family picnic. Maria played with her cousins all day. _____.
   ○ Her friend Sarah did not have fun.
   ○ She likes school.
   ● They played volleyball and went swimming.

3. Joel likes many different kinds of foods. _____. He also loves burritos filled with rice and beans.
   ○ Joel does not like sweets.
   ● His favorite meal is spaghetti with meat sauce.
   ○ His father likes only Italian food.

4. I like talking to my neighbor, Mr. Hews. Mr. Hews always has a good story to tell. _____.
   ● I like to hear about what things were like when he was a boy.
   ○ He lives by himself.
   ○ My other neighbor is not friendly.

Go over each question on this page as a class.

For Numbers 1 through 4, find the detail sentence that best completes the story. Fill in the bubble next to your choice.

Question 1
Sequence

Question 2
Added detail

Question 3
Added detail

Question 4
Conclusion

Exercise 17
CONTRACTIONS

 Go over the explanation of contractions with your class.

Explain that a contraction means the same thing as the word or words it replaces, but it is simply a shorter form.

Read the examples provided aloud or have a student read them. Write a few more examples of contractions on the board. Some you might use are:

- *do not/don't*
- *did not/didn't*
- *have not/haven't*
- *cannot/can't*
- *was not/wasn't*
- *he is/he's*
- *they are/they're*
- *we are/we're*
- *I will/I'll*
- *they will/they'll*

Then write some incorrectly written contractions on the board. Some you might use are:

- *was'nt*
- *shes'*
- *theyv'e*
- *doe'snt*

Ask students which two words the contraction shortens. Write down the words next to the contraction. Then ask students to come to the board and correct the location of the apostrophe.

 Go over the example question as a class.

Exercise 17

 ON YOUR MARK!

Contractions

A contraction is the short form of two words. An apostrophe (') takes the place of the letters that are left out when the words are combined.

She is my older sister.   George *does not* like raisins.

She's my older sister.   George *doesn't* like raisins.

Here are some more contractions:

I am → I'm   it is → it's   is not → isn't
you are → you're   we have → we've   are not → aren't

> **TIP:** Be careful not to confuse **contractions** and **possessive pronouns** that sound alike. Some confusing words are:
>
> *your* (means *belongs to you*) and *you're* (short for *you are*)
> *their* (means *belongs to them*) and *they're* (short for *they are*)
> *its* (means *belongs to it*) and *it's* (short for *it is*)

 GET SET!

Let's look at an example.

What is another way of saying the underlined word?
<u>You're</u> very good at playing tennis.
○ Your
○ You are
○ You did

(2nd) is **correct!** *You're* is the contraction of *you are*.

⭐ EXTRA ACTIVITY

Hand out copies of a paragraph filled with words that could be shortened to contractions. Have students cross out the words and substitute the appropriate contraction.

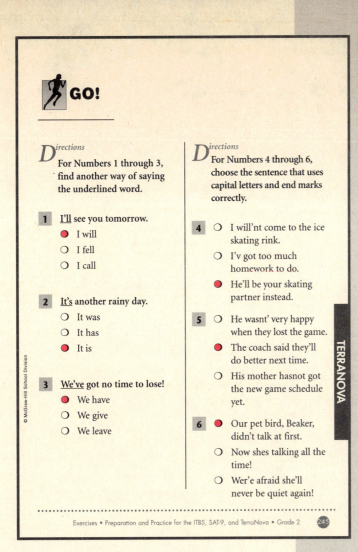

GO!

Directions
For Numbers 1 through 3, find another way of saying the underlined word.

1. <u>I'll</u> see you tomorrow.
   - ● I will
   - ○ I fell
   - ○ I call

2. <u>It's</u> another rainy day.
   - ○ It was
   - ○ It has
   - ● It is

3. <u>We've</u> got no time to lose!
   - ● We have
   - ○ We give
   - ○ We leave

Directions
For Numbers 4 through 6, choose the sentence that uses capital letters and end marks correctly.

4.
   - ○ I will'nt come to the ice skating rink.
   - ○ I'v got too much homework to do.
   - ● He'll be your skating partner instead.

5.
   - ○ He wasnt' very happy when they lost the game.
   - ● The coach said they'll do better next time.
   - ○ His mother hasnot got the new game schedule yet.

6.
   - ● Our pet bird, Beaker, didn't talk at first.
   - ○ Now shes talking all the time!
   - ○ Wer'e afraid she'll never be quiet again!

 Go over each question on this page as a class.

Questions 1, 2, and 3

For Numbers 1 through 3, find another way of saying the underlined word. Fill in the bubble next to your answer.

Point out that contractions do not work with action verbs, only with helping verbs and with forms of the verb *be*.

Questions 4, 5, and 6

For Numbers 4 through 6, find the sentence that has correct use of contractions. Fill in the bubble next to the correct sentence.

Exercise 18
PRONOUNS

 Go over the definition of a pronoun with students.

Explain that subject pronouns replace nouns that are the subject of a sentence. Object pronouns replace all other nouns in the sentence. For example, have students look at the example provided on the top of the Pupil Edition page:

WRONG: *Her* take the bus. (*Harriet* is the subject of the sentence, so a subject pronoun must replace it.)

WRONG: He walked by *she*. (*Susan* is not the subject of the sentence, so an object pronoun must replace it.)

Although it is not mentioned on the Pupil Edition page, explain that *he, she,* and *it* replace singular nouns (one person, place, or thing), while *they* replaces plural nouns (more than one person, place, or thing).

Explain that *I* and *me* always come last when telling about another person (or other people) and yourself.

 Go over the example question as a class.

 Exercise 18

ON YOUR MARK!

Pronouns

A **pronoun** is a word that you use instead of one or more nouns.
Subject Pronouns: *I, you, he, she, it, you, we, they*
Harriet takes the bus.   **She** takes the bus.
Object Pronouns: *me, you, him, her, it, you, us, them*
He walked by **Susan**.   He walked by **her**.

Always name yourself last when telling about another person (or other people) and yourself.
CORRECT: *Bonnie Jean and I are watering the plants.*
WRONG: *I and Bonnie Jean are watering the plants.*

CORRECT: *The cat sits with grandma and me.*
WRONG: *The cat sits with me and grandma.*

 GET SET!

Let's look at an example.

Find the answer choice that can take the place of the underlined word.

<u>Kathy</u> liked that drawing the most.
○ They
○ Her
● She

(1st) is **wrong.** *They* is a plural subject pronoun, but the subject, *Kathy*, is singular.

(2nd) is **wrong.** *Her* is a singular object pronoun, but because *Kathy* is the subject, it must take a subject pronoun.

(3rd) is **correct!** *Kathy* is a singular subject, so it can only be replaced by a singular subject pronoun. *She* can take the place of *Kathy*.

 EXTRA ACTIVITY

Create a handout of sentences that contain underlined nouns. Have students replace the underlined nouns with the appropriate pronoun. For each replacement, have students write whether the pronoun is a subject pronoun or an object pronoun.

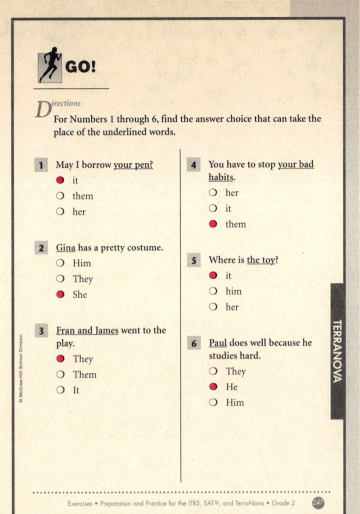

 Go over each question on this page as a class.

For Numbers 1 through 6, find the answer choice that can take the place of the underlined words. Before you make your selection, be sure to figure out whether the underlined words are the subject of the sentence or the object of the sentence, and whether the underlined words are singular or plural. Then fill in the bubble next to your answer.

Question 1
Singular object

Question 2
Singular subject

Question 3
Plural subject

Question 4
Plural object

Question 5
Singular object

Question 6
Singular subject

Exercise 19

BE SURE TO READ ALL OF THE ANSWER CHOICES

 Go over the explanation of why it is important to read all of the answer choices when taking the TerraNova.

Read the On Your Mark! section of the Pupil Edition page aloud or ask a student to read it for you. Stress that moving too quickly through the test and selecting the first tempting answer leads to careless mistakes.

 Go over the example question as a class. Again, stress the importance of going beyond the first tempting answer.

Exercise 19

 ON YOUR MARK!

Be Sure to Read All of the Answer Choices

Sometimes when you read a question, you might think the first answer choice you read is correct. It may be correct, but you should always read *all* of the answer choices before you decide. If you mark the first answer choice you think is correct, you might miss a better answer that comes later.

> **TIP:** Always get rid of the wrong answer choices first. Put a finger over the wrong choices as you rule each one out. It will help you remember to read *all* of the answer choices before you mark your answer.

 GET SET!

Find the word with the same vowel sound as the underlined word.

<u>barn</u>	bare	bat	car
	○	○	●

(1st) is **wrong.** *Bare* might look like *barn*, but they sound different.

(2nd) is **wrong.** *Bat* might be spelled with some of the same letters as *barn*, but *bat* sounds different than *barn*.

(3rd) is **correct!** *Car* has the same vowel sound as *barn*.

If you had picked the first answer choice without reading all of the answer choices, you would have missed the correct answer.

 TEACHING TIP

Make sure to emphasize the tip in the dotted box on the Pupil Edition page.

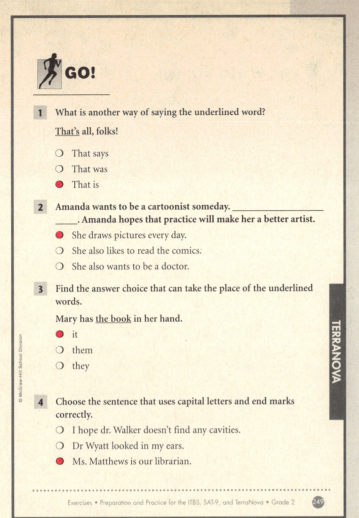

 Go over each question on this page as a class.

This page tests skills that students learned in Exercises 13 through 18. Students should make sure to read all of the answer choices carefully for Numbers 1 through 4.

🔊 *For Numbers 1 through 4, make sure you read all of the answer choices before selecting your final answer choice. Remember to always get rid of wrong answer choices first. Fill in the bubble next to your final answer.*

Question 1

Contractions are used with pronouns and with the verb *be*.

Question 2

Tell students that they must choose the detail sentence that best fits in the paragraph. Detail sentences tell more about the main idea in the topic sentence.

Question 3

Replace *the book* with a singular object pronoun.

Question 4

Terms of respect must begin with a capital letter and end with a period.

Exercise 20

ALWAYS CAPITALIZE THE PRONOUN *I*

 Go over the rules for the pronoun *I*.

Write a few sentences on the board with errors in the capitalization of the pronoun *I*. Have students come to the board and correct the errors. Some sentences you might use are:

- *Joe and i are best friends.*
- *i am on the soccer team.*
- *Next week i will start school.*

 Go over the example question as a class.

 Exercise 20

ON YOUR MARK!

Always Capitalize the Pronoun *I*

Use *I* to tell about yourself in the subject of a sentence.

I looked into the mirror to see my new haircut.

The pronoun *I* is always capitalized.

You and I can eat a whole pizza together.

I am the captain of my soccer team.

 GET SET!

Let's look at an example.

Fill in the circle under the part of the sentence that has an error in capitalization. If there are no mistakes in the sentence, fill in the circle under "None."

Mark and i | built a snowman.   None
  ○   ○   ○

(1st) is **correct!** There is an error in the first part of the sentence. The pronoun *I* should always be capitalized.

(2nd) is **wrong.** There is no error in the second part of the sentence.

(3rd) is **wrong.** There is an error in the first part of the sentence.

 TEACHING TIP

Tell students that *I* is the subject pronoun used to refer to yourself in the subject of a sentence. When referring to yourself in other parts of the sentence, use the object pronoun *me*. *Me*, unlike *I*, does not need to be capitalized.

GO!

Directions

For Numbers 1 through 8, find and then mark the part of the sentence that needs to be changed. If no part needs to be changed, mark "None."

1. Sandra and i | went to the park.   None
   ●   ○   ○

2. i like it when | I do not have a cold.   None
   ●   ○   ○

3. Larry and I | raced home.   None
   ○   ○   ●

4. Armond and I | like horses.   None
   ○   ●   ○

5. I'm not sure | if i want to go.   None
   ○   ●   ○

6. Deshawn and i | went to the store.   None
   ●   ○   ○

7. Manuel and I | play the drums.   None
   ○   ○   ●

8. I said | that i am a pitcher.   None
   ○   ●   ○

Go over each question on this page as a class.

For Numbers 1 through 8, fill in the circle under the part of the sentence that has an error in capitalization. If there are no mistakes in the sentence, fill in the circle under None.

Remind students that the pronoun *I* is always capitalized no matter where it appears in a sentence.

Exercise 21

SILENT LETTERS

 Go over the explanation of silent letters with your students.

Say aloud the example words for each pronounced consonant sound noted on the top of the Pupil Edition page. Have students repeat the words. Then write the example words with the silent letters on the board. Circle the silent consonants. Say aloud the example words for each silent consonant. Have students repeat the words. By hearing the words, students will better grasp the concept of silent letters.

 TEACHING TIP

Make sure students understand that a "silent letter" is called silent because it is not pronounced.

Ask students to provide extra examples of words with silent letters. Write their suggestions on the board.

 Go over the example question as a class. Make sure to write the correct spelling of *fight* and *white* on the board so that students can become familiar with the words.

 Exercise 21

ON YOUR MARK!

Silent Letters

Most consonant letters, such as *l, b, k, w, g,* and *h,* are pronounced.

- l → look, lip, love
- k → king, keep, kite
- g → go, get, give
- b → boy, bat, ball
- w → win, wish, wall
- h → he, house, hat

Sometimes these consonant letters have no sound at all. They are called **silent letters**.

- silent *l* → talk, walk
- silent *k* → know, kneel
- silent *g* → sign, gnaw
- silent *gh* → night, light
- silent *b* → comb, lamb
- silent *w* → write, wrong
- silent *h* → when, white

 GET SET!

Let's look at an example.
Which underlined word is spelled correctly?
○ a bad <u>fite</u>
○ the <u>right</u> answer
○ a <u>wite</u> horse

(1st) is **wrong.** *Fight* is not spelled correctly.
(2nd) is **correct!** *Right* is spelled correctly.
(3rd) is **wrong.** *White* is not spelled correctly.

 EXTRA ACTIVITY

Have students write a short paragraph on a topic of their choice that includes at least five words with silent letters. Check papers for correct spelling.

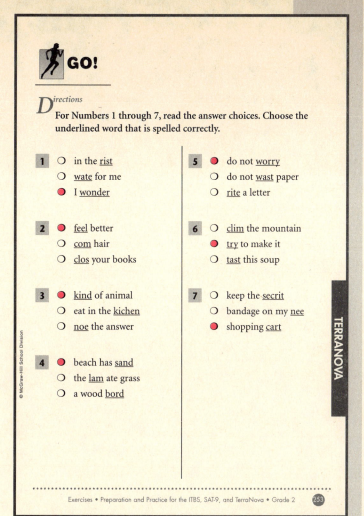

 Go over each question on this page as a class.

For Numbers 1 through 7, read the answer choices. Choose the underlined word that is spelled correctly. Fill in the bubble next to the correctly spelled answer. Don't forget to consider silent letters!

After students have completed the questions, go over the answers as a class. Write the correct spelling of all of the answer choices on the board so that students can become familiar with the words.

Question 1

wrist, wait

Question 2

comb, close

Question 3

kitchen, know

Question 4

lamb, board

Question 5

waste, write

Question 6

climb, taste

Question 7

secret, knee

Exercise 22

LONG E AND SHORT E SOUNDS

 Go over the explanation of long and short /e/ sounds.

Write the letters *e* and *ea* on the board. Read the example words from the Pupil Edition page aloud. Begin with the words with the short /e/ sound, and then write the words on the board. Ask students to list all of the words they can think of with a short /e/ sound. As they list them, spell them correctly on the board next to the *e* or the *ea*. Some words they might suggest are:

- With *e*: *rest, met, step*
- With *ea*: *weather, leather, sweater*

Then go over the long /e/ sound words. Write the letter combinations for long /e/ on the board. Read the example words with the long /e/ sound, and then write the words on the board. Ask students to list all the words they can think of with a long /e/ sound. As they list them, spell them correctly on the board next to the appropriate letter combination. Some words they might suggest are:

- With *y*: *friendly, happy*
- With *ey*: *monkey, money*
- With *ee*: *teen, wheel*
- With *ie*: *belief, chief*
- With *ea*: *meal, dream, clean*

 Go over the example question as a class.

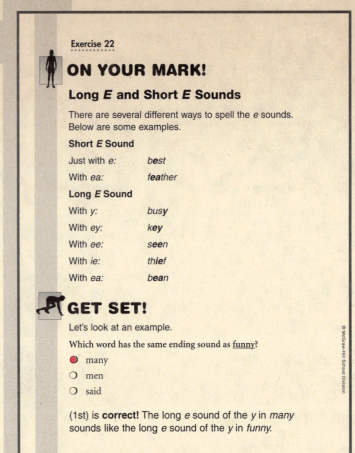

Exercise 22

ON YOUR MARK!

Long E and Short E Sounds

There are several different ways to spell the *e* sounds. Below are some examples.

Short E Sound

Just with *e*: best
With *ea*: feather

Long E Sound

With *y*: busy
With *ey*: key
With *ee*: seen
With *ie*: thief
With *ea*: bean

GET SET!

Let's look at an example.

Which word has the same ending sound as <u>funny</u>?

● many
○ men
○ said

(1st) is **correct!** The long *e* sound of the *y* in *many* sounds like the long *e* sound of the *y* in *funny*.

 EXTRA ACTIVITY

Divide students into small groups and give each group alphabet cards. Call out a spelling word from today's exercise. Using the cards, the groups must spell out the word. Correct spellings earn the group one point.

Go over each question on this page as a class.

For Numbers 1 through 6, read the directions carefully. Find the word with the same sound described in the directions. You will be matching up middle sounds and ending sounds. Fill in the bubble next to your answer.

After students have completed the questions, go over the answers as a class. Read aloud the correct pronunciation of all of the answer choices and have students repeat them.

GO!

1 Which word has the same middle sound as <u>measure</u>?
- ○ sat
- ○ mean
- ● ready

2 Which word has the same ending sound as <u>money</u>?
- ● hungry
- ○ finger
- ○ get

3 Which word has the same middle sound as <u>feed</u>?
- ○ head
- ○ said
- ● seed

4 Which word has the same middle sound as <u>grief</u>?
- ● leaf
- ○ weight
- ○ grit

5 Which word has the same middle sound as <u>neat</u>?
- ○ great
- ● wheat
- ○ friend

6 Which word has the same ending sound as <u>mostly</u>?
- ○ kept
- ○ bet
- ● lastly

Exercise 23

THE SOUND OF THE LETTERS *C* AND *G*

 Go over the different sounds the letters *c* and *g* make.

Explain that *c* and *g* can make different sounds depending on the surrounding letters.

Have students look at the lists on the top of the Pupil Edition page that compare the different sounds of /c/ and /g/.

Have one student say the words *cat, car,* and *clip* aloud. Then have another student say the words *race, space,* and *trace.* Discuss how the hard /c/ and soft /c/ sounds are different, even though they are made by the same letter.

Follow this routine with the hard and soft /g/ sounds.

 TEACHING TIP

Make sure students understand that:

- When the /s/ sound (soft /c/) is spelled with a *c*, the *c* is always followed by *e, i,* or *y*

- When the /j/ sound (soft /g/) is spelled with a *g*, the *g* is always followed by *e, i,* or *y*

 Go over the example question as a class.

 Exercise 23

ON YOUR MARK!

The Sound of the Letters *C* and *G*

Hard *c* and hard *g* sounds are heard in words such as:
- *c* → cat, car, clip
- *g* → gas, grow, give

Soft *c* and soft *g* sounds are heard in words such as:
- *c* → race, space, trace
- *g* → page, stage, cage

When the *s* sound is spelled with a *c*, the *c* is always followed by *e, i,* or *y*.
    fa**ce**   la**cy**   **ci**ty

When the *j* sound is spelled with a *g*, the *g* is always followed by *e, i,* or *y*.
    ju**dge**   **gi**ant   **gy**m

 GET SET!

Let's look at an example.

Find the word that has the same consonant sound as the underlined letter in the word below.

ge<u>m</u>

○ game
○ badge
○ egg

(1st) is **wrong**. *Game* has a hard *g* sound.

(2nd) is **correct!** *Gem* has a soft *g* sound, and the *dge* in *badge* makes a soft *g* sound.

(3rd) is **wrong**. The *gg* in *egg* makes a hard *g* sound.

 EXTRA ACTIVITY

Have students write two sentences. In one sentence, they must include a word with a soft /c/ consonant sound and a word with a hard /c/ consonant sound. In the second sentence, they must include a word with a soft /g/ consonant sound and a word with a hard /g/ consonant sound. For example:

- *The blue* car *won the* race.

- *I* gave *water to my bird in the* cage.

Students may share their sentences with the class.

GO!

1. Find the word that has the same consonant sound underlined in the word gra<u>p</u>e.
   - ○ giant
   - ● guide
   - ○ judge

2. Find the word that has the same consonant sound underlined in the word <u>g</u>as.
   - ● get
   - ○ just
   - ○ jet

3. Find the word that has the same consonant sound underlined in the word pa<u>c</u>e.
   - ○ fuse
   - ○ rise
   - ● mice

4. Find the word that has the same consonant sound underlined in the word ri<u>c</u>e.
   - ○ his
   - ● fuss
   - ○ buzz

5. Find the word that has the same consonant sound underlined in the word en<u>g</u>ine.
   - ○ golf
   - ● just
   - ○ grid

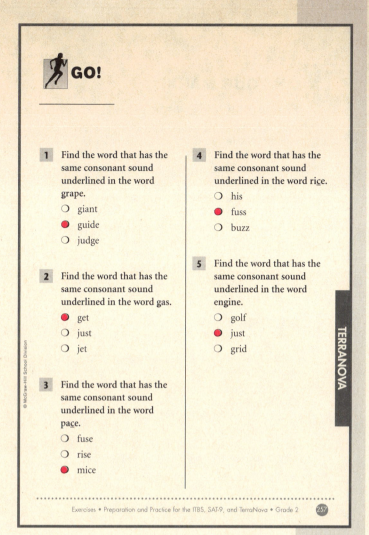

Go over each question on this page as a class.

For Numbers 1 through 5, read the directions carefully. Find the word that has the same consonant sound as the underlined part in the example word. Remember that the letters c and g each have two different sounds. Fill in the bubble next to the correct answer.

After students have completed the questions, go over the answers as a class. Read aloud the correct pronunciation of all of the answer choices and have students repeat them orally.

Exercise 24

PH, CH, AND TCH SOUNDS

 Go over the explanation of the /ph/, /ch/, and /tch/ sounds.

Explain that certain consonants make different sounds when combined with other consonants.

As a class, look at the explanations for each sound discussed on the Pupil Edition page. Have one student say the word *pot*. Have another student say the word *hot*. Then as a class, say the word *phone*. Discuss how the sounds are different, even though they contain the same letters. Follow this routine with the /ch/ and /tch/ sounds.

Have students think of several words that contain the /ph/, /ch/, and /tch/ sounds. Write their suggestions on the board.

 Go over the example question as a class.

Exercise 24

 ON YOUR MARK!

Ph, ch, and tch Sounds

Consonants by themselves make certain sounds. For example, *p* in the word *pot* and *h* in the word *hot* each have their own sound.

Putting certain consonants together changes the consonants' sounds.

phone The sound made by putting *p* and *h* together is not *p* in *pot* or *h* in *hot*. It is *f* in *fan*.

inch The sound made by putting *c* and *h* together is not *c* in *cat* or *h* in *hot*. It is a different sound—*ch* in *chin, chicken, chart, charm*.

catch The sound made by putting *t, c,* and *h* together is not *t* in *top, c* in *cat,* or *h* in *hat*. It is the same *ch* sound in *chin, chicken, chart*.

 GET SET!

Let's look at an example.

Find the answer that contains an underlined word that is spelled correctly.

○ a tree <u>brantch</u>
○ play <u>fetch</u>
○ answer the <u>fone</u>

(1st) is **wrong**. The word is spelled *branch*, not *brantch*.
(2nd) is **correct!** The word *fetch* is spelled correctly.
(3rd) is **wrong**. The word is spelled *phone*, not *fone*.

 TEACHING TIP

Point out to students that /tch/ is not used as the beginning sound of any English words.

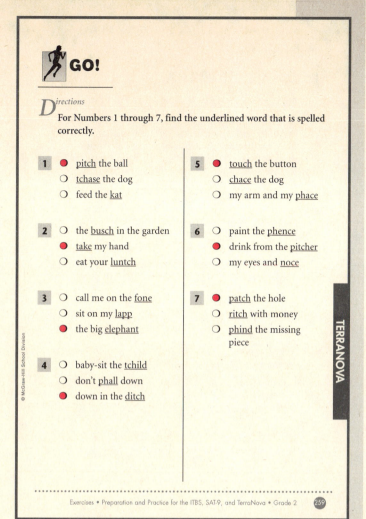

GO!

Directions

For Numbers 1 through 7, find the underlined word that is spelled correctly.

1. ● pitch the ball
   ○ tchase the dog
   ○ feed the kat

2. ○ the busch in the garden
   ● take my hand
   ○ eat your luntch

3. ○ call me on the fone
   ○ sit on my lapp
   ● the big elephant

4. ○ baby-sit the tchild
   ○ don't phall down
   ● down in the ditch

5. ● touch the button
   ○ chace the dog
   ○ my arm and my phace

6. ○ paint the phence
   ● drink from the pitcher
   ○ my eyes and noce

7. ● patch the hole
   ○ ritch with money
   ○ phind the missing piece

TERRANOVA

 Go over each question on this page as a class.

For Numbers 1 through 7, find the underlined word that is spelled correctly. Fill in the bubble next to the correct answer.

After students have completed the questions, go over the answers as a class. Write the correct spelling of all of the answer choices on the board so that students can become familiar with the words.

Question 1
chase, cat

Question 2
bush, lunch

Question 3
phone, lap

Question 4
child, fall

Question 5
chase, face

Question 6
fence, nose

Question 7
rich, find

Exercise 25
PACING YOURSELF

 With your class, read the *Pacing Yourself* explanation on the Pupil Edition page.

Write the three tips from the middle of the Pupil Edition page on the board. Keep them on the board as students work through the questions in the Go! section as a reminder.

 Go over the example question with the class.

Exercise 25

 ON YOUR MARK!

Pacing Yourself

When you take the TerraNova, you should not rush through the test or spend too much time trying to answer the questions. Instead, you should pace yourself. **Pacing yourself** means taking the time you need to answer the test questions as best as you can without racing through the test or wasting too much time trying to answer difficult questions.

- **Do not get stuck on one question.** If you cannot answer a question and you have been trying for a while, take your best guess and move on.
- **Know the directions.** When you take the practice tests, listen to the directions that your teacher reads so that you will already know them when you take the real exam.
- **Relax.** Don't worry if you don't know an answer. The TerraNova is just one way to measure your skills. The calmer you are, the more likely you are to answer the questions correctly!

 GET SET!

Let's practice pacing yourself on this example.

Find the word with the same vowel sound as h<u>ear</u>d.

   fear   were   let
    ○   ○   ○

(1st) is **wrong.** *Fear* has a long *e* vowel sound.

(2nd) is **correct!** The vowel sound in *heard* is like the vowel sound in *were*.

(3rd) is **wrong.** *Let* has a short *e* sound.

 EXTRA ACTIVITY

Create a handout with three language arts questions of similar difficulty. Give students the opportunity to experience different paces by controlling their answering with these guidelines:

- **For question 1, give the students a very long amount of time and ask them to read the question and answer choices through at least two or three times.**

- **For question 2, give students a very short amount of time (almost too little).**

- **For question 3, let students answer the question at their own pace.**

Discuss how each pace felt.

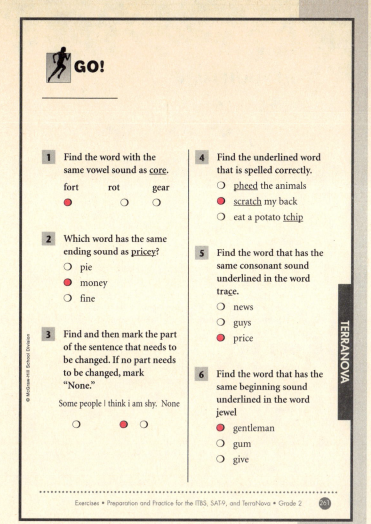

 Go over each question on this page as a class.

This page tests skills that students learned in Exercises 20 through 24. Students should remain conscious of their pace as they complete the questions on this page.

For Numbers 1 through 6, read the directions carefully and select the best answer to each question. Fill in the bubble next to your choice. Remember to set a good pace for yourself as you move through the questions.

Question 1
Vowel sounds with the letter *r*

Question 2
Long /e/ sound

Question 3
The pronoun *I* is always capitalized.

Question 4
Correct spellings: feed, chip

Question 5
Soft /c/ sound—*c* followed by *e*

Question 6
Soft /g/ sound—*g* followed by *e*

Exercise 26
SPELLING TRICKY WORDS

 Read the list of tricky words to the class or go around the room having students read them aloud.

Have students point out the strange letter combinations in each word.

 TEACHING TIP

If students are keeping spelling journals, add the words from the tricky words list to their journals. If not, start spelling journals with your students using the tricky word list. Tell students to add words they have trouble spelling. Remind students to go back to their lists regularly and practice spelling the words.

 Go over the example question with the class.

Exercise 26

ON YOUR MARK!

Spelling Tricky Words

Some words are difficult to spell. You can use this list to check your spelling. You can also practice spelling these words correctly.

again	been	early	money	said	tired
along	before	family	myself	school	together
also	buy	finally	o'clock	soon	until
always	charge	first	off	started	upon
another	clothes	friend	once	sure	were
any	color	heard	our	than	when
anything	could	hurt	please	their	which
around	dear	know	pretty	they	while
balloon	decide	little	really	third	would
because	does	might	right	through	write

> **TIP:** Keep a word list in your spelling journal. Write down all of the words you have trouble spelling.

 GET SET!

Let's look at an example.

Find the answer choice that contains an underlined word that is spelled correctly.

○ <u>aerly</u> in the morning
○ <u>our</u> hometown
○ <u>wonce</u> upon a time

(1st) is **wrong**. The word *early* is not spelled *aerly*.
(2nd) is **correct!** The word *our* is spelled correctly.
(3rd) is **wrong**. The word *once* is not spelled *wonce*.

 EXTRA ACTIVITY

Have a spelling bee with the class. Call out words from the *Tricky Words* list on the Pupil Edition page. If an individual misspells a word, he or she must sit down. The last person left standing is the Spelling Bee Champ of the day.

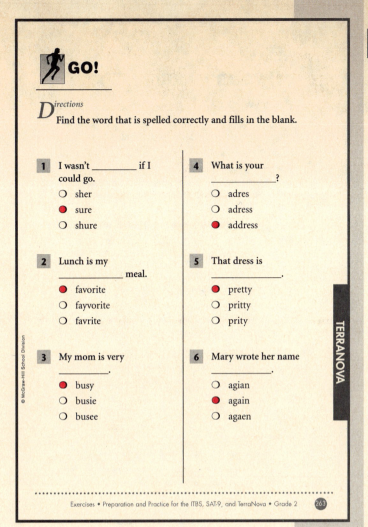

 Go over each question on this page as a class.

For Numbers 1 through 6, find the word that is spelled correctly and fills in the blank. Fill in the bubble next to the correct answer.

Exercise 27

ROOT WORDS

 Go over the definition of a root word with the class.

Write the example *small + est = smallest* on the board. Add a few more examples of a root word + *-est*. Some you might use are:

- *old + est = oldest*
- *short + est = shortest*

Write on the board the other common endings *-ing*, *-ed*, *-es*, *-s*, and *-ly* and the examples listed on the middle of the Pupil Edition page. Draw a vertical line between the root words and the endings in the examples. Ask students to come up with some examples of their own. Have students come to the board and draw a line between the root words and the endings in their examples.

TEACHING TIP

Make sure students understand the difference between root words and compound words. Review compound words (Exercise 8) if necessary.

 Go over the example question as a class.

Exercise 27

ON YOUR MARK!

Root Words

A **root word,** or base word, is a word that you can add endings to in order to make another word. For example:

small + est = smallest

The word *small* is the **root word**. The ending *-est* is not a word by itself. It is an ending added to the **root word** *small*. Adding *-est* to the word *small* changes the meaning from "little" to "the most little."

Here are some common endings: *-ing*, *-ed*, *-es*, *-s*, and *-ly*.

Root word	Other words formed with endings
walk	walking
pick	picked
teach	teaches
play	plays
love	lovely

 GET SET!

Let's look at an example.

What is the root word in the word <u>talking</u>?

   tal   king   talk
   ○   ○   ●

(1st) is **wrong.** *Tal* is not a word.

(2nd) is **wrong.** The letters *-king* are not an ending.

(3rd) is **correct!** *Talk* is a word that you can add endings to in order to make another word.

 EXTRA ACTIVITY

Play a listing game with the class. *Round 1:* Select a letter of the alphabet. Have students come up with as many root words as they can that begin with that letter. The student with the most root words gets to select one root word from his or her list to use in Round 2. *Round 2:* Write the selected root word on the board and see who can come up with the most new words by adding endings to that root word.

Go over each question on this page as a class.

For Numbers 1 through 6, find the root word in the underlined word. Fill in the bubble under the correct answer.

Encourage students who are having trouble identifying the root to draw a vertical line between the root word and the ending.

Remind students that a root word can be a word on its own—without an ending.

Tell students to try using each answer choice in a sentence. The only choice that can be used in a sentence is the root word.

Exercise 28

SPELLING

Changing *y* to *i* and Adding *-es*

 Go over the rule for changing a *y* to *i* and adding the ending.

Write the first example for the word *berry* on the board. Make sure that students understand the steps in the rule.

Ask students to explain how the words in the list were spelled. As they explain, write the steps on the board. For example:

- *hurry* ➔ change the y to i ➔ hurri + ed = hurried

Repeat this process with all of the words on the list.

 Go over the example question as a class. Ask students to explain how the two incorrect answers fail to meet the steps in the rule.

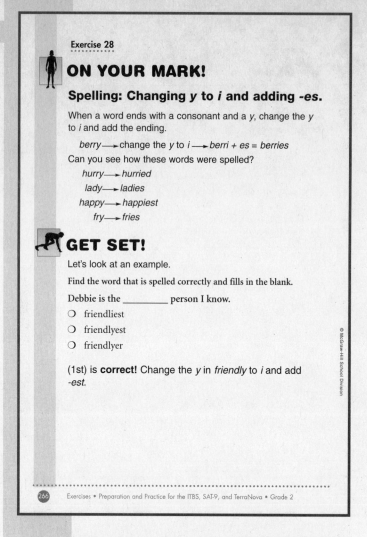

Exercise 28

ON YOUR MARK!

Spelling: Changing *y* to *i* and adding -es.

When a word ends with a consonant and a *y*, change the *y* to *i* and add the ending.

berry ⟶ change the y to i ⟶ berri + es = berries

Can you see how these words were spelled?

hurry ⟶ hurried
lady ⟶ ladies
happy ⟶ happiest
fry ⟶ fries

GET SET!

Let's look at an example.

Find the word that is spelled correctly and fills in the blank.

Debbie is the _____ person I know.
○ friendliest
○ friendlyest
○ friendlyer

(1st) is **correct!** Change the *y* in *friendly* to *i* and add *-est*.

 TEACHING TIP

Suggest that students add this spelling rule to their spelling journals. It might help them with some of the words on their lists. Along with the rule, they should list a few example words.

GO!

Directions

For Numbers 1 through 4, find the underlined word that is spelled correctly.

1.
   - ● Brian has a lot of buddies.
   - ○ Ryan ate too many candys.
   - ○ The fairries in this story are pretty.

2.
   - ○ I like to read the funnyes in the Sunday paper.
   - ● The princess always marries the hero.
   - ○ Can I read the storys?

3.
   - ○ My bird always flys around the house.
   - ○ Mary dryes the dishes.
   - ● The pennies are in my piggybank.

4.
   - ○ Many famileys were at the concert.
   - ● Scott is petting the bunnies.
   - ○ The night skyes are pretty here.

Directions

For Numbers 5 and 6, fill in the blank with the word that is spelled correctly.

5. Tom _____ every night.
   - ○ studyies
   - ○ studys
   - ● studies

6. My mom always _____ about me.
   - ● worries
   - ○ worrys
   - ○ wories

TERRANOVA

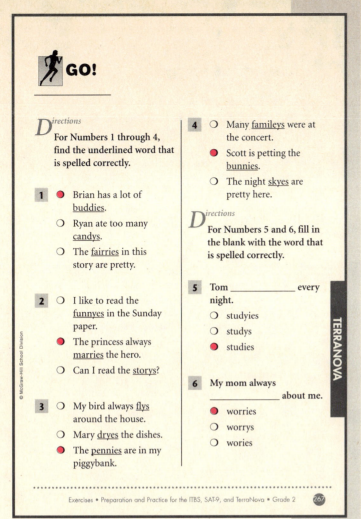 **Go over each question on this page as a class.**

Questions 1, 2, 3, and 4

For Numbers 1 through 4, find the underlined word that is spelled correctly. Fill in the bubble next to the correct answer.

Encourage students who are having difficulty to keep repeating the spelling rule to themselves as they consider all of the answer choices.

Questions 5 and 6

For Numbers 5 and 6, fill in the blank with the word that is spelled correctly. Fill in the bubble next to your selection.

Exercise 29
WORDS WITH A SILENT *E*

 As a class, go over the definition of silent letters and the rule for adding endings to words that end in silent /e/.

Ask students to take turns saying aloud the words with silent /e/ listed at the top of the Pupil Edition page. Discuss how you cannot hear the /e/ when the word is pronounced correctly.

Write the spelling rule for adding endings to words that end in silent /e/ on the board. Then go over the examples provided. Make sure students understand that the *e* must be dropped before adding the endings.

 Go over the example question as a class. Ask students to explain how the two incorrect answers fail to meet the steps in the rule.

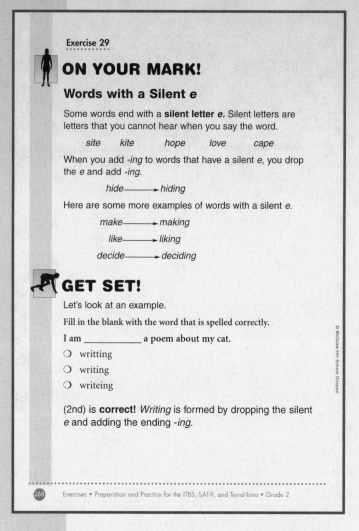

Exercise 29
ON YOUR MARK!
Words with a Silent e

Some words end with a **silent letter e.** Silent letters are letters that you cannot hear when you say the word.

   site   kite   hope   love   cape

When you add *-ing* to words that have a silent *e*, you drop the *e* and add *-ing*.

   hide ⟶ hiding

Here are some more examples of words with a silent *e*.

   make ⟶ making
   like ⟶ liking
   decide ⟶ deciding

GET SET!
Let's look at an example.
Fill in the blank with the word that is spelled correctly.
I am _____ a poem about my cat.
○ writting
○ writing
○ writeing

(2nd) is **correct!** *Writing* is formed by dropping the silent *e* and adding the ending *-ing*.

 TEACHING TIP

Suggest that students add this spelling rule to their spelling journals. It might help them with some of the words on their lists. Along with the rule, they should list a few example words.

GO!

Directions
Fill in the blank with the word that is spelled correctly.

1 Tina is _____ at me.
○ stareing
○ starring
● staring

2 I am _____ Jim and Bobby.
○ inviting
● invitting
○ inviteing

3 We are _____ fish for dinner.
○ haveing
○ havveing
● having

Directions
For Numbers 4 and 5, find the underlined word that is spelled correctly.

4 ○ The cat is biteing the string.
○ I like liveing in the country.
● Mom sliced the apple.

5 ● Marcy likes riding in the truck.
○ I lovved swimming in the ocean.
○ Hanna thinks that math is boreing.

TERRANOVA

Exercises • Preparation and Practice for the ITBS, SAT-9, and TerraNova • Grade 2   269

Go over each question on this page as a class.

Questions 1, 2, and 3

For Numbers 1 through 3, fill in the blank with the word that is spelled correctly. Fill in the bubble next to your selection.

Remind students that when words end in silent /e/, they must drop the *e* before adding *-ing*.

Questions 4 and 5

For Numbers 4 and 5, find the underlined word that is spelled correctly. Fill in the bubble next to the correct answer.

Exercise 30

USING RHYMING WORDS TO HELP YOU SPELL

 Go over the explanation of rhyming.

Explain that once students have successfully learned how to spell one word, it might help them to spell many more that sound the same.

Write a list of words on the board. Have students come up with as many words as they can that rhyme with the words in the list. Some examples you might use are:

- *night*—*light, sight, fight*
- *tone*—*phone, cone*
- *date*—*late, hate, state*

 Go over the example question as a class.

Exercise 30

ON YOUR MARK!

Using Rhyming Words to Help You Spell

When you are not sure if a word is misspelled, think of a word that rhymes with it that you do know how to spell. Look at this word:

stick

Do you think *stick* is spelled correctly? If you're not sure, think of another word with the same ending. It might be a rhyming word, like this one:

pick

Compare the letters in the two words. You will find that they both end with an *ick*. This is a clue that *stick* is spelled correctly.

 GET SET!

Let's look at an example.

Find the underlined word that is spelled correctly.

○ My dog likes to <u>growell</u>.
○ Don't you feel <u>wel</u>?
● I feel just <u>fine</u>.

(1st) is **wrong**. If you think of the word *owl*, you will find that this word is spelled wrong.

(2nd) is **wrong**. *Well* is misspelled. If you think of the word *sell*, you will find that there should be a second *l* at the end of *wel*.

(3rd) is **correct!** If you think of the word *mine*, you will find that this word is spelled correctly.

 EXTRA ACTIVITY

Make copies of some poems that contain many rhyming words to hand out to the class. Ask students to volunteer reading the poems. Then as a class, compile a list of some of the rhyming words that are spelled the same. Students may add these words to their spelling journals if they wish.

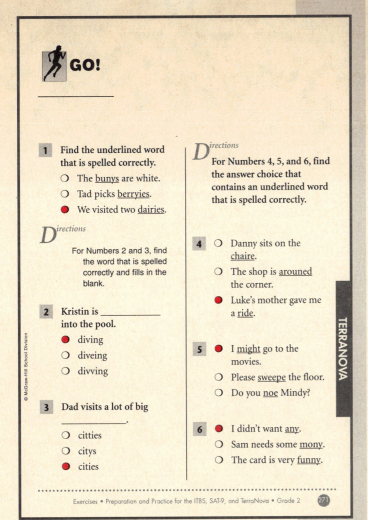

GO!

1 Find the underlined word that is spelled correctly.
- ○ The <u>bunys</u> are white.
- ○ Tad picks <u>berryies</u>.
- ● We visited two <u>dairies</u>.

Directions
For Numbers 2 and 3, find the word that is spelled correctly and fills in the blank.

2 Kristin is _____ into the pool.
- ● diving
- ○ diveing
- ○ divving

3 Dad visits a lot of big _____.
- ○ citties
- ○ citys
- ● cities

Directions
For Numbers 4, 5, and 6, find the answer choice that contains an underlined word that is spelled correctly.

4
- ○ Danny sits on the <u>chaire</u>.
- ○ The shop is <u>arouned</u> the corner.
- ● Luke's mother gave me a <u>ride</u>.

5
- ● I <u>might</u> go to the movies.
- ○ Please <u>sweepe</u> the floor.
- ○ Do you <u>noe</u> Mindy?

6
- ● I didn't want <u>any</u>.
- ○ Sam needs some <u>mony</u>.
- ○ The card is very <u>funny</u>.

 Go over each question on this page as a class.

This page tests skills students learned in Exercises 25 through 29.

Read each set of directions carefully. Think about the spelling rules you have learned so far as you read the answer choices. Use rhyming words to help you choose your answer. Fill in the bubble next to the answer you choose.

Question 1
For a word ending in *y*, drop the *y* and add *-ies* to make it plural.

Question 2
Rhyming word: driving

Question 3
Rhyming word: kitties

Question 4
The spelling words in these answer choices have tricky spellings that must be memorized. Rhyming words: hair, stair, pound, hound, hide, side

Question 5
Rhyming words: light, beep

Question 6
Rhyming words: many, honey, runny

Practice Test

Part 1

> Please bear in mind that the Practice Test contains reading comprehension passages and questions in addition to language arts questions. The reading comprehension questions were included because the actual TerraNova combines these two sections. You will not, however, find annotations for any of the questions involving reading comprehension skills except the correct answer choices.

Growing Every Day

Have you noticed that you are growing up a little every day? Each day you learn something new. Learning is the key to growing. In this section, you will learn about some other people who are learning and growing.

Directions

> Read the directions and poem carefully.

This is a poem about a young tree. Read the poem and answer the questions that follow.

I'm a Tree

I push my head up through the dirt
To see what I can see.
I'm just a tiny seedling now,
But soon I'll be a tree.
The sun shines bright and warms me
From my tip down to my roots.
My leaves turn light into food I need
To sprout new tender shoots.
The grown-up trees are high above me
Moving in the breeze.
I wonder if I'll ever be
A tree as tall as these.
I dig my roots into the soil
And soak up some more sun.
I stand beside the grown-up trees
Pretending I am one.

📢 *Read the directions for Numbers 1 and 2 and answer them by filling in the bubble under the picture you choose.*

1 What helps the tree turn sunlight into food?

● ○ ○

2 What are the grown-up trees doing in the poem?

○ ● ○

 For Numbers 3 and 4, fill in the circle next to the sentence that is complete.

3
○ Drawing a picture.
● He is talented.
○ On the blackboard.

(1st) Missing a subject
(2nd) Complete sentence
(3rd) Missing subject and verb

4
○ Studying for the test.
○ Many correct answers.
● I stayed home yesterday.

(1st) Missing subject and helping verb
(2nd) Missing verb
(3rd) Complete sentence

Go On ➡

5 **Trees need water to survive. _____. That is how they grow.**

- ● Their roots soak up water from the soil.
- ○ People need a lot of water each day.
- ○ It is often very dry in the mountains.

> For Numbers 5 and 6, find the sentence that best completes the story. Fill in the bubble next to the sentence you choose.

6 **The little tree looks up at the grown-up trees around it. They are very big. _____.**

- ○ The little tree grew from a tiny seed.
- ● The little tree hopes to be that big one day.
- ○ Soon it will be summer.

> Both 5 and 6 need a detail sentence. Detail sentences tell more about the main idea in the topic sentence.

Directions

Read the directions and the poem carefully.

Below is a poem about how a child has fun in his attic. Read the poem. Then answer the questions that follow.

I walk
Up ten steps,
Around a corner,
Then up ten more—
Through
A little
Door
And into a room
Just under my roof.
The room is my attic—
Stacked with boxes and boxes
Of books.

It smells like dust,
And time,
And yellow autumn leaves.
I am a pirate.
The books are my
Treasure.
They tell me about
Places I will see,
Things I will do,
And
What I might grow up to be.

> For Numbers 7 through 10 on this page and 11 through 14 on the next page, read the directions and the questions carefully. Fill in the bubble next to the answer you choose.

7 Why does the boy like the attic?
- ● He likes to read.
- ○ He likes to hunt for treasure.
- ○ He likes to hide in boxes.

Directions
Read the sentence. Then choose the best sentence to follow it.

8 I took swimming lessons this summer.
- ○ I played baseball last year.
- ○ My brother is too young to swim.
- ● I learned how to dive into the pool.

Need a detail sentence. Detail sentences tell more about the main idea in the topic sentence.

A word made up of two words is called a COMPOUND WORD.

---

9 Which one of these words is a compound word?
- ○ window
- ● baseball
- ○ rocket

Only the second answer choice can be separated into two words: base and ball.

10 Choose the words that have the same vowel sound.
- ● <u>steep</u> and <u>lean</u>
- ○ <u>leap</u> and <u>wear</u>
- ○ <u>stem</u> and <u>steam</u>

Steep and lean both have a long /e/ sound.

11 Which one of these words is a compound word?
- ○ basement
- ● notebook
- ○ sweaters

Only the second answer choice can be separated into two words: note and book.

12 Find the sentence that is complete and that is written correctly.
- ● She ate a big lunch.
- ○ I with her at lunch.
- ○ In the living room.

(1st) Complete sentence
(2nd) Missing a verb
(3rd) Missing a subject and a verb

Directions

Read each sentence. Then choose the answer choice that contains a mistake. If both sentences are correct, choose "No mistake."

13
- ○ I have to study for the test.
- ● my dad will help me.
- ○ No mistake

The first letter of a sentence is always capitalized.

14
- ○ I went fishing with Mary and Randy.
- ○ Mom asked me to clean my room.
- ● No mistake

Directions

Read the directions and the passage carefully.

Below is a story about two friends who are looking for something to do. Read the story. Then answer the questions that follow.

Day with Mr. Lu

Amy and Ben lived near a costume shop. Mr. Lu owned the shop.

One day, Amy and Ben were bored. They went to visit Mr. Lu.

"We're bored, Mr. Lu," said Ben.

"What can we do?" asked Amy.

Mr. Lu scratched his head. "I have an idea," he said. "Come with me."

Amy and Ben followed Mr. Lu to a big room. They looked around. The two friends were amazed. They saw hats and coats. They saw dresses and capes. They saw masks and wigs.

"Wow!" said Amy.

"Gosh!" said Ben.

All day, they tried on costumes.

"Rrrooowwwwrrr!" growled Ben the Bear.

"Stop thief!" cried Amy the Officer.

"Woof! Woof!" barked Ben the Dog.

"I'll save you!" yelled Amy the Firefighter.

Amy and Ben knew they would never be bored again.

> For Numbers 15 and 16, find the word that fits best in the blank. Fill in the bubble next to the answer you choose.

15 Ben tried on the clown shoes. _____ were too big.
- ○ Them
- ○ It
- ● They

Pronoun refers to the clown shoes. Need a plural subject pronoun.

16 Amy visited the costume shop. _____ had fun.
- ○ It
- ○ Him
- ● She

Pronoun refers to Amy. Need a singular subject pronoun.

> For Numbers 17 and 18, find the sentence that best completes the story. Fill in the bubble next to the sentence you choose.

17 I like to go camping. _____. I stay warm in my sleeping bag.
- ○ I just learned how to swim.
- ● It is fun to sleep outdoors.
- ○ I am afraid of the dark.

18 My brother is not nice. _____. He keeps his toys to himself.
- ● He doesn't like to share.
- ○ He is in the fourth grade.
- ○ I like to play in his room.

Both 17 and 18 need a detail sentence. A detail sentence tells more about the main idea in the topic sentence.

Part 2

> Have students read this short paragraph.

The Best I Can Be

Everyone wants to be good at something. The best way to become good at something is to practice doing it. The stories in this section are about learning how to be good at something.

Directions *Read the directions and the passage carefully.*

The story below is about a girl who wants to do something special for her father's birthday. Read the story. Then answer the questions that follow.

The Special Gift

When Angel came home from school, he saw a worried look on his little sister's face.

"What's the matter, Rosie?" Angel asked.

Rosie sighed and said, "I want to get Dad something extra special for his birthday, but I don't have any money."

"I know what you can do for Dad that won't cost any money," replied Angel. "Wait here." Angel left the room, leaving Rosie wondering what her brother was up to.

Angel soon returned with a big box. The box held ribbons, glitter, glue, scissors, and paper of every color. Angel said that he was going to help Rosie make a special gift for their father.

"Parents always like homemade gifts better than a gift from the store," Angel said. "Mom always says that homemade gifts are held together with love."

Rosie's face lit up. "I'm going to make Dad the best birthday card ever!" she exclaimed. Rosie rushed to the box and began sorting through the things inside.

Suddenly, Rosie thought of something she forgot to do. She stopped for a moment, looked at Angel, and said, "Thanks, Angel. You're a pretty neat brother."

19 You can tell that Rosie thinks Angel is
- ○ strong
- ○ foolish
- ● helpful

20 Rosie and Angel's parents probably think that
- ○ gifts from the store are better
- ● homemade gifts are more thoughtful
- ○ Angel should let Rosie do her own work

21 What does Rosie think she needs before she hears Angel's idea?

● ○ ○

22 Find the sentence that is complete and that is written correctly.
- ● Rosie worked hard on the gift.
- ○ Her big brother's name is angel?
- ○ they are good Friends.

(1st) Correct

(2nd) A statement needs to end with a period, not a question mark. Peoples names should be capitalized.

(3rd) The first letter of a sentence is always capitalized.

> Read the directions for each question and the answer choices carefully. Fill in the bubble for the answer you choose.

23 What is the past tense of the word <u>eat</u>?
- ○ eating
- ○ eats
- ● ate

24 Rosie wanted to make a gift. _____ made a birthday card.
- ○ Her
- ○ It
- ● She

Pronoun refers to Rosie. Need a singular subject pronoun.

25 Which word has the same vowel sound as <u>first</u>?
- ○ mist
- ● herd
- ○ fight

Vowel sound with the letter r

26 Which of these is the root word of <u>studying</u>?
- ○ studied
- ○ studies
- ● study

A root word is a word that you can add endings to in order to make another word. Only the third answer choice is a root word. The first and second answer choices already have endings added: -ed and -es.

Go On

Directions *Read the directions for each question and the answer choices carefully. Fill in the bubble for the answer you choose.*

For Numbers 27 and 28, read the sentence. Then complete the sentence with the answer choice that is written correctly.

27 Today is my second day at _____
- ○ Camp Green River?
- ○ camp green River.
- ● Camp Green River.

Capitalize all major words in a proper noun, and end a statement with a period.

28 I was born on _____
- ● November 20, 1997.
- ○ november 20, 1997.
- ○ November 20 1997.

A comma always goes between the day of the month and the year, and months must always be capitalized.

Directions

Read the directions and the passage carefully.

Below is a story about a girl who wants to help her sister. Read the story. Then answer the questions that follow.

Emma Helps Out

Emma stood in the garden. She watched her big sister Carolyn plant flowers. "Can I help?" she asked.

"You're too little," said Carolyn.

Emma did not think she was too little. She wanted to help.

"Dad, will you help me plant flowers?" Emma asked.

Dad thought for a while. "Follow me," he said.

Dad and Emma went outside. They planted seeds in a pot. They put the pot in a window.

Emma watered the seeds. She watched and waited. Soon, daisies began to grow.

One day, Carolyn saw the daisies. "Come help me, Emma," she said.

They took the daisies outside. They planted them in the garden.

Carolyn smiled. "You are a good helper," she said.

Emma smiled, too.

29 What is Carolyn probably thinking when she says, "You're too little"?

- ○ Emma is not nice.
- ○ Emma is not tall enough.
- ● Emma is not old enough.

30 Who is probably the youngest person in Emma's family?

- ○ Carolyn
- ○ Dad
- ● Emma

31 Who does Emma help at the end of the story?

 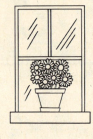 

● ○ ○

32 Why does Emma smile at the end of the story?

- ○ She is little.
- ● She feels proud.
- ○ She likes flowers.

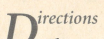
Read the directions for each question and the answer choices carefully. Fill in the bubble for the answer you choose.

Directions Choose the pair of words that shares the same vowel sound.

33
- ● glove and dove
- ○ broom and cook
- ○ tore and top

34 Which word has the same middle sound as star?
- ○ tame
- ● far — Vowel sound with the letter r.
- ○ take

35 What is another way of saying, "I will do the dishes"?
- ● I'll do the dishes. — I'll is the contraction form of I will. The apostrophe shows where the letters were left out.
- ○ I's do the dishes.
- ○ I've do the dishes.

Directions *Read the directions for each question and the answer choices carefully. Fill in the bubble for the answer you choose.*

For Numbers 36 and 37, choose the pair of words that shares the same vowel sound.

36
● tore and roar
○ foot and tooth
○ choose and those

37
○ drape and trap
● braid and made
○ late and cat

This is the end of the Reading and Language Arts section of the test. Give students a break. Then have them turn to page 294 to begin the Language Mechanics section of the test.

Language Mechanics

Directions 📣 *Read the directions and each question carefully. Fill in the bubble next to the punctuation mark you choose.*

For Numbers 1 through 4, find the punctuation mark that should go at the end of the sentence.

1 Watch out
- ○ ,
- ○ ?
- ● ! *An exclamation ends with an exclamation mark.*

2 Please close the door
- ○ ?
- ○ , *A command ends with a period.*
- ● .

3 Are you going to the play
- ● ? *A question ends with a question mark.*
- ○ .
- ○ !

4 Stop
- ● ! *An exclamation ends with an exclamation mark.*
- ○ ?
- ○ ,

Directions

> Read the directions and the answer choices carefully. Fill in the bubble next to the sentence you choose.

For Numbers 5 through 9, choose the sentence that uses capital letters correctly.

5
- ● I will be back later.
- ○ I think mr. martin's class is fun.
- ○ My brother and i do not like meatloaf.

(1st) Correct
(2nd) *Mr.* is a title and should be capitalized.
(3rd) The pronoun *I* is always capitalized.

6
- ○ terri said, "It's almost time for dinner."
- ○ "Have you seen my pen?" asked mrs. Frank.
- ● "Please print your name," said Mr. Martin.

(1st) The first letter of a sentence is always capitalized.
(2nd) *Mrs.* is a title and should be capitalized.
(3rd) Correct

7
- ○ I live in Austin, texas.
- ○ We visited orlando, florida.
- ● My mom is from Tucson, Arizona.

(1st) States are always capitalized.
(2nd) Cities and states are always capitalized.
(3rd) Correct

8
- ● Where is the lunch room?
- ○ we have a test today.
- ○ Today is lisa's birthday.

(1st) Correct
(2nd) The first letter of a sentence is always capitalized.
(3rd) A person's name is always capitalized.

9
- ○ I have gym class on wednesday.
- ● School ends in June.
- ○ I went to camp in july.

(1st) Days of the week are always capitalized.
(2nd) Correct
(3rd) Months are always capitalized.

Go On

Directions *Read the directions and the answer choices carefully. Fill in the bubble next to the answer you choose.*

For Numbers 10 through 12, fill in the blank with the answer choice that uses capital letters and end marks correctly.

10 My parents were married on _____.
- ○ March, 2 1989
- ○ march 2, 1989
- ● March 2, 1989

A comma always goes between the day of the month and the year, and the month should always be capitalized.

11 We all wore red shirts on _____.
- ○ Valentine's day
- ● Valentine's Day
- ○ valentine's Day

Holidays are always capitalized.

12 We visited _____ last summer.
- ○ Mount rushmore
- ● Mount Rushmore
- ○ mount Rushmore

Capitalize all major words in a proper noun.

Directions *Read the directions and the answer choices carefully. Fill in the bubble next to the answer you choose.*

Read the postcard. Then find the answer choices with the correct capital letters and end marks for each missing part.

_____(13)_____

Dear Dad,

Aunt Ida's house is huge! The bedroom I sleep in is the size of our _____(14)_____ combined! I've got plenty of room for all of my things.

_____(15)_____

Mary Claire

13
- ○ july 10 2000
- ○ July, 10 2000
- ● July 10, 2000

A comma always goes between the day of the month and the year, and the month should always be capitalized.

14
- ● living room, kitchen, and dining room
- ○ living room, kitchen, and dining room,
- ○ living room, kitchen and, dining room

Commas are used to separate items in a series. Do not put a comma after the and *or after the last word in a series.*

15
- ● Much love,
- ○ much, love
- ○ Much Love.

The closing in a letter always begins with a capital letter and ends with a comma.

Go On →

Practice Test • Preparation and Practice for the ITBS, SAT-9, and TerraNova • Grade 2

16 Choose the correct end mark for this sentence.

What time is it

○ .
● ?
○ !

> A question ends with a question mark.

17 Choose the sentence that uses capital letters and end marks correctly.

● We learned our lesson.
○ dr. Rollins is nice.
○ Here it is

> (1st) Correct
> (2nd) *Dr.* is a title and should be capitalized. In addition, the first letter of a sentence is always capitalized.
> (3rd) A statement ends with a period.

> This is the end of the Language Mechanics section of the test. Give students a break. Then have them turn to page 299 to begin the Spelling section of the test.

Spelling

Directions — For Numbers 1 through 10, read the directions and the answer choices carefully. Fill in the bubble next to the answer you choose.

Fill in the blank with the word that has the correct spelling.

1 I like to _____ my grandpa.
- ● visit
- ○ viset
- ○ visut

2 My big brother is _____.
- ○ lazey
- ○ lazie
- ● lazy

3 My _____ is going on a trip.
- ● family
- ○ famuly
- ○ famely

4 I _____ all of my art projects.
- ○ savd
- ● saved
- ○ savved

Go On

5 She is always _____.
- ○ smileing
- ○ smilling
- ● smiling

> When you add *-ing* to words that have a silent /e/, you drop the *e* and add *-ing*.

6 The _____ kitten was cute.
- ● little
- ○ littel
- ○ littal

7 Jose _____ his foot.
- ○ hert
- ● hurt
- ○ hirt

8 Susan's mom is _____ us home.
- ○ drivving
- ○ driveing
- ● driving

9 She collected _____ stamps.
- ● ninety
- ○ ninty
- ○ nintey

10 Brenda likes _____.
- ○ bakeing
- ○ bakking
- ● baking

> For Numbers 8 and 10, when you add *-ing* to words that have a silent /e/, you drop the *e* and add *-ing*.

Directions  For Numbers 11 through 20, read the directions and the answer choices carefully. Fill in the bubble next to the answer you choose.

For Numbers 11 through 20, read the sentences. Then find the underlined word that is spelled correctly.

11
- ○ I am going outside <u>agen</u>.
- ● <u>There</u> is my house.
- ○ I <u>mayled</u> the letter.

12
- ● I <u>thought</u> I knew the answer.
- ○ Tom knew he <u>coud</u> do it.
- ○ I didn't know <u>wich</u> one to choose.

13
- ○ I let go of my <u>baloon</u>.
- ○ Dad made me get up <u>erly</u>.
- ● Kenneth's room is <u>always</u> clean.

14
- ○ Nathan was <u>tirred</u> of the game.
- ○ Dad <u>mooved</u> the furniture.
- ● My brother is <u>driving</u> to school.

15
- ● Our pet duck had <u>babies</u>.
- ○ Mr. Barry tells good <u>storyies</u>.
- ○ I have a jar of <u>pennys</u>.

> When a word ends with a consonant and a *y*, change the *y* to *i* and add the ending.

16
- ○ Henry was there <u>befor</u>.
- ● Marcus is smart <u>because</u> he studies hard.
- ○ Betsy <u>reelly</u> likes to read.

17
- ○ What <u>coud</u> I do?
- ○ He is a good <u>frend</u>.
- ● Sparky jumped <u>through</u> the hoop.

18
- ○ I do not <u>beleive</u> you.
- ● <u>Tomorrow</u> we'll go to the record store.
- ○ Pierre has ten <u>dolars</u> to spend.

19
- ● The <u>library</u> is five blocks away.
- ○ Tom is my little <u>brothor</u>.
- ○ <u>Poeple</u> came from everywhere.

20
- ○ Grace feels <u>allright</u> today.
- ○ Why haven't we <u>benn</u> there?
- ● The rain falls <u>quietly</u> to the ground.

On Your Mark, Get Set, Go! Review

REVIEW

The following pages offer a list of the skills that students should be familiar with after completing the exercises in this book.

Sentences

Students should know:

- A sentence is a complete thought
- An incomplete sentence is not a complete thought
- How to tell the difference between a sentence and an incomplete sentence

Compound Words

Students should know:

- A compound word is made up of two words
- How to recognize and form a compound word

Punctuation

Student should know:

- Periods are used at the end of a statement
- Periods are used at the end of a command
- Question marks are used at the end of a question
- Exclamation marks are used at the end of a statement of excitement
- Commas always separate the month and day from the year
- A period follows an abbreviation
- Commas are used between the name of a city and state
- Commas follow letter greetings and closings

Spelling

Students should know:

- How to add suffixes such as -*ies*, -*ied*, -*iest*, -*s*, -*ing*, and -*es*
- How to recognize and spell words with silent letters
- How to spell tricky words such as *because, please, early, were,* and *could*

Sounds

Students should know:

- The difference between the sounds of long and short vowels
- How vowel sounds change when followed by the letter *r*
- The different spellings for the short /e/ and long /e/ sound
- The difference between the sound of a soft /c/ and a hard /c/
- The difference between the sound of a soft /g/ and a hard /g/
- The sounds that result from *ph, ch,* and *tch*

Verbs

Students should know:

- The difference between a subject and a verb
- The difference between a singular and a plural subject or verb
- How to make subjects and verbs agree
- How to recognize a past and a present tense verb
- What a helping verb is and how it is used

Capitalization

Students should know:

- A capital letter always begins a sentence
- Names of people and pets should be capitalized
- Days of the week, months of the year, and holidays should be capitalized
- Specific names of places should be capitalized
- Terms of respect (e.g., *Mr., Dr.*) should be capitalized
- The first word of a letter greeting or closing is capitalized
- The pronoun *I* is capitalized

Contractions

Students should know:

- A contraction is a short form of two words
- Where to place an apostrophe in a contraction
- Contractions are words that are combined with *not*, *be*, and *have*

Paragraphs

Students should know:

- What a main idea is
- A topic sentence is the first sentence in a paragraph and tells the main idea
- What makes a good topic sentence
- How to recognize a good detail sentence

Pronouns

Students should know:

- A pronoun is used to replace a noun
- A subject pronoun takes the place of a noun in a subject
- *I, you, she, he, it, we,* and *they* are subject pronouns
- An object pronoun takes the place of a noun after a verb
- *Me, you, him, her, it, us,* and *them* are object pronouns
- The pronoun *I* is always capitalized and always goes last when there is more than one subject

Root Words

Students should know:

- What a root word is
- How to recognize the root word of a longer word
- Common endings that are added to a root word to form a longer word

ITBS Index

SKILLS

Capitalization
- first word of sentence — 38
- letters — 46
- proper nouns
  - dates — 44
  - people — 42
  - places — 40
- quotations — 38, 50

Contractions — 56

Expression
- fragments — 66
- paragraphs
  - detail sentences — 72
  - main idea — 70, 72
  - sentence order — 72
  - time-order — 70
  - topic sentences — 70
- run-on sentences — 66
- sentence clarity — 68
- verb tense agreement — 64, 76

Possessive Nouns — 54

Punctuation
- abbreviations — 58
- apostrophes — 54, 56
- colons — 60
- commas
  - addresses — 60
  - dates — 60
  - letters — 60
  - quotations — 50
- end marks — 50, 52
- quotation marks — 50
- time — 60

Spelling
- /c/ sounds — 30
- /g/ sounds — 30
- /s/ sounds — 30
- letter combinations — 32
- silent letters — 28
- tricky words — 34
- word endings — 26

Usage
- double negatives — 76
- irregular verbs — 82
- pronouns — 78
- subject-verb agreement — 80
- verb tense agreement — 76

TECHNIQUES
- answer bubbles — 12
- asking questions — 15
- fixing mistakes — 62
- learning from mistakes — 15
- listening to yourself — 84
- pacing — 11, 48
- paying attention — 9, 15
- preparing for ITBS — 84
- process of elimination — 10, 36
- reading carefully — 9
- sharing writing — 74
- word game — 14
- working carefully — 9

SAT-9 Index

SKILLS

Capitalization
- first word of sentence — 168
- letters — 169
- pronoun I — 168
- proper nouns — 168
- quotations — 154, 168
- terms of respect — 168
- titles — 152, 168

Comparisons — 160

Conjunctions — 174, 178

Contractions — 156

Finding Information
- almanac — 194
- atlas — 194
- dictionary — 194
- encyclopedia — 194
- index — 194
- newspaper — 194
- textbook — 194
- thesaurus — 194

Paragraphs
- audience — 186
- definition — 182
- main idea — 182, 184, 188
- purpose — 186
- supporting details — 182, 184, 188
- time-order words — 182
- topic sentences — 184

Possessive Nouns — 158

Pronouns — 166

Punctuation
- abbreviations — 170
- apostrophes — 156, 158
- commas
  - addresses — 170
  - compound
  - dates — 170
  - letters — 170
  - sentences — 178
  - series — 170
- end marks — 170
- quotation marks — 154

TerraNova Index

Sentences
combining sentences	178
complete sentences	174
compound sentences	178
fragments	176
run-on sentences	174

Spelling
adding endings	146
confusing sounds	144
silent letters	140
tricky spellings	148
two-letter sounds	142

Using a Dictionary
definition	192
entry words	192
guide words	192
pronunciation key	192
pronunciation	192

Verbs
irregular verbs	162
verb tense	162, 164
verb tense agreement	164

TECHNIQUES
answer bubbles	126
asking questions	129
fixing mistakes	172
learning from mistakes	129
pacing	125, 190
paying attention	123, 129
process of elimination	124, 150
reading answer choices	198
reading carefully	123
sharing writing	180
word game	128
working carefully	123

SKILLS

Capitalization
dates	264
first word of sentence	272
holiday	264
letters	268
places	270
quotations	262
terms of respect	266

Comparisons 288
Conjunctions 298
Contractions 292

Paragraphs
main idea	300
supporting details	302
topic sentences	300, 302

Pronouns
object pronouns	290
subject pronouns	290

Punctuation
abbreviations	256, 266
apostrophes	292
commas	
compound sentences	258
dates	264
introduction	258
letters	268
pause	258
quotations	262
series	260
set-off name	258
end marks	256
quotation marks	262
terms of respect	266

Sentences
complete sentences	296
definition	296
fragments	296
predicates	276, 296
run-on sentences	298
subjects	276, 284, 296
topic sentences	300

Spelling
/f/ sound	248
/ie/ and /ei/	248
silent /e/	248
tricky spellings	252
words that must be memorized	250
words with q	248

Verbs
action verb	278
helping verbs	282
irregular verbs	278
subject-verb agreement	282, 284
verb tense agreement	280
verb tense	278, 280

TECHNIQUES
answer bubbles	234
asking questions	237
key words	304
learning from mistakes	237
pacing	233, 294
paying attention	231, 237
preparing for the test	306
process of elimination	232, 254
reading carefully	231
word game	236
working carefully	231